Slow Tourism, Food and Cities

T0330684

Slow Food began in the late 1980s as a response to the spread of fast food establishments and as a larger statement against globalization and the perceived deterioration of modern life. Since then, slow practices have permeated into other areas, including cities and territories and travel and tourism.

This book provides an in-depth examination of slow food, tourism and cities, demonstrating how these elements are intertwined with one other as part of the modern search for "the good life." Part 1 locates the slow concept within the larger social setting of modernity and investigates claims made by the slow movement, examining aesthetic and instrumental values inherent to it. Part 2 explores the practices and places of slow, containing both conceptual and empirical chapters in Italy, the birthplace of the movement. Part 3 provides a comparative perspective by examining the practices in Spain, the UK, Germany and Canada.

Slow Tourism, Food and Cities offers key theoretical insights and alternative perspectives on the varying practices and meanings of slow from a cultural, sociological and ethical perspective. It is a valuable text for students and scholars of sociology, geography, urban studies, social movements, travel and tourism, and food studies.

Michael Clancy is Professor of political science in the Department of Politics, Economics, and International Studies at the University of Hartford, USA. He is the author of two books on tourism and development in Mexico and Ireland, respectively, and has written on various aspects of tourism and political economy.

Routledge Advances in Tourism
Edited by Stephen Page
School for Tourism, Bournemouth University

For a full list of titles in this series, please visit www.routledge.com/series/
SE0258

Slow Tourism, Food and Cities

Pace and the Search for the "Good Life"

Edited by Michael Clancy

Routledge
Taylor & Francis Group

LONDON AND NEW YORK

First published 2018
by Routledge

2 Park Square, Milton Park, Abingdon, Oxfordshire OX14 4RN
52 Vanderbilt Avenue, New York, NY 10017

Routledge is an imprint of the Taylor & Francis Group, an informa business

First issued in paperback 2019

British Library Cataloguing in Publication Data
A catalogue record for this book is available from the British Library

Library of Congress Cataloging in Publication Data
A catalog record for this book has been requested

ISBN: 978-1-138-92091-0 (hbk)
ISBN: 978-0-367-24528-3 (pbk)

Typeset in Times New Roman
by diacriTech, Chennai

For Max, Nico, and Patrick

Contents

Figures

Tables

Contributors

Viviana Calzati, PhD in sociology, has also lectured in territorial management and marketing at the University of Siena, Italy. Her research interests are in the field of the territorial sociology, with particular reference to tourist development models in rural areas and specifically slow tourism. Her recent publications include *Nuove Pratiche Turistiche e Slow Tourism* (2016), *Sustainability and the Small Destination: The EDEN Project in Italy* (2014), *Turista Slow e Stile di Vita: Una Prima Indagine sul Territorio di Todi in Umbria* (2012), and *Territorial Brands for Tourism Development: A Statistical Analysis on the Marche Region* (2011).

Ana María Campón-Cerro is a professor in the Department of Business Management and Sociology, School of Business, Finance and Tourism at the University of Extremadura, Spain. She received her PhD from the University of Extremadura, and she is the author of various papers in Spanish and international journals and chapters in edited volumes. Her research interests include marketing and tourism management.

Michael Clancy is a professor of political science in the Department of Politics, Economics, and International Studies at the University of Hartford, Connecticut, USA. He is the author of two books on tourism and development in Mexico and Ireland, respectively, and has written on various aspects of tourism and political economy.

Paolo Corvo is the director of the Sociology Laboratory at University of Gastronomic Sciences in Bra, Italy, where he teaches sociology of consumption and gastronomy and social research. His research interests include food and consumption, slow and sustainable tourism, happiness and quality of life. He is the author of *Food Culture, Consumption and Society*, Palgrave MacMillan, 2014.

María de Obeso worked at Ikiam University of Regional Amazon (Ecuador) at the time of this research.

Paola de Salvo is an assistant professor in sociology of territory in the Department of Political Sciences, University of Perugia, Italy. Her research focuses on the study of local development and tourism, in particular to the study of the territorial development as a process that links socioeconomic and cultural aspects to sustainable development.

Elide Di-Clemente recently obtained her PhD from the University of Extremadura (Spain). She is graduated in economics for tourism from the University of Perugia (Italy) and holds two Masters degrees, in management of tourism organizations and resources and in social sciences research. She is author of various publications in scientific journals and book chapters in the fields of slow tourism, experiential marketing and culinary tourism.

Michael B. Duignan is a senior lecturer in tourism and events and a research fellow at the Institute for International Management Practice (IIMP), Lord Ashcroft International Business School (LAIBS), Anglia Ruskin University, UK. He is published in the area of mega-event impact analysis, host community and regional development and slow tourism, situating much of his research in the context of both smaller, regional grassroots events and festivals in the UK, right through to the analysis of mega-events, including the London 2012 and Rio 2016 Olympic Games. Mike is working on several papers in the context of Rio, centered on (i) the democratization of urban mega-event spaces, (ii) the strategic leverage value of core and ancillary event spaces for micro and small entrepreneurs, (iii) mega-event tourism behaviors and movement, and (iv) policy-level study, working with major stakeholder bodies in Rio de Janeiro to understand the tourism impact of the Rio 2016 Games. He is a critically oriented academic, whose major objective over the coming years is to consider how best to redistribute economic benefits of mega-events back in to host communities and for small businesses.

José Antonio Folgado-Fernández is a professor in the Department of Financial Economics and Accounting at the University of Extremadura, Spain. Prior to his academic career, he worked in managing several service companies. He was given a PhD Extraordinary Award and has published several papers in specialized journals. His research is focused on tourism events, branding and destination management.

Jennie Germann Molz is an associate professor of sociology at the College of the Holy Cross in Worcester, Massachusetts, USA. She is an editor of the journal *Hospitality & Society* and the author of *Travel Connections: Tourism, Technology and Togetherness in a Mobile World* (Routledge, 2012), co-author of *Disruptive Tourism and Its Untidy Guests* (Palgrave Macmillan, 2014), and co-editor of *Mobilizing Hospitality: The Ethics of Social Relations in a Mobile World* (Ashgate, 2007). She has published extensively on the topics of tourism mobilities, mobile technologies, cosmopolitanism, and the ethics of hospitality.

José Manuel Hernández-Mogollón is a professor in the Department of Business Management and Sociology, School of Business, Finance and Tourism, University of Extremadura, Spain. He holds a PhD in economics and business management, and he authored several publications in national and international journals and books. His research interests are marketing and tourism management.

Colleen C. Myles is an assistant professor in the Department of Geography at Texas State University in San Marcos, Texas (USA). She is a rural geographer and political ecologist with specialties in land and environmental management, (ex)urbanization, (rural) sustainability and tourism, wine and beer geographies (aka "fermented landscapes"), and agriculture (urban, peri-urban, and sustainable).

John S. Hull is an associate professor of tourism management at Thompson Rivers University, British Columbia, Canada. His research addresses the sustainability of tourism in peripheral regions focused mainly on planning and development of creative tourism, cruise tourism, culinary tourism, geotourism, Arctic tourism, mountain tourism, indigenous tourism, and wellness tourism. He is a visiting professor at the University College of Southeast Norway and at the Harz University of Applied Sciences, Germany. He is also a member of the International Competence Network for Tourism Research and Education (ICNT), the Sonnino Working Group, Italy, and the New Zealand Tourism Research Institute (NZTRI).

Roberto Lavarini is a professor of sociology of tourism at IULM (Università di Lingue e Comunicazione a Milano) in Milan, Italy, where he also offers courses in data analysis and demography. He has headed workgroups and associations for the study of tourism and personal relationships. He is particularly interested in the evolution of touristic habits from infancy to the elderly; he carried out many research projects in pilgrimage, religious tourism, seaside tourism and slow travel. Among his positions, he was member of the board of directors of APT (Tourist Promotion Agency of Milan and province) and was the scientific secretary of the Observatory on Tourism and Cultural Resources of the Chamber of Commerce in Milan.

Gabriele Manella is an assistant professor of sociology of territory and environment at Alma Mater Studiorum–Università di Bologna, Italy, where he is also a member of Ce.P.Ci.T. (Centro Studi sui Problemi della Città e del Territorio). He has served as secretary of the Mediterranean Association for the Sociology of Tourism since 2008.

Raffaele Matacena is a PhD candidate in Urban and Local European Studies (URBEUR) Department of Sociology and Social Research–University of Milan Bicocca, Italy. His doctoral research focuses on small-scale agri-food producers selling their product through alternative food channels in Western European contexts.

Peter McGrath has both a professional and personal interest in slowness. While co-writing the chapter for this edited book, Peter was employed as a lecturer at the University of Central Lancashire (UCLan), UK, and working towards a PhD in this area but has since taken up a position at the Open University, UK. His personal interest in slowness has taken precedence within his life and he is currently fully engaged with the slow ethos.

Filippo Randelli is a tenure-track researcher in the Department of Economic and Management at the University of Florence, Italy. He completed a PhD in economic geography at the University of Rome, Italy, "La Sapienza." He carries out research on sustainable tourism, economic geography and geography of innovations, publishing in several international journals and participating in conferences and workshops worldwide. He is a member of the board of the Società di Studi Geografici and has been an invited scholar in Utrecht University, Netherlands (2010), and Cambridge University, UK (2011).

Rosantonietta Scramaglia is a professor of sociology at IULM University (Università di Lingue e Comunicazione a Milano) in Milan, Italy, since 2005 and has also taught urban sociology at Politecnico University (Milan, Italy) since 2003. She has directed many research projects for private and public institutions (European Social Fund; Italian Ministry of University and Research; Cities of Verona and Milan, etc.) and has authored essays and articles about tourism, elderly and young values, feelings, consumer habits, housing, and social life, the sharing economy, and cities and their inhabitants.

Donna Senese is an associate professor of geography at the University of British Columbia Okanagan, Canada. Her research and teaching interests are in the geographies of tourism, parks and protected areas, food systems and wine. She is the director and founder of the Sonnino Working Group, an international transdisciplinary research collective, and is the North American director of academics at the Sonnino Centre for International Studies at Castello Sonnino in Montespertoli, Tuscany, Italy, where she continues her research in rural landscape change and instructs experiential courses in rural sustainability, tourism, food and wine.

Richard Sharpley is a professor of tourism and development at the University of Central Lancashire, UK. His research focuses primarily on tourism and development and the tourist experience, and he has published widely in these areas.

Katia Laura Sidali is a professor of sustainable tourism and faculty researcher at the Free University of Bozen/Bolzano, Italy. Previously, she worked as a PhD candidate at the University of Bologna (Italy) and as a post-doc researcher at the University of Göttingen (Germany) as well as at the Ikiam University of the Regional Amazon in Ecuador. Her research focuses on marketing of food and tourist services, certification schemes, consumer behavior and collective action along agro-industrial supply-chains. Her research has appeared in many peer-reviewed journals such as *Journal of Sustainable Tourism, British Food Journal, International Food and Agri-Business Management*, and *Leisure/Loisir.*

Giovanni Tocci is an assistant professor of sociology of environment and territory in the Department of Social and Political Science at the University of Calabria, Italy. Since 2007, he has taught in the Bachelors and Masters degree programs in tourism. His main research fields concern urban sociology, tourism, territorial governance and local development.

Chris Wilbert is a senior lecturer in tourism and geography at Anglia Ruskin University in Cambridge, England. His current research focuses on sustainable rural and urban tourism, heritage, memory and landscapes, and animal geographies and tourism. He is the author of numerous journal articles and book chapters, and is the coeditor of a number of books, including *Technonatures: Spaces Places Environments in the 21st Century*, with Damian White (Wilfred Laurier University Press, 2008); *Animal Spaces, Beastly Places: New Geographies of Human-Animal relations*, with Chris Philo (Routledge, 2000); and *Killing Animals*, with the Animal Studies Group, University of Illinois Press, 2007).

Moreno Zago is an associate professor at the University of Trieste, Italy, in sociology of tourism and sociology of international relations. His research primarily focuses on the determinants in tourism supply and demand and on the identity and cross-border cooperation. He served as scientific coordinator of the EU project "Slow Tourism: Valorization and Promotion of Slow Tourist Itineraries between Italy and Slovenia" (2010–2014).

Acknowledgments

It is perhaps fitting that the evolution and ultimate completion of this volume was, well, slow in coming. It is the product of many debts I have incurred and many contributions made by others. In many ways its original genesis came with a two-day conference in 2012 sponsored by Cittàslow International and the University of Perugia in Italy and organized by Viviana Calzati, Paola de Salvo and Pier Giorgio Oliveti. The conference theme, "The Value of Slowness for Future Tourism," brought together a number of scholars addressing the slow movement and its connection to food, cities and travel and tourism and many of them are contributors to this volume.

That same year I first presented my own research on slow tourism as a form of ethical consumption at the Association of American Geographers annual conference in New York on a panel organized by Clare Weedon and Karla Boluk. I gained from the feedback I received there and later from both editors and reviewers when that work became a book chapter in a volume edited by Weedon and Boluk.

I was able to meet a number of scholars who participated in the 2012 slow tourism conference in Italy a year later, where the original idea for this edited volume emerged. In addition to several of the contributors here, Pier Giorgio Oliveti, Director General of Cittàslow International, Giuseppe Roma, and Asterio Savelli also welcomed me. I also benefitted from participation in a conference on slow food and tourism associated with Frantoi Aperti in Assissi, Umbria, in November 2014.

At Routledge, Faye Leerink and Priscilla Corbett were both encouraging and immensely patient. Thanks to them as well as to reviewers there. I was also supported by my institution, the University of Hartford (Connecticut, USA), especially through two separate Vincent B. Coffin grants, money from the Dean's Travel funds, and importantly a sabbatical during the 2014–15 academic year. Thanks also to Liel Asulin for his editorial work. While on sabbatical I was warmly welcomed as a scholar in residence at Rollins College (Florida, USA) where much work for the volume took place. Finally, my family was, as always, highly supportive of me while I was away or had my gaze fixed on my laptop. I am immensely grateful to them.

1 Introduction

The rise of slow in a fast world

Michael Clancy

Introduction

Over the past several years the Slow Movement has emerged as an alternative set of personal practices juxtaposed with the rapid pace associated with modern life. Originating with the Slow Food movement in Italy in the late 1980s, the modern slow movement has not only spread horizontally to more than 150 nations, but has also grown to encompass new activities and spaces such as locales (cities and territories), travel and tourism, design, medicine, finance, architecture, television, gardening, education, media, sex, television, parenting – even religion (Honoré, 2004, 2013; Parkins & Craig, 2006; Smith & Pattison, 2014). How do we best understand the slow phenomenon itself, its timing, and what it represents as part of the broader politics of everyday life?

The overall slow philosophy and set of practices owe their origin to the Slow Food movement. Started by the Associazione Ricreativa Culturale Italiana (ARCI), the recreation association of the Italian left, Arcigola, the precursor to the Slow Food movement, was created in 1986. Led by Carlo Petrini, the movement famously protested the planned establishment of a McDonald's restaurant that year at the foot of the Spanish Steps by handing out bowls of pasta (Lindholm & Lie, 2012). Three years later the Slow Food Manifesto was signed in Paris. The manifesto made both aesthetic and ethical claims. Today Slow Food is global in scope and highly institutionalized. It boasts more than 150,000 members in 150 countries. It has 2000 local chapters, sponsors networks of food communities, works to protect biodiversity and sponsors a massive global conference on slow food biannually in Turin. Even when not branded explicitly as "slow," the effects of the movement are seen daily in the form of farm-to-table restaurants, locavores, the proliferation of farmers markets, pop-up restaurants, farm shares, and the revitalization of craft-made food and drink.

Inspired in part by the Slow Food movement, the mayors of five small Italian towns met in October 1999. Shortly thereafter they produced a Slow Cities (Cittàslow) agreement in an effort to revitalize and protect public spaces and urban life. Their effort was to reclaim public spaces in cities and towns to make them more livable for citizens and visitors alike. By 2017, 238 cities in 30 countries had become members of the Cittàslow network. Cittàslow also became institutionalized, with a formal application process, site visit and assessment for would-be slow cities. The Slow Cities manifesto contains six separate categories with nearly 60 separate criteria upon which cities are assessed. These include environmental policy, infrastructure policy, technology and design for urban quality, promotion of local production, support for Slow Food activities, hospitality and adherence to Cittàslow (Manella, this volume).

Slow tourism first emerged early in the twenty-first century and while influenced by Slow Food and cities, experienced a more organic origin. Many trace the named activity to a website, slowtravel.org, where users shared their experiences traveling more deliberately and with self-awareness (McGrath and Sharpley, this volume). Heitmann et al. (2011, 117) describe slow tourism as "a form of tourism that respects local cultures, history and environment, and values social responsibility while celebrating diversity and connecting people (tourists with other tourists and host communities)." This definition places slow tourism directly under the umbrella of ethical tourism in that it contains a social component to it directed toward an "other." While one might argue that the activity is not at all new, it has only appeared under the name "slow tourism" beginning shortly after the turn of the century when this virtual community began to appear. Soon one market summary produced in 2007 predicted that slow tourism would grow by at least 10 percent annually over the next five years and "become a significant alternative to 'sun and sea' and cultural tourism" (Euromonitor International, 2007, quoted in Lumsden and McGrath 2011, 266).

These better-known movements have spawned additional slow activities, including slow money, parenting, gardening, design, fashion, and art. Parkins and Craig (2006, 1) suggest a deeper social purpose of the movement in that it "declare[s] the value of slowness in our work, in our personal life, in public life, is to promote a position counter to the dominant value system of 'the times.'" Although Slow proponents primarily make individualistic claims involving quality (slow is better), there are also important social, ethical and aesthetic issues at stake. How do we best understand the rise of slow and the ethical claims it makes? Is it best understood as a new form of "life politics" (Giddens, 1991; Rojek, 2010), and if so, what are the implications in terms content and consequences of this new form of politics, particularly within the realm of citizenship?

In order to answer these questions we need to (1) place the rise of the slow movement within a specific socio-historical moment, (2) examine the rhetoric associated with the movement, (3) describe the larger set of practices of which the slow movement is a part, and (4) examine slow on the ground – in other words, how it manifests itself in action. *Slow Food, Tourism and Cities* aims to do just that through its various contributions. The remainder of the chapter will discuss not just the rise of the slow movement itself, but do so within a larger backdrop of modernity and the cult of speed. This speed has produced, among other things, a crisis of traditional politics and practices of citizenship. Following this backdrop the chapter closes with a brief summary of the chapters to come.

Locating slow

The Slow movement is contentious, not simply in its desirability but in its very nature and what it signifies. On one side are those who see the set of slow practices lacking social significance, being "bourgeois" (Cresswell, 2010 on slow tourism) or confined to a small set of urban elites (DuPuis & Goodman, 2005; Veseth, 2006 on slow food). Similarly, writing on Slow Food, Tomlinson views it as a narrow Luddite movement that "defends existing enclaves of interest" (2007, 148). At the other sit observers such as Schneider (2008), who places it within the larger contemporary social movement category, suggesting it shares important political and organizational features as other social movements. Similarly Haenfler et al. (2012) and Parkins and Craig (2006) categorize it as a lifestyle movement in that it reclaims the nature of everyday individual activities. Lindholm and Zúquete (2010) go even further. They refer to slow as an anti-globalization "aurora movement" on par with al Qaeda, the Zapatista rebels in Mexico and the neo-fascist National Front in France! The point here is that *how* we classify this movement directly affects what we think of its ultimate promise. An additional caveat: slow is not a single unified movement; various aspects of it started at different times. Some elements (food, tourism) relate directly to consumption habits while others (cities, homes, regions) to spatial organization and still others (parenting, religion) to daily personal and family practices. As a result we need to be careful in our generalizations.

Modernity and the cult of speed

Despite those caveats, we, as social scientists, still need to gain a deeper understanding of collective social activities whatever they may be. One way to begin is locate a social phenomenon within a larger social and historical context, and in addition, to think about what it is not or what it is against. In this case the answer is simple: speed. Following Virilio, Mark Taylor (2014) argues that velocity has been *the* core value of modernity. The promise of speed has been totalizing, lying at the heart of values of utility, productivity, efficiency, competition and consumption. Tomlinson (2007) also places the origin of acceleration at the emergence and subsequent domination of capitalist society and urbanization. Speed has not just permeated market relations, but also social and political ones. Weber (1978) defines modern bureaucracy partially on its precision and efficiency. The point of all this is that the promise of speed under modernity has always been the promise of the good life. Taylor shows that early promoters of speed promised more leisure time and relatedly, more happiness. Richard Nixon predicted a four-day workweek in 1956 and in the mid-1960s a U.S. Senate subcommittee heard expert testimony that by the end of the twentieth century, Americans would be working only 14 hours per week.

Writing on the same topic, Duffy (2009) points out that speed as both a desirable means and end arose with capitalist relations but itself became a product of the market in the twentieth century. As such modernity no longer promised speed directly, but rather the possible *access* to speed. Speed became valued not just simply within production, particularly the clock time under Taylor's scientific management, but also a commodity unto itself. As with many other commodities, however, public discourse regarding speed has continued to emphasize not just its desirability but also its widespread accessibility. Nowhere has this been felt more than in the typical household in post-industrial countries. The twentieth century brought such labor-saving (read speed) appliances as the washer/dryer, microwave, and convection oven, to say nothing of new food products such as cake mixes and frozen dinners. Michael Pollan (2014) reports that today the average American household spends just 27 minutes daily preparing meals, down some 50 percent from the 1960s. Major technological advances today involve speed and efficiency, whether it is broadband, smart objects, or delivery times for products or services.

The promise of ever-increasing speed and efficiency has changed our primary values. Waiting or moving slowly is to be avoided, whether at the checkout at the supermarket, the highway, security at the airport. In fact many of our social inventions are created in order to avoid just these time bottlenecks – witness the express lane in the store, fast track through airport security, the fast lane on highways and urgent care health-care facilities. Behind all of this is the promise that spending less time in producing and reproducing life will give us more leisure time, thus making us happier. And therein lies the problem. By most accounts, people living in the lap of late modernity are working a great deal *more* than expected, and they report being not all together happy.

Certainly recent studies from the Organization for Economic Cooperation and Development (OECD) suggest the promises of speed and efficiency for happiness have not been realized. Among the findings are that on average OECD workers who have full-time jobs work roughly 1765 hours per year (which averages out to just under 34 hours per week on a 52-week workweek annually), although that figure varies significantly, ranging from the average full-time worker in Mexico (2226) to the Netherlands (1381) (OECD, 2014a). An alternative measure is the percentage of full-time workforce working very long hours (defined as more than 50 hours per week). Here the OECD average is just nine percent but again with wide variation. In Turkey 43 percent or workers exceed the 50-hour-per-week threshold while in Mexico the figure is 29 percent. At the other end of the spectrum are Sweden (1.1 percent) and the Netherlands (0.5 percent) (OECD, 2014a). Some of this is due to the re-blurring of clock time. Disappearing is the clear demarcation between work time and non-work time, but as Taylor (2014) points out people also internalize the imperative of work. According to the U.S. Travel Association, in 2015 American workers failed to use 222 million paid days off and more than half of all workers (55 percent) left at least some allotted vacation time unused. On average they took 16 vacation days, down from an average of 20.3 between 1976 and 2000 (USTA, 2016). In short, if one promise of speed was less time at work, there is little evidence this has come to be the case.

The other implicit promise of modernity has been achievement of the good life through speed. Directly this was to come in the form of more leisure time, and indirectly in the form of abundance. And to be sure, most measures of abundance show vast material improvement over time (OECD, 2014b). Yet whether this has translated into happiness, especially as of late, is not at all clear.[1] In fact, many contemporary studies of happiness indicate otherwise. The OECD, interested in quality of life for its residence, here creates a 10-point scale for comparative purposes. In a 2013 survey it reports "very high happiness" on average for residents of Canada, Norway, Denmark and Switzerland (7.4 or higher on the scale), while countries with very low happiness include Estonia, Greece, Hungary, Portugal and Turkey (5.5 or lower) (OECD, 2013). The well-known Easterlin Paradox found that self-reported happiness is not correlated with economic growth or well-being[2], and the OECD study tends to confirm that. In Mexico, for example, with one of the lower GDP per capita figures among the 36 OECD nations, and also among those with a high percentage of people living long hours, happiness levels ranked eighth. In contrast much wealthier Japan ranked 28th.

More revealing are findings that relative happiness levels among residents in affluent countries have remained flat or declined over time. De Neve et al. (2014) show that among several Western European countries reported life satisfaction improved slightly in Sweden and Denmark between 1970 and 2013 but they were the outliers. More common were countries like France, the UK, Germany and the Netherlands, which experienced almost no change in self-reported happiness from residents. More surprising were the experiences of Spain and Ireland – which experienced major economic and political transformations during that time but again saw no real change in reported happiness – and Portugal and Greece, which showed significant *declines* in life satisfaction despite making major material gains.

Separately the *World Happiness Report* comes to similar conclusions, though its longitudinal span is from only 2007 from 12, a period coinciding with the global financial crisis. That study shows increases in the average level of self-reported subjective wellbeing (happiness) in many countries in the world but also absolute declines in Western Europe, the U.S., Canada, Australia and New Zealand (Helliwell Layard & Sachs, 2013). From this, De Neve et al. (2014) hypothesize that happiness levels are as much as eight times more susceptible to negative economic factors as positive ones.

The crisis of citizenship

It should come as no surprise that accompanying this failure to deliver on the promise of the "good life" as evidenced by the self-reporting of life satisfaction in many of the world's wealthiest societies has been a decline in traditional forms of civic participation associated with civic republicanism.

That traditional forms of civic participation are in decline is not in question. Voter turnout among OECD countries declined by eight percentage points between 1980 and 2011 (OECD, 2014a). In the U.S. the most recent (2014) midterm election saw a turnout of eligible voters at 36.4 percent, the lowest since World War II (Washington Post, 2014). Preliminary figures for the US Presidential election in 2016 show turnout to be the lowest since 1996. Low voter turnout is consistent with declines in other forms of traditional participation such as party membership, attendance in political meetings and campaigns, writing letters to politicians and taking part in political rallies (Putnam, 2000; Macedo et al., 2005).

An alternative measurement, trust in government, also highlights the perceived relationship between citizen and state. Van der Meer and Dekker (2011) argue trust is a manifestation of people's evaluation of the relationship between the citizen and state. It contains four elements: competence, care, accountability and reliability. In the OECD countries, trust levels fell to 39 percent in 2013, although it declined much more in countries hit by the global financial crisis. In Spain, for example, the percentage of people who had trust in their national government was at 58 percent in 2008 but just 18 percent five years later. Results from the Eurobarometer 80, published in 2013, showed similar trends among EU respondents. It showed that levels of trust in EU institutions had fallen from 50 percent approval in 2004 to 31 percent in 2013. During the same period the proportion of respondents who indicated their voice did not count in the EU increased from 52 to 66 percent (Standard Eurobarometer, 2013). Indeed the rise and success of nontraditional populist parties on both the right and left is testament to this distrust (Goodwin, 2011; Bröning, 2016).

In the United States pollsters from Pew now ask about trust in government meaning conviction that the government will do what is "right." When first asked about trust in 1958, 73 percent of respondents answered that they trust government to do what is right either just about always or most of the time. More recently that figure was between 10 and 22 percent (reported in Baiocchi et al., 2014, 6). Utilizing a different set of measurements, the American National Election Service has come to similar conclusions. Years 1994 and 2008 produced the lowest scores in more than a half-century (Baiocchi et al., 2014). The role of money in politics, especially in the United States, has undoubtedly exacerbated this disaffection. Supreme Court cases such as *Citizens United* have made American electoral politics, already awash in money, a veritable casino for big donors. Meanwhile voters are opting out.

While decline in traditional practices of republican citizenship are not in dispute, exactly what they mean remains in question. For some this signals a dangerous signal for the health of democracy. Developmental democrats argue that citizens develop civic virtue and a sense of community *through participation*. Failure to do so, therefore, signals dangerous times for democracy (Putnam, 2000). Crouch (2004) argues that in many post-industrial democracies we are moving steadily toward what he calls "post-democracy," where the shell of the system remains but "[t]he energy and innovative drive pass away from the democratic arena and into small circles of a politico-economic elite." Undoubtedly the recent rise in populism – from countries as diverse as The Philippines, Thailand, the United Kingdom, Hungary, Turkey and the United States – is connected to this broader distrust and dismay with traditional democratic tools. Others, following Beck (1992, 1997; Beck Giddens & Lash, 1997), contend that people have instead found new ways to participate in ways that they find meaningful and even political, but that are outside mainstream democratic participatory politics (Giddens, 1991; Ingelhart, 1997; Bennett, 1998; Rojek, 2001; Micheletti, 2003; Bennett et al., 2013). For them, the very *locale* of politics moves from the public realm to that of everyday practice. Stolle and Micheletti (2013, 35) refer to the everyday-maker as "a citizen involved with issues in a very local and specific way who may work alone or in ad hoc networks organized outside the formal system of politics and across traditional political ideological boundaries."

The rise of Slow, therefore, is best understood within the context of these crises—the crisis of modernity, the speed it brings with it, and the crisis of democratic citizenship. The Slow Food movement arose not only within this general period of time but more specifically during a period of intensified neoliberal globalization. Slow Food went so far as to state that it was reacting against speed, both in the form of fast food but also within the larger cult of speed that marks late modernity. The call was not for a return to tradition, but rather a reemphasis on time as a path toward intense and authentic experience. That its very creation came as a reaction to a fast-food restaurant is not accidental. Fast food restaurants represent not only the logical end of modernity defined as speed but also as a powerful symbol of neoliberal globalization (Ritzer, 1993). Slow Food and slow tourism are also manifestations of the ethical consumption movement that includes ethical tourism. While ethical or political consumption has deep historical roots, the contemporary consumer phenomenon is directly connected to the crises or late modernity and of citizenship. Related, the Cittàslow movement aims to recapture public spaces of the everyday and better the quality of life for residence. All three, as lifestyle movements, seek to recapture aspects of ordinary, daily routines in the face of long-term, deep-seated forces.

Outline of the book

The remainder of the volume is made of up three sections. The first, "Locating Slow: the philosophical and sociological roots of the Slow movement," investigates the rhetoric of Slow through examination of aesthetic and instrumental values inherent to the movement. In Chapter 2, Jennie Germann Molz takes up the politics of pace. Starting from the so-called mobilities turn, Germann Molz examines how the continuum between fast and slow is socially constructed. She introduces four concepts – stillness, waiting, deceleration and rhythm – that mobilities scholars have introduced and debated, and relates them to pace and more specifically slow mobilities. Viviana Calzati and Paola de Salvo (Chapter 3) locate slow tourism within a larger sea change in global tourism (and global consumption) that has come to emphasize individual experience. They create three separate theoretical models for placing slow tourism: the first emphasizes experience and active consumption; the second focuses on the personal link between consumption, territory and sustainability while implicitly criticizing pro-growth policies; the third focuses on well-being also, but on tourism, pace and subjective quality of life assessment. Peter McGrath and Richard Sharpley provide a genealogy of slow travel and tourism in Chapter 4, tracing their rise to much earlier critiques of modern tourism, particularly those in the works of Jost Krippendorf. At the same time they argue that slow travel and tourism do not share the fundamental counterculture critique of mainstream values inherent in the Slow Food and Cittáslow movements. Their chapter outlines the differences between slow tourism and slow travel as a means of explaining why this is the case. Michael Clancy takes up the links between consumption, lifestyle, ethics and citizenship in Chapter 5. Clancy's focus is on Slow Food and slow tourism as forms of ethical consumption. He looks critically at the 'other' orientation of both, arguing they ultimately reflect a neoliberal rather than cosmopolitan ethic.

Part 2, "Places and practices of Slow," looks at new forms of lifestyle practices, from active tourism to renewed focus on food and the remaking of territories. Roberto Lavarini and Rosantonietta Scramaglia connect slow tourism with the concept of creative tourism in Chapter 6. Here tourism is connected to learning or practicing a skill – such as regional cooking, music or art – and thus such tourism is also connected to broader cultural tourism. The authors also discuss how suppliers and destinations (cities, regions) have jumped on board of this niche market in recent years. In Chapter 7 Paolo Corvo and Rafaelle Matacena examine the connections between Slow Food and slow tourism in greater depth. Following Appadurai and others they detail the sociological and symbolic basis of food and eating historically and in a contemporary context. They also remind us that because food and cuisine make up a core element of culture, they have long been the subjects of tourism. Corvo and Matacena point to a growing percentage of international tourists who focus on gastronomy on their holidays. Because slow tourism centers on knowledge and integration with the local territory, this form of tourism frequently centers on local food production, where "geography, place and identity are intertwined."

In Chapter 8 Giovanni Tocci makes the connection between slow cities and smart cities. The chapter demonstrates parallels between the two, in particular features of inclusive governance, a focus on quality of life for residents, economic vitality, sustainability and the use of technologies to deliver services. Tocci also reminds us that "Slow" can be applied to places we often think of as fast – large metro areas. He highlights this through consideration of neighborhoods in Namyangju, South Korea and Barcelona. Moreno Zago's detailed case study examines the results of a European Union initiative on transborder cooperation through slow tourism between regions in Italy and Slovenia in Chapter 9. Zago argues the multiyear initiative, aimed at increased regional and cross-border integration, has thus far produced mixed results. Although it funded and coordinated multiple slow tourism projects along the upper Adriatic focusing on ecotourism, cycle tourism, food and wine tourism, bringing together some 600 stakeholders, overall results in attracting new tourists to the region have been modest. A survey of operators found that coordination is still lacking and more still needs to be done in successful promotion of the "Slow" brand. In Chapter 10 Gabriele Manella examines the Cittàslow movement within the north-central Emilia-Romagna region of Italy. The region contains some 13 designated Slow Cities. Manella finds that the most common motivation for joining the Cittàslow network is to promote tourism in the name of economic development. Despite this, preliminary evidence suggests that many merchants are unaware of their town's Cittàslow status. Similar to Zago, Manella finds more needs to be done on the marketing side.

Part 3, "Comparative perspective," provides just that: a series of chapters that examines the ways in which the slow concept travels across borders. In Chapter 11, Katia Laura Sidali and María de Obeso, first locate slow tourism within the larger literature on sustainability, and then investigate food tourism revolving around Algovian Emmentaler cheese from Southern Germany. They trace early tourism to the region back to the 1880s and suggest that today the dairy and tourism industry work in a complementary manner that has allowed the area to become a center of food tourism. The authors conducted a small-scale, open-ended set of interviewers with key informants revolving around the three pillars of sustainability: economic, environmental and sociocultural. Their findings show that while some tensions exist, ultimately the region has found a balance between resident lifestyle, economic viability and sustainability. Chapter 12, by José Manuel Hernández-Mogollón, Elide Di-Clemente, Ana María Campón-Cerro, and José Antonio Folgado-Fernández, examines slow tourism and travel in Spain. Their chapter discusses the academic literature emerging from the country as well as practices of slow tourism and travel. They find the Spanish scholarly approach to slow travel and tourism to be consistent with literature elsewhere. Their chapter also gives examples of both public and private initiatives toward promoting slow tourism.

Michael Duignan and Chris Wilbert integrate the Slow Cities model with Slow Tourism in their in-depth study of the small city of Cambridge, UK in Chapter 13. They show that this university city currently draws most of its visitors via day trippers from London. Whether Londoners themselves or travelers who have made the capital the center of their visit, most visitors to Cambridge spend just hours and focus their stay in the main city center. The authors argue the reasons behind the "one day" challenge are multiple, but one important one is the homogenization of entertainment and shopping districts associated with corporate globalization. Duignan and Wilbert discuss how a new private/public destination management organization might make use of the Slow concept as a means of overcoming this trend toward "clone towns" while simultaneously meeting their goals of increasing visitor length of stay and making use of a broader array of attractions. They introduce the concept of "Slow Phases" and demonstrate how the model can work inclusively toward these goals of alternative tourism growth, economic sustainability and increased livability for city residents. Chapter 14, a collaboration between Donna Senese, Filippo Randelli, John S. Hull and Colleen C. Myles, examines the linkages between food and wine, tourism and lifestyle migration in a comparative study of Tuscany, Italy, and the Okanagan Valley, British Columbia, Canada. The authors utilize an evolutionary economic geography (EEG) in order to trace the spatial evolution in each region as they have emerged into centers of oeno gastronomic tourism. Senese et al. argue that this process is driven by behavior of individuals and firms at the micro level – especially lifestyle migration by wine and food entrepreneurs into each region – along with macro opportunities and constraints shaped primarily by broader economic change and institutional policies. Ultimately, they argue the two regions experienced similar paths but were driven by a different mixture of factors. Finally, a concluding chapter by Michael Clancy discusses the promises and pitfalls of slow food, cities and tourism.

Notes

1 This is not the place to enter into key debates in happiness studies, the most basic of which are defining and measuring the phenomenon. For a representative sample see Kahneman et al. (1999); Di Tella et al. (2003); Bruni and Porta (2005); Griffin (2007); McCloskey (2010).
2 Easterlin's original claim has since been challenged (e.g., see Deaton, 2008). The debate is a fairly complex one I take no position on. Also see De Neve et al. (2014).

References

Baiocchi, G., Bennett, E. A., Cordner, A., Taylor Klein, P., & Savell, S. (2014). *The Civic imagination: Making a difference in American political life*. Boulder, CO: Paradigm Publishers.
Beck, U. (1992). *Risk society: Toward a new modernity*. London: Sage.
Beck, U. (1997). *The reinvention of politics: Rethinking modernity in the global social order*. Oxford: Polity Press.
Beck, U., Giddens, A., & Lash, S. (1997). *Reflexive modernization: Politics, tradition and aesthetics in the modern social order*. Cambridge, MA: Polity Press.
Bennett, E. A., Cordner, A., Taylor Klein, P., Savell, S., & Baiocchi, G. (2013). Disavowing politics: Civic engagement in an era of political skepticism. *American Journal of Sociology, 119*(2), 518–548.
Bennett, W.L. (1998). The un-civic culture. Communication, identity and the rise of lifestyle politics. *PS: Political Science and Politics, 31*(4), 740–761.
Bröning, M. (2016). The rise of populism in Europe. *Foreign Affairs*. N.p., June 3, 2016. Retrieved from www.foreignaffairs.com/articles/europe/2016-06-03/rise-populism-europe.
Bruni, L., & Porta, P. L. (Eds.). (2005). *Economics and happiness: Framing the analysis*. Oxford: Oxford University Press.

Cresswell, T. (2010). Towards a politics of mobility. *Environment and Planning D: Society and Space, 28*(1), 17–31.

Crouch, C. (2004). *Post-Democracy.* London: Polity Press.

Deaton, A. (2008). Income, aging, health and wellbeing around the world: Evidence from the Gallup world poll. *Journal of Economic Perspectives, 22*(2), 53–72.

De Geus, M. (2009). Sustainable hedonism: The pleasures of living within environmental limits. In K. Soper, M. Ryle & L. Thomas (Eds.), *The politics and pleasures of consuming differently* (pp. 113–129). London: Palgrave.

De Neve, J-E., Ward, G., De Keulenaer, F., Van Landeghem, B., Kavetsos, G., & Norton, M. (2014). *Individual experience of positive and negative growth is asymmetric: Global evidence using subjective well-being data.* (LSE CEP Discussion Paper No. 1304). Retrieved from London School of Economics, Centre for Economic Performance website: http://cep.lse.ac.uk/pubs/download/dp1304.pdf

Di Tella, R., MacCulloch, R. J., & Oswald, A. J. (2003). The macroeconomics of happiness. *Review of Economics and Statistics, 85*(4), 809–827.

Duffy, E. (2009). *The speed handbook: Velocity, pleasure, modernism.* Durham, NC: Duke University Press.

DuPuis, E. M., & Goodman, D. (2005). Should we go "home" to eat?: Toward a reflexive politics of localism. *Journal of Rural Studies, 21*(3), 359–371.

Euromonitor International. (2007). *WTM global trends report 2007.* London: Author.

Giddens, A. (1991). *Modernity and self-identity: Self and society in the late modern age.* Stanford, CA: Stanford University Press.

Goodwin, M. (2011). *Right response. Understanding and countering populist extremism in Europe.* (Chatham House Report, September) Retrieved from Chatham House website: www.chathamhouse.org/sites/files/chathamhouse/r0911_goodwin.pdf

Griffin, J. (2007). What do happiness studies study? *Journal of Happiness Studies, 8,* 139–148.

Haenfler, R., Johnson, B., & Jones, E. (2012). Lifestyle movements: Exploring the intersection of lifestyle and social movements. *Social Movement Studies, 11*(1), 1–20. https://doi.org/10.1080/14742837.2012.640535.

Heitmann, S., Robinson, P., & Povey, G. (2011). Slow food, slow cities and slow tourism. In P. Robinson, S. Heitmann and P. Dickey (Eds.), *Research themes for tourism* (pp. 114–127). London: CAB International.

Helliwell, J., Layard, R., & Sachs, J. (Eds.). (2013). *World happiness report 2013.* New York, NY: U.N. Sustainable Development Solutions Network.

Honoré, C. (2004). *In praise of slowness. How a worldwide movement is changing the cult of speed.* San Francisco, CA: HarperCollins.

Honoré, C. (2013). *The slow fix: Solve problems, work smarter, and live better in a world addicted to speed.* New York, NY: HarperOne.

Ingelhart, R. (1997). *Modernization and postmodernization: Cultural, economic and political change in 43 societies.* Princeton, NJ: Princeton University Press.

Kahneman, D., Diener, E., & Schwarz, N. (Eds.). (1999). *Well-being: The foundations of hedonic psychology.* New York, NY: Russell Sage Foundation.

Lindholm, C., & Lie, S. (2012). You eat what you are: Cultivated taste and the pursuit of authenticity in the Slow Food movement. In N. Osbaldiston (Ed.), *Culture of the slow: Social deceleration in an accelerated world* (pp. 52–70). London: Palgrave MacMillan.

Lindholm, C., & Zúquete, J.P. (2010). *The struggle for the world: Liberation movements for the 21st century.* Palo Alto, CA: Stanford University Press.

Lumsden, L.M., & McGrath, P. (2011). Developing a conceptual framework for slow travel: A grounded theory approach. *Journal of Sustainable Tourism, 19*(3), 265–279.

Macedo, S., Alex-Assensoh, Y., Berry, J., Brintnall, M., Campbell, D., Fraga, L.R., ... Cramer Walsh, K. (2005). *Democracy at risk: How political choices undermine citizen participation and what we can do about it.* Washington, DC: Brookings Institution Press.

McCloskey, D. (2010). *Bourgeois dignity: Why economics can't explain the modern world.* Chicago, IL: University of Chicago Press.

Micheletti, M. (2003). *Political virtue and shopping: Individuals, consumerism, and collective action.* London: Palgrave MacMillan.

OECD (Organization for Economic Cooperation and Development). (2013). *How's life? 2013: Measuring well-being.* Paris: OECD.

OECD (Organization for Economic Cooperation and Development). (2014a). *Better life index.* Retrieved from www.oecdbetterlifeindex.org. Paris: OECD.

OECD (Organization for Economic Cooperation and Development). (2014b). *How was life?: Global well-being since 1820.* Paris: OECD.

Parkins W., & Craig, G. (2006). *Slow living.* Oxford: Berg.

Pollan, M. (2014). *Cooked: A natural history of transformation.* New York, NY: Penguin.

Putnam, R. (2000). *Bowling alone: The collapse and revival of American community.* New York, NY: Simon & Schuster.

Ritzer, G. (1993). *The MacDonaldlization of society.* Thousand Oaks, CA: Pine Forge Press.

Rojek, C. (2001). Leisure and life politics. *Leisure Sciences*, 23(2), 115–125.

Rojek, C. (2010). *The labour of leisure.* London: Sage.

Schneider, S. (2008). Good, clean, fair: The rhetoric of the slow food movement. *College English, 70*(4), 384–402.

Smith, C., & Pattison, J. (2014). *Slow church: Cultivating community in the patient way of Jesus.* Downers Grove, IL: IVP Press.

Standard Eurobarometer (2013). *Public opinion in the European Union: First Results. Brussels: European Commission-Directorate General for Communication.* Retrieved from http://ec.europa.eu/public_opinion/archives/eb/eb80/eb80_first_en.pdf

Stolle, D., & Micheletti, M. (2013). *Political consumerism: Global responsibility in action.* Cambridge: Cambridge University Press.

Taylor, M. (2014). *Speed limits: Where time went and why we have so little left.* New Haven, CT: Yale University Press.

Tomlinson, J. (2007). *The culture of speed: The coming of immediacy.* London: Sage.

USTA (United States Travel Association). (2016). *The state of American vacation 2016: How vacation became a casualty of our work culture.* (USTA Project Time Off Report). Retrieved from USTA website: www.ustravel.org/system/files/Media%20Root/Document/PTO_SoAV%20Report_FINAL.pdf

van der Meer, T. & Dekker, P. (2011). Trustworthy state, trusting citizens? A multilevel study into objective and subjective determinants of political trust. In S. Zmerli, and M. Hooghe (Eds.), *Political trust: Why context matters* (p. 95–116). Colchester, UK: ECPR Press.

Veseth, M. (2006). *Globaloney: Unraveling the myths of globalization.* Oxford: Rowman and Littlefield Publishers.

Washington Post. (2014). *Voter turnout in 2014 was the lowest since WWII.* Retrieved from www.washingtonpost.com/blogs/post-politics/wp/2014/11/10/voter-turnout-in-2014-was-the-lowest-since-wwii/

Weber, M. (1978). *Economy and society.* Berkeley, CA: University of California Press.

Part I

Locating Slow

The philosophical and sociological roots of the Slow movement

2 "Travel too fast and you miss all you travel for"

Slower mobilities and the politics of pace

Jennie Germann Molz

Introduction

On my office wall is a framed quote by Louis L'Amour: "Travel too fast and you miss all you travel for." The quote, set in bold white letters against a photo of an antique Airstream trailer, intrigues me. Without telling us precisely why we travel, the message suggests that travel is not entirely instrumental. If mere transportation from point A to point B were the goal, then traveling too fast wouldn't matter. But this quote suggests that there is another desire embedded in travel that cannot be satisfied by speed. So what do we travel for? And how does slow travel get us there?

The image of the Airstream trailer, that aluminum emblem of baby boomer nostalgia for the open road, intrigues me, too. This mobile home, in all its silvery glory, encapsulates the intersection of movement and stasis. Mobilities scholars are fascinated by the dialectic of mobility and immobility, and especially by the way it maps onto hierarchies of access and power and privilege (Hannam, Sheller, & Urry, 2006). On one end of the spectrum, the Airstream trailer symbolizes American retirees comfortably crossing the country while nestling into their mobile homes-away-from-home. On the other end, it conjures up images of trailer parks that amount to little more than "canned labor being preserved between shifts," as Barbara Ehrenreich (2001, p. 40) puts it, housing the working poor who are both stuck and precarious. Who gets to travel, who is forced to travel, who is blocked or stuck or gets to stay home – these are the mobilities, immobilities, and moorings around which contemporary social life revolves.

The anxiety expressed in L'Amour's quote – that we might miss something if we travel too fast – animates another set of debates that revolve, instead, around pace. What are the tempos and temporalities at stake in this mobile world? When are speed or deceleration valorized; and when are they framed as a problem? Why do some people move rapidly and seamlessly while others seem to be continually waiting, slowed down, or stuck? Jamaica Kincaid writes eloquently about the way tourists turn the "native's boredom" into an object of tourist fascination and desire. In those places where meaningful, livable work is all but nonexistent, the tourist mistakes the native's "life of overwhelming and crushing banality and boredom" for the charm of an unhurried lifestyle (Kincaid, 1988, p. 18). The mistake may pivot on the wealthy tourist's association of boredom not with slowness, but with speed. In moderation, the frantic pulse of western modernity may foster excitement, but too much of it leads to numbness and ennui. And that goes for travel, as well, as John Ruskin wryly noted: "All traveling becomes dull in exact proportion to its rapidity" (cited in Urry, 2000, p. 60).

In other words, it is not just a question of who moves or who doesn't move, but of pace. The purpose of this chapter is to highlight the way pace has been explored within the "new mobilities paradigm" (Hannam et al., 2006; and see Urry, 2000, 2008). In the sections that follow, I review the work of some of the key scholars in mobilities studies to see what they have to say about the temporal aspects of mobility and to draw out themes that contribute to a more nuanced theorization of slowness.

Slow and slower mobilities

When we talk about a "mobilities turn" in the social sciences, we are talking about a turn away from sedentarist modes of analysis and towards metaphors like networks, scapes, flows, and liquidity that better capture the mobile qualities of contemporary life (Castells, 1996; Appadurai, 1990; Bauman, 2000). These metaphors tend to conjure up a sense of incessant movement and global acceleration. Indeed, the dominant discourse that ushered in late modernity was all about speed. Theorists predicted that the pace of life in the network society would accelerate, temporal horizons would collapse, and time would become instantaneous – even timeless (Harvey, 1990; Castells, 1996; Virilio, 2000; Hassan, 2009). These forecasts were summed up nicely in the title of James Gleick's book *Faster: The Acceleration of Just about Everything* (1999). Amidst the frenetic buzz about 24/7 lifestyles, high-speed computers, jet travel, and instantaneous connections, it would have been easy to overlook slowness. But mobilities scholars have consistently reminded us that all of this speed is inextricably tied to slowness. John Urry's mobility manifesto, which he outlines in *Sociology beyond Societies* (2000), doesn't just cover "instantaneous time," but also "glacial time," and he devotes as much attention to describing various forms of slow travel as he does to the acceleration of social life. Later, in their introduction to the "new mobilities paradigm," Kevin Hannam et al. (2006) emphasized the way diverse mobilities are reliant on immobile platforms, fixed infrastructures, and moorings that settle, hold, or lock people in place. Scholars have continued to develop a nuanced understanding of mobility by tuning in to the temporalities of speeding up and slowing down. In the sections that follow, I discuss four concepts – stillness, waiting, deceleration, and rhythm – that mobilities scholars have introduced to think about pace, and especially about slow and slower mobilities.

Stillness

Although an apparent paradox in terms, mobilities scholars have found stillness to be a richly evocative concept. David Bissell and Gillian Fuller inserted the concept of stillness into conversations about mobility with their edited collection, *Stillness in a Mobile World* (2011). In the introduction to the book, they argue that even against the "buzz of mobility and animation, a topology of stillness haunts the space of flows" (p. 4). They offer the following list to illustrate the way stillness punctuates everyday mobilities: "a queuer in line at the bank; a moment of focus; a passenger in the departure lounge; a suspension before a sneeze; a stability of material forms that assemble; a passport photo" (p. 3). The essays in the book go on to reveal the conceptual, political and philosophical significance of stillness, but Bissell and Fuller's volume is not a nostalgic return to sedentary metaphysics. Instead, it offers stillness as a lens through which we can understand the complexity of mobile relations. Stillness is part of the grammar of a mobile life; it is the punctuation that makes mobility legible.

Bissell and Fuller show that there is more to life than stop and go. The idea here is to use stillness to pry open a conceptual space in between mobility and immobility that allows us to acknowledge and analyze the various registers and modalities of an (im)mobile life that is both animated and suspended; both fast and slow. The contributors to Bissell and Fuller's book make sense of stillness through a mix of philosophical reflections and empirical analyses that highlight the way "stillnesses pulse" through everyday life (Bissell & Fuller, 2011, p. 3). Covering topics ranging from retreat houses and public art performances to the stilled images of World War II photography to bodies incarcerated in shipping containers or detention camps, the chapters in the book show stillness to be multiple, contingent, potent, and polyvalent.

Slowness is one of the registers through which stillness becomes meaningful in the context of mobility. It is telling that one of the themes cutting across the chapters in *Stillness in a Mobile World* is the idea of slowing down. Stillness is not equivalent to slowness, of course, but the two concepts are deeply intertwined. For one thing, both concepts have tended to be negatively associated with "stuckness" or "docility" or "passivity." Bissell and Fuller resist this implicit coding, arguing that stillness "has a capacity to do things" (Bissell & Fuller, 2011, p. 5). As many of the chapters in the book demonstrate, stillness and slowing down can be strategic and tactical, focusing attention or prompting perception in particular ways. For example, David Conradson's (2011) chapter on two spiritual retreats illustrates how stillness can produce affective dynamics that contrast with the stress and rush of people's busy lives. Detailing the subjective experiences of participants at a rural retreat community and at a Buddhist retreat house, Conradson found that stillness was not just about slowing down hectic lifestyles, but about attaining a "state of consciousness characterized by calmer mental rhythms and a shift in attention from other places and times (the 'there' and 'then') towards the present moment (the 'here' and 'now')" (p. 72). He describes this shift as a "centring" that consolidates attention through a slower rhythm of daily life. He emphasizes that "stillness is increasingly a matter of attention" (p. 74). In this sense, Conradson equates stillness to thinking and feeling differently; to inhabiting the world differently. Achieving stillness was "no simple matter," however, and required deliberate spatial and temporal orchestration on the part of retreat guides and the participants themselves. Both the physical environment (such as the scenic landscape and comfortable but basic furnishings) and the daily routines (including meditation practices) were designed for stillness.

From a slightly different perspective, Emma Cocker's (2011) chapter on public art performances also reveals how stillness can be orchestrated to focus attention differently. She describes her participation in several art projects that used stillness to reveal and disrupt the habitual mobilities of urban life. One such event, choreographed by the artist group Open City, asked participants to follow directions written on postcards. For example, one postcard instructed participants to walk along the high street during rush hour and then "suddenly and without warning, stop and remain still for five minutes ... then carry on walking as before" (cited in Cocker, p. 89). As Cocker explains, the project "explored how performed stillness and slowness could operate as tactics for rupturing or disrupting the homogenized flow of authorized and endorsed patterns of public behaviour" (p. 89). In these instances, the artists deploy stillness as an ontological experiment. Stillness is not passive acquiescence, but rather a form of resistance that disrupts the social arrangements of urban life, and in the process reveals their contingency.

Along with Conradson and Cocker, the contributors to *Stillness in a Mobile World* demonstrate that pace is interlaced with ways of being in the world that cultivate reflexivity and awareness. Through these analyses, we see how stillness and slowness can be deployed as tactics to reveal our taken-for-granted habits and wake us up to new possibilities.

Waiting

One particular form of stillness is waiting. Waiting is a common, if infrequently examined, part of everyday life. Travelers in airport lounges or train stations, commuters in traffic back-ups, urban residents in line at the bank or the coffee shop, and even scholars stranded by a volcanic eruption all experience waiting as a kind of stillness imposed on an otherwise mobile itinerary. According to popular conceptions, waiting is wasted time. But against the stereotype of waiting as dead time, mobilities scholars have highlighted the complex fullness of waiting (see Vannini, 2002; Lyons & Urry, 2005; Larsen, Urry, & Axhausen, 2006; Jain & Lyons, 2008). A salient moment for theoretical reflection came in April 2010 when the eruption of Iceland's Eyjafjallajökull volcano brought international air travel to a halt. In a special issue of Mobilities that followed soon after, scholars interrogated the disruptive effects of the volcanic eruption from various perspectives, including the personal experiences of being stranded abroad, waiting for mobility systems to get back to normal (Birtchnell & Büscher, 2011; and see Cresswell, 2012). Ole Jensen (2011), like several other contributors to the special issue, had been attending a conference in Washington, DC at the time and found himself stuck there. In his account of the experience, he describes the various "emotional eruptions" he witnessed as people dealt with the effects of the volcanic eruption. Some experienced anxiety or were disoriented by the disruption and many were reduced to tears. Some people took the unexpected stranding as an opportunity to go sightseeing while still others turned to online hospitality networks to find free lodging with local hosts while waiting out the delay. In these cases, waiting generated "different and innovative strategies to cope with this unforeseen situation of impaired mobility" (Jensen, 2011, p. 73).

These reflections on being stuck or stranded show that waiting is not "dead time," but entails its own relative and relational dynamics, a point that David Bissell and Gillian Fuller both address in their respective analyses of waiting and queuing. In an article titled "Animating Suspensions: Waiting for Mobilities" (2007), Bissell explores waiting not as a dead period to be endured nor as time out of our regularly scheduled mobilities, but rather as a constitutive temporality of everyday life. For Bissell, waiting itself is an affective and embodied performance that entails "a specific kind of relation-to-the-world" that, like stillness, "heralds a heightened sensual attentiveness to the immediate spatiality" (285–286). In some ways, waiting may entail withdrawal, perhaps into the soundscapes or social worlds that our personal technologies afford, but periods of waiting are also "incipient rich durations" (p. 279) in which the world comes into stark focus and makes itself available to be noticed.

Many of my own experiences of waiting align with Bissell's observation that waiting intensifies "corporeal attentiveness to the immediate environment" (p. 286). While reading his article, I remembered a cross-country road trip I took with my husband many years ago. As we were driving late at night, the horizon suddenly turned red with brake lights. Along with the other cars on the highway, we came to a halt. A truck had overturned and blocked the highway. While we waited for the tow trucks to clear the wreck, we sat, stopped, on the highway. I remember staring up at the night sky, black and clear, and then down at the road beneath our car. I noticed that the asphalt was actually quite rough and pocked, not smooth. Small bushes grew along the shoulder of the highway. The line of yellow paint along the margin of the road was not as straight as it had seemed at sixty miles per hour. Instead, its edges were scalloped, the paint leaking into crevices. The smoothness of the road and straightness of the line were illusions afforded by speed. While we waited, that small patch of highway became a world in itself, taking on a new quality of "here-ness" and a renewed sense of contingency.[1]

Waiting brings our attention to the environment as well as to ourselves and our own bodies. Bissell notes that "the act of bodily stillness through waiting is instrumental in heightening an auto-reflexive self-awareness" (p. 286).

He refers to Phillip Vannini's description of being contained in a waiting room and becoming deeply aware of his own sense of corporeality: "the world feels intensely present. I feel a sense of engagement-with-my-world, a long-forgotten sense of presence" (cited in Bissell, 2007, p. 286). Waiting is not just a means to an end – a temporary hiccup to getting back on the road or getting back to normal – rather it entails its own dynamics of activity and inactivity, of patience and impatience, and of withdrawal and attention. Bissell insists that our descriptions of waiting should let go of "the productivist rendering of the (singular) event-to-come" and acknowledge instead the way these hiatuses are woven into the fabric of everyday life (p. 278).

Fuller picks up on this theme in her analysis of queuing. As she puts it, "queuing is the slow dance of the everyday" (2014, p. 205). It is a habitual response to the myriad tasks of everyday life: "We queue at ATMs, ticket machines, motor registries, hospitals, at any place where traffic, in the broadest sense of the term, congregates" (p. 206). Drawing on Jean-Paul Sartre's notion of the queue as a "plurality of isolations," Fuller sees in the spatiotemporal configuration of the queue the larger tensions of social life writ small: queues are both individual and collective, visceral and habitual, coded and implicit (p. 209). She observes that amidst the flow of urban living "there seems to be an unspoken and largely unquestioned respect for queues … as a type of moral and fair mode of organisation" (p. 206). Although the practices and meanings of queuing (and not queuing) are arguably more culturally diverse than Fuller allows, this idea that queuing is a respectable and respected form of social ordering extends our understanding of what it means to wait. In other words, queues are metaphors for and performances of what it means to live together. As a reflection on fairness, the queue takes on moral weight, which means that "jumping the queue" is a significant ethical violation that can extend from the embodied context, such as waiting at the bank, to a metaphorical level in terms of the state. In the latter case, moral condemnation awaits immigrants or asylum seekers who are seen as "queue-jumpers" (p. 206), a point I will return to later.

Waiting is also a central theme in the work of Philip Vannini, whose object of investigation is the ferry lineup where cars and pedestrians wait on a first-come basis for room on the next sailing. Based on a three-year mobile ethnography of coastal and island communities in British Columbia and the ferry systems that serve them, Vannini's work offers a rich account of the complex orchestrations of rest and movement involved in waiting for the ferry. Fascinated by one respondent's comparison of the ferry system to a prison warden that holds island community residents captive and to a thief that "steals" their time, Vannini set out to discover whether waiting really is a form of stolen time, as this respondent claimed (2011, p. 277).

After spending time in ferry terminals, embarking on several hundred ferry journeys, and conducting even more qualitative interviews, what Vannini found were active and strategic performances of waiting. Drawing on the musical idea of *tempo rubato* ("stolen time") and Michel de Certeau's (1984) notion of tactics, Vannini describes how people steal time back while waiting for the ferry. He explains that "a lineup can work in an oppositional, tactical fashion ... [as] a furtive re-appropriation of time" (p. 279). He sums up the tactics he observed:

> You're here, you're waiting, you have little else to do, so might as well getting something done, right? Bills, correspondence, walking the dog, doing homework, reading the bulletin boards in the waiting room, enjoying a sunny day, doing tai-chi, practicing karate moves – all of these ways of lining up are happening somewhere at a ferry terminal as you read this.
>
> (Vannini, 2011, p. 282)

In other words, islanders and tourists co-opt the space and time created by the ferry schedule and reallocate it to their own activities. Vannini goes on to describe ferry journeys and lineups as a liminal space-time where passengers can recalibrate their temporal rhythms to the slower pace of island life, a theme he explores through the concept of deceleration.

Deceleration

If waiting slows down movement without our consent, deceleration is deliberate and chosen. Vannini even argues that we should think of slow not as an essence, but as a verb. For Vannini, slow is something we do: "to slow down nowadays means to decelerate from an ever increasingly pervasive regime built around the logic of speed" (2014, p. 116). But it is also something we desire, not least of all for its transformative potential. He explains that even kinetic elites often want to slow down because to decelerate "means to affect one's lifeworld in tactically notable ways, for desirable aims. To slow down, therefore, means to affect the way in which we dwell in the world, and in turn to be affected by it" (2014, p. 117). Deceleration, like stillness and waiting, is a way of being in the world.

This theme of deceleration as an orientation to temporality, as an object of desire, and as a way of being in the world runs through Vannini's ethnography of ferry mobilities. He describes how the slower tempo of ferry travel enables island and coastal residents, as well as tourists, to escape the faster-paced pulse of the city and instead tune into the temporal regimes of coastal life. Or as Vannini puts it, deceleration requires moving "out of time" in order to move "in time." He defines being "in time" as bringing "a sense of harmony to islanders and coasters" whereas being "out of time" refers to the sense of discordance brought on by the overwhelmingly chaotic, noisy, and frenetic "hegemonic beats of the city" (Vannini, 2012, p. 259). Moving out of time means leaving the relentless speed of urban life behind. In this regard, slowing down to move "in time" subverts the hectic temporalities of productive urban, work or family schedules and embraces the less hurried pace of coastal life.

Vannini (2012, p. 248) recounts an exchange between two of his respondents as they articulate the effects of moving "in time":

> Tony picks up again, "it's state of mind, it's a way of living your life at a slower pace." "That's true," Belinda adds, "I live in Genoa Bay. Any visitor from the mainland says there is something different about the way we relate to life. ... [T]hose who are on island time try to take the time to think, to connect with friends and neighbors, to smell the roses, to go out for a walk, or to take up time-consuming hobbies, like gardening. I am very sensitive about this idea because I grew up in Calgary and when I moved to Vancouver Island my main reason for moving was to slow down, to switch off. And at first it was incredible how much energy it took me. I had to work hard at it."
>
> (Vannini, 2012, p. 248)

For Tony and Belinda, decelerating and moving "in time" afford a different way of relating to oneself, one's social circles, and one's environment through a particular tempo. Belinda's comment about working hard at slowing down touches on another important insight: deceleration is not just about moving more slowly, but also moving from one pace of life to another. In Belinda's case, moving from Calgary to Vancouver Island entailed downshifting from a faster temporal regime to a slower one and, in the process, learning how to slow down in her everyday life. Not surprisingly, however, Vannini's respondents go on to reveal that decelerating is not always seamless or pleasurable. For example, Belinda recounts suppressing her urge to hasten a grocery store cashier along and many of the people Vannini interviewed admitted to having a love/hate relationship with the ferries. And yet despite these diverse experiences of deceleration, Vannini's respondents reproduced a very consistent narrative of island temporality as relaxed, slow, unhurried, peaceful, and quiet.

The picture Vannini's respondents paint of ferry networks and coastal lifestyles is very much interwoven with specific place temporalities, or what I have referred to elsewhere as "pace-myths" (Germann Molz, 2009, 2010). The concept of "pace-myths" is inspired by Rob Shields' (1991) "place-myths," the dominant narratives that circulate about the unique qualities of a particular place. Places take on a particular currency in the cultural imaginary based on their scenery, history, or culture, but also, I argue, based on their temporal regimes. Different places become associated with different perspectives on time or with different daily rhythms, which then constitute the "pace-myth" of a place. Shaw argues that "places have a particular pace which is part of their character" and which has "become a selling point for a number of industries, particularly ... tourism" (2001, p. 120). For example, Tokyo is described as hectic, Bali as serene, and still other places are deemed to be a "step back in time." As pace-myths circulate, they conflate places with particular temporal rhythms, such as the supposedly more elastic tempos of "Fiji time," "island time," or, in Indonesia, "jam karet" ("rubber time"). The way place and pace are interconnected, however, cannot be understood as the effect of some immanent quality of the place itself. Instead, it is often the effect of highly romanticized "pace-myths" that are widely distributed by the tourism industry, as Shaw notes. However pace-myths, especially those that represent certain places as inherently slow, tend to overlook the way these places are embedded in broader spatiotemporal constellations. As Vannini puts it, a place is not "a hermetically protected bubble" detached from the various mobilities that shape all places (Vannini, 2012, p. 250). Even island dwellers are constantly aware of other schedules and temporal pressures that infiltrate "island time," especially when they are catching a ferry that will take them to the airport in time to catch a flight. In other words, places are shaped through multiple, relational, and intersecting rhythms.

Rhythm

The mobile world we inhabit, and the specific places in which we move and live, are assembled around a panoply of rhythms, of which slowness, stillness, waiting, and deceleration are a part. Many mobilities scholars, most notably geographer Tim Edensor, have been inspired by Henri Lefebvre's *Rhythmanalysis* (2004) to understand rhythm as embedded in everyday life and therefore as part and parcel of the contested reproduction of social order. According to Edensor, Lefebvre offers a useful method for observing and analyzing the rhythms that configure social life into particular arrangements – from calendrical, diurnal, and lunar cycles to bodily or mechanical cadences to the pulse of the city (Edensor, 2010a).

Whether examining the mobile geographies of walking (Edensor, 2010b), tourism (Edensor, 2011a), the daily commute (Edensor, 2011b), or a coach excursion through Ireland (Edensor & Holloway, 2008), Edensor renders richly textured accounts of the "polyrhythmic ensemble" (Crang, 2001) of place and pace. Consider, for example, his depiction of the intersecting rhythms that compose an urban setting:

> [T]he timetabled journeys of throngs of children walking along routes that converge on schools ... intersect with ... strolling workers en route to places of employment. ... Contrast these mobile morning rhythms of walking with those of the evening, as shoppers and commuters have already drifted back home, and hedonistic crowds of evening clubbers, drinker and cinema-goers animate the streets of the city with purposive and more exuberant styles of walking. ... And these walking rhythms co-exist and intersect with a host of other mobile rhythms: the regular timetabled bus, train and tram travel, the pulse of cyclists, cars and motorcycles, and the non-human pulse of electricity, water, gas and telephony. These multiple mobile rhythms of place further supplement seasonal,

climatic and tidal rhythms ... Since places are always becoming, walking humans are one rhythmic constituent in a seething space pulsing with intersecting trajectories and temporalities.

(Edensor, 2014, p. 164)

Edensor's portrayal of pedestrian commutes, transportation timetables, daily routines, and seasonal cycles highlights the multiple "bundles, bouquets, garlands of rhythms" (Lefebvre, 2004, p. 20) that simultaneously mobilize and stabilize place. In other instances, however, Edensor emphasizes the discordant intersections of rhythm, as in the following description of a coach tour around the Ring of Kerry in Ireland:

[M]uch of the journey is experienced through the rhythms induced by cushioned, gentle motion, productive of a relaxed, somnolent state as the vehicle smoothly glides over straight, well-surfaced roads, with the regular pulses of acceleration and mild braking. At other times, however, rougher roads jar passengers out of a relaxed state, and travelling bodies become uncomfortable, feel hungry, desire physical exercise or need to stretch.

(Edensor & Holloway, 2008, p. 496)

This kind of rhythmanalysis reveals differential qualities, speeds, and modalities of movement, such as the smooth and rough, fast and slow, or soothing and jarring rhythms of bodies and buses.

Gabriel Klaeger (2012) also uses rhythmanalysis in his ethnographic study of roadside entrepreneurs who sell bread along one of Ghana's busy arterial roads. As traffic on the Accra-Kumasi road becomes congested and slows down, the touts are able to weave through the vehicles to sell their bread to drivers and passengers. When the traffic begins to gather speed, the touts must run alongside the vans and cars to hawk their goods or complete a sale. As the traffic accelerates even more, however, and the touts can no longer keep pace, they return to their roadside perches and wait for the cars to slow down so that business can pick up again. The touts' mobile lifeworlds are shaped by a variety of tempos and temporalities: the differential speeds of slow and then fast traffic; the fleeting interactions between buyers and sellers; the freshness of the bread; the touts' efforts to synchronize their running to keep up with the vehicles; and moments of idleness and inactivity. Klaeger describes these alternating rhythms as "run, rush, relax" (p. 545).

Evident in Klaeger's and Edensor's accounts of everyday mobilities are instances of harmonizing bodily movement with the speeding up or slowing down of vehicular movement as well as examples of clashing rhythms and temporal disruptions. Indeed, one of the aspects of rhythmanalysis that Edensor underscores in his work is "the mix of social ordering and disordering through which spatio-temporal patterns are laid down" (p. 2). For example, Cresswell (2010) describes how the provocative rhythms of some forms of music, such as jazz, punk, and rave, disrupted the social order. And yet in other contexts, such as "motion studies" used in early twentieth-century factories or "gait analysis" techniques deployed in airports today, rhythms have also been used to discipline workers and surveil travellers. In such distinctions between "strange" and "curious" rhythms, on the one hand, and implicitly "correct and regular movements," on the other, Cresswell identifies an "aesthetics of correct mobility that mixes with a politics of mobility" (Cresswell, 2010, p. 24).

Edensor (2014) introduces the concepts of "eurhythmia" and "arrhythmia" to explore the way rhythms can discipline and constrain or liberate and resist. He describes eurhythmia as movements that are synchronized with the dominant routines and rhythmic conventions of life. Conradson's retreat houses, discussed previously, offer one example of eurhythmia. At the retreat houses, environmental cues and bodily practice are choreographed to accord with stillness as a sense of centering attention to the "here" and "now." Likewise, Vannini's ferry passengers express a desire to move "in time," to regulate their daily and bodily rhythms to the slower temporal regimes of island life. Unlike the regulated harmonization of eurhythmia, arrhythmia is a rejection of structured temporalities. The public art projects described earlier are an example of such resistance. As Cocker notes, these projects insert stillness as a deliberate disruption to the predictable and habitual flows of urban life. Arrhythmia is not always deliberate, however. It can emerge in spontaneous interruptions to the predictable flow of the day, such as the volcanic eruption that halted air traffic (Jensen, 2011), blisters that disrupt a walk (Edensor, 2010b), traffic jams and accidents that unravel planned schedules (Edensor, 2011b), or the tempo rubato of waiting (Vannini, 2011). Arrhythmia also describes those discordant moments when individual or embodied rhythms fail to align with imposed rhythms (Edensor, 2011b, p. 192). It is not difficult to think of such instances: being roused from a deep sleep by the alarm clock, curious young children hurried along by impatient parents, feeling overwhelmed by the frantic pace of the city, or jet lag.

What Edensor's description of everyday rhythms suggests, however, is that places and people are often simultaneously eurhythmic and arrhythmic. For example, in his analysis of the pleasures and pains of commuting, he writes that "a tension emerges between the pleasures and irritation of predictability, and the delights and frustrations of disruption and improvisation" (2011b, p. 194). Like Vannini's respondents who expressed a love/hate relationship with the ferries, Edensor's commuters alternate between pleasant and frustrating experiences of pace (and see Urry, 2000). Time can drag or it can fly by; it can be boring or full. Rhythm is not an objective or inherent quality of pace or place, but rather a multiple and relational effect of embodied practices and intersubjective habits in the moment.

Given its focus on the polyrhythmic, relational, and contingent qualities of everyday temporalities, rhythmanalysis is a useful lens through which to consider slowness. First, slowness is part of a complex temporal choreography of contemporary mobility that includes a mash-up of various rhythms and tempos. Second, slowness is not an empirical measure of distance over time, but rather a relational quality. Lefebvre argues that a "rhythm is only slow or fast in relation to other rhythms with which it finds itself associated in a more or less vast unity" (Lefebvre, 2004, p. 89). For example, when tourists first began to travel by train in the nineteenth century, they considered themselves to be moving through the landscape at extraordinary speed. That is until commercial air travel made trains seem slow by comparison (see Kern, 1983; Urry, 2000). By insisting "on the relativity of rhythms," Lefebvre (2004, p. 89) highlights the fact that the pace of life in a particular place is not an objective reality, but rather is performed and made meaningful precisely through its juxtaposition with other mobilities.

It is not just pace that is relational, but also the meanings we attach to pace. Certain values come to be associated with stillness, slowness or speed depending on political, institutional, or social contexts. In their historical accounts of walking and tramping, John Urry (2000) and Tim Cresswell (2001, 2006) outline the contested discourses that framed strolling. Before the late eighteenth century in Europe, walking was seen as a sign of poverty or indigence. In the United States, as well, it was deemed to be an inappropriate and even illegal mode of travel. As Cresswell notes, in the late nineteenth century and early twentieth century, some places in the United States instituted "tramp laws" that sought to curb the mobilities of unemployed men, which were seen as threatening the social order, by criminalizing the act of roving from place to place or strolling the country (Cresswell, 2006, pp. 159–160). Later, however, once walking became a voluntary and leisurely practice among the upper classes, it took on more positive associations with freedom, education, and connection to nature (Urry, 2000, p. 51).

As the history of walking shows, neither the embodied experiences of slowness nor the meanings associated with various rhythms and speeds are absolute, rather they are relationally emergent. This is an important point to keep in mind when thinking about slow tourism or slow lifestyles, because it reminds us to interrogate the social structures that produce slowness and its meanings in the first place. When we talk about what it means to "go slow," we are venturing into a highly contested terrain that, in all likelihood, reveals more about social hierarchies and our own position in those hierarchies than it reveals about slowness itself.

The politics of pace

Mobilities scholars have been quite effective at bringing our attention to what Doreen Massey (1994) calls the "power geometries" of mobility. Within the mobilities literature, it is common knowledge that the mobility of some people is premised on the immobility of others. But the power geometry does not just diagram mobility versus immobility. It can also be used to interrogate the unequal conditions under which some people move, are moved, stay home, or are locked in place (see Hannam et al., 2006). Feminist theorists, cultural geographers and immigration scholars, in particular, have gone to great lengths to remind us that not everyone is on the road in the same way, nor is the world speeding up for everyone. For example, the accelerated modern world is actually full of friction, slow-downs and barriers for many immigrants, asylum seekers, and refugees. When we begin to examine these more nuanced conditions of mobility and immobility, it becomes clear that pace is a significant differentiating factor.

As Cresswell (2010, p. 21) argues, "speeds, slownesses and immobilities are all related in ways that are thoroughly infused with power." The frictionless traveling rhythms of some travelers frequently rely on the slowing down, stilling, or social exclusion of others. Likewise, the leisurely slowness of some travelers may depend on the efficient labor or enforced deceleration of others. Furthermore, the valorization of some people's speed or slowness as "free," "civilized" or "sustainable" is often accompanied by the disparagement of other people's speed or slowness or stillness as "irresponsible," "banal," or "primitive." In other words, some people's slowness "counts," and counts differently than other people's slowness. And this often boils down to the fact that "to travel slowly is a necessity for some people, in some circumstances, but it is also a choice for other people in other circumstances" (Vannini, 2012, p. 249).

Depending on where someone lands on the power geometry, stillness can easily slip into stuckness. Deceleration is not always deliberate. And the metaphor of waiting as tempo rubato or incarceration (Vannini, 2012) may hit far too close to home. Let's take waiting as an example. Despite efforts to recuperate a sense of dynamism to waiting, which I described earlier, scholars have argued that waiting can be a form of symbolic violence that oppresses those who already suffer from poverty and social marginalization (Harvey, 2011; Auyero, 2012). Although a seemingly banal and unremarkable part of everyday life, waiting exerts a powerful force in the lives of poor people who are most susceptible to its particular forms of subjugation and social control. As Gillian Fuller argues, "queues are a type of control architecture" (2014, p. 206). And this control is as much discursive as it is spatial or temporal. Fuller notes that "queues have a decided moral dimension," which is especially evident in public debates over immigration and border control. Calling an asylum seeker or an immigrant from the global South "a 'queue-jumper' is a form of vilification, justifying all kinds of cruel nonsense [such as] interment in offshore detention centres" (Fuller, 2014, p. 207). Patience may be a virtue, but this also means that "jumping the queue" is "indexical with impoverished moral values and antisocial civil disobedience" (2014, p. 206).

A themed issue of *Gender, Place and Culture*, edited by Deirdre Conlon (2011), brings a feminist perspective to waiting through studies of migrants from the Global South who, lacking permanent legal status, find themselves suspended in bureaucratic queues, stuck in refugee camps, and detained in political and geographical limbo. In their article on displaced people living in refugee camps, Jennifer Hyndman and Wenona Giles (2011) found that waiting is gendered in specific ways. For example, refugees who remain in the camps are feminized as passive, innocent, and therefore deserving of help, whereas those who move on are coded via masculinist assumptions as self-serving subjects who pose a threat to security. Another case focuses on asylum-seekers from Afghanistan who, in 2001, were intercepted en route to Australia and towed to the island of Lombok, Indonesia, where they were detained until 2008. In her analysis of this incident, Alison Mountz (2011) contends that the liminality of waiting gets mapped onto spatial ambiguities that reflect larger geopolitical inequalities. In this case, Australia "offshored" its responsibilities to accept the asylum-seekers as "part of a global trend to contract out asylum and detention to poorer countries" (Mountz, 2011, p. 384). Their precarious legal and political status, coupled with uneven power relations between wealthier and poorer nations, makes the asylum seekers more vulnerable to waiting, and to a particularly pernicious form of waiting that amounts to never-ending imprisonment (Mountz, 2011, p. 388). Nevertheless, waiting is ambivalent. Here, the dynamics of everyday life – "sickness, marriage, childbirth" (Mountz, 2011, p. 390) – unfold even amidst perpetual incarceration. So, too, do strategies for survival and attention. Mountz describes the asylum seekers' efforts to secure legal representation and bring their plight to public attention, highlighting in the process the possibilities for activism and political agency that open up in these liminal spaces of waiting.

Like waiting, slowness is morally coded along the axes of gender, race, class and nationality, for example by ascribing value to relatively wealthy tourists from the global North choosing a slow tourism experience that, for the poor residents of the global South, is a fact of life. In his critique of the Slow Food and Slow Culture movements, Cresswell (2010) points out that it is usually only members of the elite class who have the time and resources to be slow by choice. Indeed, slower forms of tourism – from canal boating to walking vacations to yoga retreats – have become an increasingly popular way for relatively wealthy tourists to escape the frantic speed of modern life (see Dickinson & Lumsdon, 2010; Fullagar, Markwell, & Wilson, 2012). But is the potential for slow tourism to contribute to the "good life" limited only to those who can afford it?

Zygmunt Bauman's (1998) distinction between "tourists" and "vagabonds" offers a useful framework for thinking about the politics of pace and the power of choice. Both tourists and vagabonds are on the move, but under vastly different conditions. Tourists travel for fun; vagabonds because they have no other choice. Tourists have the cultural and financial resources to travel slowly if they want to, or quickly if they so desire. Vagabonds have little say over the speeds at which they move. As Vannini reminds us, "most of the world's seven billion passengers are more prone to experience, say, slow inter-city bus travel than jet speed" (Vannini, 2014, p. 117). Furthermore, while the tourist's slow mobility gets coded as eco-friendly or ethical or authentic, the vagabond's slowness gets coded as banal. The slow travel of the vagabond is not the kind we find featured in glossy travel magazines.

Travel writer Carl Hoffman (2010) presents precisely this paradox in *The Lunatic Express*, a memoir that chronicles his five-month journey on the world's most dangerous – and, not coincidentally, slowest – transportation. Hoffman describes ferries in Indonesia, buses in South America, and trains in India that take days to travel the distance an airplane could cover in mere hours. Whereas middle-class tourists pay more to go slower, Hoffman's fellow passengers have little choice in the matter. With safe flights and regulated railways out of reach for most of the world's travelers, the slow ferry or bus is the only option. Unlike eco-conscious travelers from the Global North, these passengers, among the poorest people in the world, are not rejecting a hegemony of materialism and speed; they are just trapped on the other side of it. If slow tourism is to achieve the goals of sustainability attached to it by tourists and researchers alike, we must not romanticize slowness, but politicize it. We must examine slow tourism and slow lifestyles as an opportunity to further develop a politics of pace that underscores the ways in which the risks and pleasures of slow travel are unequally distributed.

Conclusion

As we have seen throughout this chapter, the slow mobilities implicit in acts of stillness, waiting, deceleration, and the rhythms of everyday life afford something more than mere transportation. More than an objective measure of distance divided by time, pace is a discursive, relational, and political construct that can be interrogated to reveal deeper assumptions about who and what matters in this world. As mobilities scholars work their way through the temporal qualities of travel, they propel our understanding of what slowness it is, what it does, and where it takes us.

We can distill several insights from this discussion. First, we have seen that pace is multiple and relational. There is not just one form of stillness or one way to decelerate. Instead, we find plural stillnesses and manifold ways of being or going slow. Rhythmanalysis, especially, emphasizes the extent to which our daily lives are choreographed around constellations of fast and slow rhythms. Furthermore, pace is relational, but not just in terms of measuring one speed as slower or faster than another. The meanings we ascribe to pace are also relational, contingent on the contexts in which people travel. Whether fast is seen as a valuable attribute of the productive citizen or slow is seen as a more centered or sustainable mode of travel has less to do with speed itself, and more to do with the way experiences and representations of pace are shaped by race, class, gender, and nationality.

Second, ethnographic accounts of stillness, waiting, deceleration, and rhythm show us that pace is entwined with attention. We have seen how stillness can center attention or how waiting can attune us to the self and the environment. While the studies outlined here bring out rich details about attention and reflexivity, the relationship between pace and attention requires additional theoretical interrogation. Related to this is a third insight: pace is a way of being in the world that is both subjective and externally imposed. When our interior and external pulses march to the same drumbeat, we experience a sense of synchronicity or flow. When they don't, we experience arrhythmia. In both cases, focusing on pace uncovers deeper questions about discipline, resistance, order, and disorder. Rhythm can habitually reproduce the social order, or it can trouble it. Slowing down lets us see how social arrangements are put together. Like my experience of seeing the rough asphalt and uneven margin lines while stopped on the highway, slowing down can be an opportunity to see the seams and sutures that hold together a socially constructed world. In fact, some activists and artists deliberately deploy this quality of slowness and stillness to disrupt the habitual ticking-over of daily life and remind us of other possibilities. Waiting may be "part of the fabric of everyday life" (Bissell, 2007, p. 281), but it also promises (or threatens) to disrupt our ontological comfort by puncturing the thrall of constant mobility. As Bissell observes, waiting is "alive with the potential of being other than this" (p. 277).

In light of these insights, we might conclude that what we "travel for" is not necessarily to arrive at a particular destination, but to be on the road and in the world in a particular way. It is a cliché, of course, that the journey is the destination, but that seems to be the point. Or perhaps we should say that pace is the destination. What matters is not how fast or how slow we travel, but how we orient ourselves within the complex temporal landscapes of travel, and how we harness pace as a way of making sense of ourselves, of our travel companions, and of the world.

Note

1   Marc Augé (1995) has written about motorways and motels and airports as non-places; but they are only non-places to those just passing through. For people who live, work and inhabit these places, gas stations, highways, motels, and the like are rich anthropological worlds. Perhaps Augé ascribes to place qualities that are actually produced by pace. See critiques of Augé, and vignettes similar to my own experience on the highway, in Edensor (2003) and Merriman (2004).

References

Appadurai, A. (1990). Disjuncture and difference in the global cultural economy. *Theory, Culture & Society*, 7(2–3), 295–301.

Augé, M. (1995). *Non-places: An introduction to supermodernity*. London, UK: Verso.

Auyero, J. (2012). *Patients of the state: The politics of waiting in Argentina*. Durham, NC: Duke University Press.

Bauman, Z. (1998). *Globalization: The human consequences*. New York, NY: Columbia University Press.

Bauman, Z. (2000). *Liquid modernity*. Cambridge, UK: Polity Press.

Birtchnell, T., & Büscher, M. (2011). Stranded: An eruption of disruption. *Mobilities*, 6(1), 1–9.

Bissell, D. (2007). Animating suspension: Waiting for mobilities. *Mobilities*, 2(2), 277–298.

Bissell, D., & Fuller, G. (2011). Stillness unbound. In D. Bissel & G. Fuller (Eds.), *Stillness in a mobile world* (pp. 1–17). London, UK: Routledge.

Castells, M. (1996). *The rise of the network society*. Cambridge, MA: Blackwell.

Cocker, E. (2011). Performing stillness: Community in waiting. In D. Bissel & G. Fuller (Eds.), *Stillness in a mobile world* (pp. 87–106). London, UK: Routledge.

Conlon, D. (2011). Waiting: Feminist perspectives on the spacings/timings of migrant (im)mobility. *Gender, Place and Culture, 18*(3), 353–360.

Conradson, D. (2011). The orchestration of feeling: Stillness, spirituality and places of retreat. In D. Bissel & G. Fuller (Eds.), *Stillness in a mobile world* (pp. 71–86). London: Routledge.

Crang, M. (2001). Rhythms of the city: Temporalised space and motion. In J. May & N. Thrift (Eds.), *Timespace: Geographies of temporality* (pp. 187–208). London: Routledge.

Cresswell, T. (2001). *The tramp in America*. London: Reaktion.

Cresswell, T. (2006). *On the move: mobility in the modern Western world*. London: Routledge.

Cresswell, T. (2010). Towards a politics of mobility. *Environment and Planning D: Society and Space, 28*(1), 17–31.

Cresswell, T. (2012). Mobilities II: Still. *Progress in Human Geography, 36*(5), 645–653.

de Certeau, M. (1984). *The practice of everyday life*. Berkeley and Los Angeles: University of California Press.

Dickinson, J., & Lumsdon, L. (2010). *Slow travel and tourism*. Oxon: Earthscan.

Edensor, T. (2003). Defamiliarizing the mundane roadscape. *Space and Culture, 6*(2), 151–168.

Edensor, T. (Ed.). (2010a). *Geographies of rhythm: Nature, place, mobilities and bodies*. Aldershot: Ashgate.

Edensor, T. (2010b). Walking in rhythms: Place, regulation, style and the flow of experience. *Visual Studies, 25*(1), 69–79.

Edensor, T. (2011a). The rhythms of Tourism. In C. Minca & T. Oakes (Eds.), *Real tourism: Practice, care, and politics in contemporary travel culture* (pp. 54–71). London: Routledge.

Edensor, T. (2011b). Commuter: Mobility, rhythm and commuting. In T. Cresswll & P. Merriman (Eds.), *Geographies of mobilities: Practices, spaces, subjects* (pp. 189–204). Aldershot: Ashgate.

Edensor, T. (2014). Rhythm and arrhythmia. In P. Adey, D. Bissell, K. Hannam, P. Merriman, & M. Sheller (Eds.), *The Routledge handbook of mobilities* (pp. 163–171). London & New York: Routledge.

Edensor, T., & Holloway, J. (2008). Rhythmanalysing the coach tour: The ring of Kerry, Ireland. *Transactions of the Institute of British Geographers, 33*(4), 483–501.

Ehrenreich, B. (2001). *Nickel and dimed: On (not) getting by in America*. New York, NY: Henry Holt.

Fullagar, S., Markwell, K., & Wilson, E. (Eds.). (2012). *Slow tourism: Experiences and mobilities*. Bristol: Channel View Publications.

Fuller, G. (2014). Queue. In P. Adey, D. Bissel, K. Hannam, P. Merriman, & M. Sheller (Eds.), *The Routledge handbook of mobilities* (pp. 205–213). London & New York: Routledge.

Germann Molz, J. (2009). Representing pace in tourism mobilities: Staycations, slow travel and "The Amazing Race." *Journal of Tourism and Cultural Change, 7*(4), 270–286.

Germann Molz, J. (2010). Performing global geographies: time, space, place and pace in narratives of round-the-world travel. *Tourism Geographies, 12*(3), 329–348.

Gleick, J. (1999). *Faster: The acceleration of just about everything*. New York, NY: Pantheon.

Hannam, K., Sheller, M., & Urry, J. (2006). Mobilities, immobilities and moorings. *Mobilities, 1*(1), 1–22.

Harvey, D. (1990). *The condition of postmodernity.* Cambridge, MA: Blackwell.

Harvey, D. C. (2011). Comments on Javier Auyero's Chuck and Pierre at the welfare office. *Sociological Forum, 26*(1), 183–184.

Hassan, R. (2009). *Empires of speed.* Leiden: Brill.

Hoffman, C. (2010). *The lunatic express.* New York, NY: Broadway Books.

Hyndman, J., & Giles, W. (2011). Waiting for what? The feminization of asylum in protracted situations. *Gender, Place and Culture, 18*(3), 361–379.

Jain, J., & Lyons, G. (2008). The gift of travel time. *Journal of Transport Geography, 16*(1), 81–89.

Jensen, O. (2011). Emotional eruptions, volcanic activity and global mobilities – Afield account from a European in the US during the eruption of Eyjafjallajökull. *Mobilities, 6*(1), 67–75.

Kern, S. (1983). *The culture of time and space: 1880–1918.* Cambridge, MA: Harvard University Press.

Kincaid, J. (1988). *A small place.* New York, NY: Farrar, Straus and Giroux.

Klaeger, G. (2012). Rush and relax: The rhythms and speeds of touting perishable products on a Ghanaian roadside. *Mobilities, 7*(4), 537–554.

Larsen, J., Urry, J., & Axhausen, K. (2006). *Mobilities, networks, geographies.* Aldershot: Ashgate.

Lefebvre, H. (2004). *Rhythmanalysis: Space, time, and everyday life* (S. Elden & G. Moore, Trans.). London: Continuum.

Lyons, G., & Urry, J. (2005). Travel time use in the information age. *Transportation Research Part A, 39*, 257–276.

Massey, D. (1994). *Space, place and gender.* Cambridge: Polity.

Merriman, P. (2004). Driving places: Marc Augé, non-places, and the geographies of England's M1 motorway. *Theory, Culture & Society, 21*(4–5), 145–167.

Mountz, A. (2011). Where asylum-seekers wait: Feminist counter-topographies of sites between states. *Gender, Place and Culture, 18*(3), 381–399.

Shaw, J. (2001). "Winning territory": Changing place to change pace. In J. May & N. Thrift (Eds.), *Timespace: Geographies of temporality* (pp. 120–231). London: Routledge.

Shields, R. (1991). *Places on the margin: Alternative geographies of modernity.* London: Routledge.

Urry, J. (2000). *Sociology beyond societies.* London: Routledge.

Urry, J. (2008). *Mobilities.* Cambridge: Polity.

Vannini, P. (2002). Waiting dynamics: Bergson, Virilio, Deleuze, and the experience of global times. *Journal of Mundane Behavior, 3*(2), 193–208.

Vannini, P. (2011). Mind the gap: The tempo rubato of dwelling in lineups. *Mobilities, 6*(2), 273–299.

Vannini, P. (2012). In time, out of time: Rhythmanalyzing ferry mobilities. *Time & Society, 21*(2), 241–269.

Vannini, P. (2014). Slowness and deceleration, In P. Adey, D. Bissell, K. Hannam, P. Merriman, & M. Sheller (Eds.), *The Routledge handbook of mobilities* (pp. 116–124). London & New York: Routledge.

Virilio, P. (2000). *Polar inertia.* London: Sage.

3 Slow tourism

A theoretical framework

Viviana Calzati and Paola de Salvo

Introduction

Since the 1970s, the global tourism industry has been characterized by numerous changes. These include globalization, the diffusion of new information technologies and changes in consumer preferences. With reference to this latter aspect, the principal transformations have occurred in lifestyle expectations and in the buying habits of tourists. A return to nature and a renewed awareness of the environment, the rediscovery of local identity, and the search for both physical and psychological well-being have resulted in a crisis in mass tourism. Replacing it has been the de-standardization of consumer choices and the confirmation of what has been defined as the post-tourism era (Urry, 1990). New tourism has become an active experience where many tourists rediscover the spiritual and cultural dimensions of travel, fed by an increasing demand for variety, quality and emotional experience. This practice of alternative tourism is also found in the expression of critical consumerism, where the responsible consumer/tourist is the expression of the typology of consumer described as a "producer consumer" (Codeluppi & Paltrinieri, 2007).

In this light, "consumers appear to be the co-creators of social value and actively participate in creation of a social ideal" (Paltrinieri, 2008, p. 102). The tourist no longer accepts being the passive recipient of decisions made by others but transforms him or herself into an active protagonist in their own experience. Savoja (2009) proposes some "responsible" actions that tourists can take, for example, within the model of stakeholder responsibility, particularly in the limitation of consumption and the diffusion of feedback in relation to the tourist experience undertaken.

The demand for quality in the tourist's experience is driven be the desire for reacquiring natural rhythms and a rediscovering local communities and territories. In this reinvented context, slowness has become one positive way of performing tourism (Savoja, 2011). Here slowness as a tourism product emerges, increasingly influenced by the tourist's heightened sense of responsibility towards the environment and the search for a meaningful experience. The growing demand for quality is the result of a transformation of industrialized societies where quality becomes a fundamental element of post-modern society, as has already occurred with reference to the environment. Post-modern tourism, articulated in its slow form, assumes importance in the realm of the conscience, where awareness of self and others become foremost in a revised relationship between guest, host and visited locations.

This chapter will highlight how sustainability, territory, well-being, quality of life, experience and consumption are essential aspects of slow tourism. The work examines existing academic work on slow tourism and from them proposes three alternative theoretical paradigms. These, in turn, offer a framework for future research on the subject. The three proposed paradigms are (a) experience – slow tourism and consumption; (b) sustainability – slow tourism and territory; and (c) well-being – slow tourism and quality of life.

Tourism's relationship with slowness

The new cultural and behavioral model of "slowness" implies a fundamental change in the concept of the consumption of goods and services as part of a lifestyle that is characterized by commitment, through a strong sense of responsibility and the search for well-being in both home and work. The slow philosophy should not be interpreted as a temporary phenomenon, a fashion or an innovative touristic product, but rather as a life philosophy and a worldwide social movement that in recent years has characterized many social-economic elements in local communities (Honoré, 2004). Slowness does not merely refer to stillness (Bissell & Fuller, 2011) but instead creates places, rhythms and social and experiential realities for daily life, offering alternatives to those of the fast and advanced manifestations of capitalistic society (Osbaldiston, 2013). Several authors have demonstrated that within Western society many people have started to exchange materialistic values in favor of a new lifestyle characterized by more time, less stress and a better equilibrium in daily life (Hamilton, 2004). In fact, "the beauty of the slow devolution is the counter-punch it could, in the long term, inflict on the culture of speed" (Osbaldiston, 2013, p. 6). In some literature however, there is skepticism in considering slowness as an actually manifested way of living (Lindholm & Lie, 2013), while others describe slowness as having the potential to confront the problems of contemporary life (Parkins & Craig, 2006; Honorè, 2004). Still others underline the idea of slowness as an ideal type, but suggest the existence of different lifestyles and different social relationships make it difficult to define (Vannini, 2014).

The Slow philosophy also brings with it the opportunity to construct a slow society, or rather, a society which gives greater attention to quality of life, ethical responsibilities and the value of solidarity between diverse social groups. The subject of slowness holds promise for different lifestyle models, intelligent consumerism and a new concept of wellness that could lead to the affirmation of a new humanism for a more supportive society (de Salvo, 2011). This concept presumes, however, that responsibility and awareness become collective ideals, creating real, significant relationships between people, culture, work, food and new touristic practices. To this end, the future challenge is to attempt to give a concrete response to the question already indicated by Honoré (2004, p. 14) "When will the many personal acts of deceleration occurring across the world reach critical mass? When will the slow movement turn into a slow revolution?"

Tourism is characterized by collective consumption, and the promise of slow tourism is that slow use on the part of some allows the same form of consumption by others, so as to activate a virtuous cycle of responsible touristic behavior. Slow tourism is aimed to contrast with the negative externalities of mass tourism, which is characterized by the extensive structural and infrastructural development of a territory based principally on economic interests, with an inadequate consideration of environmental and social factors. This form of tourism is also characterized by seasonality and the absence of a sharing (redistribution) of the socioeconomic benefits derived from the tourism itself (Weaver, 2000). Hence, in the economy of the intangible, slow tourism results in attributing value to the genius loci, the spirit of place, establishing active relationships with the local community, promoting slower rhythms and consumption of the touristic product with a vision of actual, not presumed, sustainability (Hall, 2009, 2010).

Within the academic literature, no clear and unequivocal definition of slow tourism exists even though some writers have attempted to present a definition of the phenomenon through the identification of various principles, ideas and behaviors (Babou & Callot, 2009; Blanco, 2011; Conway & Timms, 2010; Dickinson & Lumsdon, 2010; Dickinson, Robbins, & Lumsdon, 2010; Lumsdon & McGrath, 2011; Matos, 2004; Savoja, 2011). Conway and Timms (2010) connect slow tourism to sustainable development of Campbell (1996) in which the noted triangle of sustainability identifies three elements: environment (the protection of environmental resources), economy (the conditions for stable economic growth and efficiency in the allocation and use of resources) and equity (social justice to the end of a fair distribution of income and an equality of social and economic opportunity and outcome). In a recent article, the same authors (2012) maintain that the objectives established for their model of slow tourism are based on alternative forms to mass tourism, for example eco-tourism, responsible tourism and community tourism which are all initiatives which develop from local resources and thus have sustainability in their original approach.

Matos (2004) also affirms that sustainable development, intended as economic, environmental and social-economic inclusive, should be perceived as a pillar of slow tourism. Savoja (2011) investigates the relationship that connects slow tourism with the question of sustainability by introducing "necessary capacity," in contrast to the noted concept of "carrying capacity" in which slow tourism results as being sustainable but unsatisfying for the tourist. Lumsdon and McGrath (2011), in laying out a conceptual framework for the slow traveler, identify four distinct cornerstones: slowness and the value of time, the destination and on-location activities, transport and the travel experience, and environmental ethics. The authors individualize in slow travel a voyage mentality, characterized by slow pace and an environmentally aware experience that involves an alternative concept of a tour. The slow tourist is defined as a hard or a soft traveler based on the importance given to environmental responsibility and sensitivity, which influences the preparation and planning of a voyage; these typologies do not constitute two distinct characteristics but rather two extremes of a continuum (Dickinson et al., 2010, 2011).

Gardner (2009) emphasizes that slow tourism represents the frame of mind of the traveler who spends the time necessary to discover a landscape, interact with the people and to consider transport not as a simple means of arriving at a destination but as an opportunity for experience. Babou and Callot (2009) define slow tourism as the perfect convergence of two fundamental resources of the tourism industry: space and time. In this way, a new bond between tourism and slowness requires a redefining of the procedures and habits of the actual tourists, who see themselves as increasingly influenced by a new sense of the environmental responsibility. They prefer activities, destinations and means of transport, which allow them to limit the impact of their journey on society and on the environment (Bobou & Callot, 2009).

In contrast to the external motivations for slow tourism, Nocifora (2011) suggests the practice of slow tourism is characterized by an attempt to give an answer to the needs that characterize contemporary life. These include the need to find psychological and physical well-being through a form of tourism that offers a relaxed pace; to get to know/to live in/to visit ever new locations through the construction of authentic relationships and to make the most of local spaces. The UNWTO (2012, p. 24) focuses on the exchange relationship between host and guest: "Slow tourism allows a different set of exchanges and interactions than those available in the hurried contexts of mainstream tourism, with economic benefits to the host and cultural benefits to the tourist." Savoja (2011, p. 99) similarly defines slow tourism as "a form of tourism of quality if it satisfies all the stakeholders involved not only the tourists by means of an appeal to a form of selective limitation of consumption as occurs in all forms attributable to the idea of sustainable tourism." According to the author, slowness in tourism corresponds to a limitation in consumption, limitations which are evident in axiom to which the author makes reference that is "to do fewer things but do them well" (Savoia 2011, p. 100). The author maintains, therefore, that slow tourists are more capable of considering acceptable the imposed limits and are more convinced by the importance of seeking quality in their experience. Blanco (2011) argues slow tourism, as an alternative form of tourism to traditional tourism, requires responsibility from all parties in the tourist market to determine a significant change in both economical and cultural behavior. Heitmann et al. (2011) maintain the most significant principle in slow tourism is attributable to a different concept of vacation, which is no longer characterized by the number and quantity of experiences but is distinguished by living fewer experiences but of quality. Quality for Heitmann constitutes a form of tourism that respects local culture, history and environment and exercises socially responsible values of diversity and relationship between all the parties involved (tourists with other tourists and with the local community).

Using a more multifaceted approach, Zago (2012) considers the *experience* of slow tourism. In order to be defined as such, he argues the activity must satisfy contemporaneously six dimensions: relationship, authenticity, sustainability, time, slowness and emotion, which for the author constitute the castle model. Zago's work is based on the results of the European territorial trans-border cooperation project between Italy and Solvenia 2007–2013, "Slow Tourism." The project established a network of slow tourism operators and compiled a guideline document in which the six dimensions of slow tourism were transformed in defined criteria for the operators who decided to participate in the network. In contrast with other purely theoretical approaches, Zago (2012) attempts to make the six dimensions of slow tourism operative factors, clearly stating for each dimension the general requisitions required of operators who offer slow services.

The theoretical contributions summarized here highlight various attempts to establish a conceptual framework of the phenomenon of slow tourism, presenting common recurring conceptual elements though not without factors of difference. The three principal dimensions cited by researchers are environmental sustainability, modality and experience. Table 3.1 summarizes these contributions.

Table 3.1 Dimensions of slow tourism based on a review of the literature

Dimensions	Literature
Sustainability/environment	Blanco (2011); Babou and Callot (2009); Conway and Timms (2010, 2012); Dickinson and Lumsdon (2010); Lumsdon and Mcgrath (2011); Matos (2004); Savoja (2011); UNWTO (2012)
Modality	Babou and Callot (2009); Lumsdon and Mcgrath (2011)
Experience	Gardner (2009); Heitmann et al. (2011); Lumsdon and Mcgrath (2011); Nocifora (2011); Zago (2012)

Source: Authors.

Slow tourism: a theoretical framework

The previous section outlines the various theoretical approaches researchers have proposed. From them we have organized three paradigms that may frame future research projects into the phenomenon of slow tourism. The authors identify in the *experience* in relation to pace and in the *consumption* and exchange in relation to responsibility as the central axis to slow tourism. This constitutes the first paradigm proposed. In contrast, *territory* (defining their more noted characteristics of slowness and quality) and *sustainability* (articulated in a multidimensional perspective) constitute the second of the paradigms. Sustainability, which includes social, cultural and ethical aspects indicating *quality of life* and *well-being*, represents the third paradigm. The paradigms formulated are (a) experience – slow tourism – consumerism; (b) sustainability – slow tourism – territory; and (c) well-being – slow tourism – quality of life.

Experience – slow tourism– consumerism

Some researchers place individual tourist experience, especially slowness and responsible (minimal) consumerism as fundamental to slow tourism. Immateriality appears to be a central aspect of post-modernity in which experiences have taken on a key role and leisure time increases and acquires a social and economic value. Studies of consumer behavior since the 1980s have generally highlighted the emergence of a hedonistic and experiential dimension in the consumption of goods and services (Holbrook & Hirschman, 1982). The importance of the symbolic significance of the consumption of goods and services creates new relationships between producers and consumers, and as a result, new ways of organizing the processes of distribution, which are analyzed based on the experiential economy (Pine & Gilmore, 1999).

Consumption here is densely packed with social and cultural significance; experience itself becomes an instrument for the observation and understanding of consumption. Pine and Gilmore (1999) define experiential economy as a new source of values and new market, considering it as a natural evolution of the process initiated with an economy based on commodities, as one of its own products and successively as an economy of services and finally as an economy of transformations. The experiences are defined as events which engage the individuals at a personal level; hence the solicitation of experiences is the result of a planned process which determine a "cultural pathway" capable of engaging in a significant way the potential beneficiaries of the "experiential solicitation."

It is commonly accepted that the touristic experience is an individual perception in an interactive and integrative context between various resources (Björk & Sfandla, 2009). The concept of experience has been studied for more than 40 years (Cohen, 1979), and recent studies (Ritchie, Wing Sun Tung, & Ritchie, 2011) have drawn attention to the theme of experience in touristic literature. The touristic experience is a subject that involves people, services and locations (Westwood, Morgan, & Pritchard, 2006). With reference to people, tourists are the ultimate creators of their personal experience, the experience being perceived as an interior, individual and subjective process. The service is always accompanied by an experience and the touristic experience is created in the course of the service (service processes) and in the interaction with the provider of the service, the other clients and all the stakeholders. Finally, with reference to locations, it is underlined that the touristic experience must be contextualized. Service experiences come about through the complex interactions between clients and society's offers and the processes of co-creation, in which the company offers a service-scape. Björk and Kauppinen-Räisänen (2014) explains the relationship between the touristic experience and life satisfaction, drawing attention to the interaction between the two aspects, both being highly influenced and integrated with the quality of life, with well-being and with happiness. Behind this affirmation is the consideration that tourism is one of the aspects of life that contributes to overall life satisfaction. Attention to the theme of touristic experience is the product of a transformation of the tourists who have become ever more responsible and ethical in their consumption. In fact, the tourist cannot accept being the passive terminal of the decisions of consumption made by others but has to transform themselves into an active protagonist of models of touristic fruition.

In this context, the slow tourist can be a responsible consumer in that they express the consumer type defined as a "producer consumer" (Codeluppi & Paltrinieri, 2007). This definition:

> [D]emonstrates the affirmation of a "productive" dimension of consumption, within which reside the categories of empowerment, creativity, awareness, participation, concurrence, which are not in contradiction with either the market dominance or with the potential structure of the supply. In this light, the consumer emerges as a co-creator of social value and participates actively in the production of social conscience.
>
> (Paltrinieri, 2008, p. 102)

In fact, the affirmation of the practice of critical consumption has permitted the visibility of the social significance of consumption and of goods (Leonini & Sassatelli, 2008), bringing with it heterogeneous practices that propose alternative ways of life. "Alternative consumption is social (in that it tends to urge a widespread practice) and ethically motivated" (Clancy, 2014, p. 59). The affects of the practice of critical consumption are ascribable at two levels, one subjective and one systematic. The first involves the consumer's expectations and satisfactions while systematic effects involve the culture of consumption as well as production and on through to political participation which are dimensions not immediately attributable to the act due to the fact that they are part of organizational principles with an identity and series of networks with seemingly independent relationships (Sassatelli, 2008). Once identified, they expose that the experiential and symbolic aspects of consumption are inseparable. This is important for ethical tourism generally, but above all for slow tourism (Clancy, 2014). Slow tourism becomes a practice that consciously contrasts itself with the recurring consumerist bulimia, which finds in tourism privileged time, spaces and modality of expression. Savoja (2009) maintains that this responsibility (accountability) must be considered as a fundamental element of the touristic supply as well and not simply the result of a collection of behaviors of ethical consumerism. It outlines, therefore, the affirmation of the positive value of slow tourism as the characterization of a more ethical and responsible model of touristic fruition.

Sustainability – slow tourism – territory

Despite many decades of academic debate about sustainability, its implementation is difficult due to the inadequacies of the global community to address the environmental crisis and to adopt an economic development model that embraces sustainability. In fact, to talk of sustainability requires consideration of the relationship between economic growth and development and the continued availability of resources. In the course of the debate about sustainability as it is related to global tourism, at the beginning of the 1990s five principal criteria for sustainable tourism were defined: economic, environmental and social responsibility of tourism as well as its responsibility towards the tourist (visitor satisfaction) and global justice and equity (Inskeep, 1991). Nevertheless, due to the differences and the multidimensionality of the concepts (Sharpley, 2000), no unequivocal definition of sustainability in tourism exists. As a result, the concept of sustainable tourism has at times been understood as being an ideology rather than an exact operative definition.

The postmodern evolution of consumption, with its focus on experience, constitutes part of the framework useful in understanding sustainable tourism, and defining new consumers identified as new tourists or responsible tourists. These new forms of tourism (slow tourism, ecotourism, responsible tourism, rural tourism, community-based tourism, pro-poor tourism etc.) should be directed to overcoming the difficulties in relation to the inadequate economic, social and environmental sustainability typical of mass tourism and promote contextually pro-environmental attitudes and behaviors which are responsible and ethical (Fennel, 2003; Savoja, 2009). Slow tourism is characterized by taking initiatives of development from the bottom up, thus instigating sustainability in the very foundation of their practices (Conway & Timms, 2012).

The change in the tourist behavior that characterizes slow tourism leads to the acquisition of individual awareness through a change in one's lifestyle: it is necessary to start from this characteristic if one wishes to understand the "silent" relationship that unites sustainability, responsibility and slow tourism. Slow tourism can therefore be connected to *sustainability* and the *quality of life* aspects of development as opposed to simply development as economic growth. This notion of growth has often been utilized as a synonym for "development" while, in reality, development is much a broader concept, involving cultural and ethical aspects which lead back directly to an amplification of the quality of life (Calzati, 2011; Layard, 2005; Stiglitz et al., 2009; Sen, 1999).

More recently the development as growth model has come under criticism, and in particular "degrowth" and "a-growth" have been established as alternative concepts to the paradigm of growth. Though lacking a uniform definition, degrowth goes further than the concept of sustainable development (Latouche, 2011; Bayon et al., 2010; Fournier, 2008), which sees economic growth compatible with environmental protection if done right. The objectives of degrowth may be summed up as the satisfaction of fundamental human needs guaranteeing an elevated quality of life and reducing to a sustainable level the impact on the global economy, while at the same time promoting a society based on quality rather than material abundance, co-operation rather than competition. Sustainable degrowth can therefore be defined as an equable *downscaling* of production and consumption that raises human well-being and improves ecological conditions at a local and at a global level, both in the short and the long term (Kallis, 2011; Schneider, Kallis, & Martinez-Alier, 2010). On the other hand, a-growth, an indifferent or agnostic approach to economic growth, considers the gross domestic product (GDP) an unreliable measurement of social well-being (Layard, 2005; van den Bergh & Kallis, 2012).

In this vision of development, the concept of degrowth is applied to tourism by Hall (2009), who identifies the possibility of slow consumption. This involves a reduction in the personal demand for travel and the preference towards local destinations so as to reduce the energy and environmental consumption associated with long transfers. This also implies the search for ecologically efficient production, the payment of a higher price for the quality of sustainability and the orientation towards a model of steady-state tourism, assuming that the exponential demand for travel generates significant damage and is therefore unsustainable. This approach identifies in slow tourism a form of avant-garde practice characterized as being ethical and responsible and capable of activating a new politics of consumption. Here the Slow Food movement acts as a significant model for slow tourism. Therefore, if for slowness we intend a responsible and conscious use of touristic resources in such a way as to achieve satisfaction, it is evident that there is a connection between slow tourism and the question of touristic sustainability and the characteristics of the territorial supply.

In fact, some territories more than others seem to be destined to slowness, offering a nonconformist tourism which is self directed and self motivated and difficult to standardize (Manella, this volume; Savoja, 2011). These territories, described as "slow," are characterized by attention for the environment and the landscape, a high quality of life, a little known historical and architectural patrimony of quality, a strong local identity, the presence of local produce and products of quality, a hospitable local community and finally an accommodation model where the structures are integrated into the local landscape (Calzati, 2011; Lanzani, 2005; Savoja, 2011). "Slow" territories with these qualities are able to set themselves up as locations that combine economic growth, social cohesion and environmental protection on a pathway capable of giving rise to innovative and realistic programs for tourist development, through the introduction of alternative forms of tourism.

In the face of a recognized distance between well-being and economic growth, some territories have attempted to embrace the elements of sustainability or even degrowth, orienting development towards themes that concern subjective well-being, the quality of life of the community, and highlighting the territory's particular identity (Beeton, 2006). In these territories local governments have implemented political and social initiatives that attempt to apply principles of sustainability or degrowth to the city/territory by orienting touristic development towards these principles. In these contexts "smart cities," "slow cities" and "transition towns" all represent these practices.

The first of these aspires to the paradigm of sustainable development while the other two are more orientated towards the principle of degrowth (Forni, 2013). In reference to smart cities there is not a convergence of a common definition of the phenomenon. In fact, the term "smart cities" is used with various different meanings and significance, not only in the published literature, but also in other contexts (Harrison et al., 2011). In general, the term "smart," in the last decade of discussions, has identified a digital city, a socially inclusive city, as well as, more extensively, referring to the city that guarantees a better quality of life for its residents, attracting advantages from the opportunities and knowledge that can be derived from the world of research, technological innovation and citizen engagement. Slow Cities emphasize to distinctive local characteristics in a context of globalization and attempts to improve the quality of life at a local level (Pink, 2008). The Slow City's program represents a practical model of alternative urban development, sensitive to the complex interdependence of economics, environmental protection and social equality (Mayer & Knox, 2006).

Lastly, the Transition town movement, based on the concepts of resilience and permaculture, is instrumental to the realization of a virtuous relationship between the city and its territorial and environmental patrimony (Hopkins, 2008). An important factor of interest in this experience is that the system of Transition acts at an intermediary level between personal actions and the actions of public politics – that is the actions of the community. The key to activating the Transitional model is communal operation. In fact, the ideas and the initiatives taken by transition come from the actual community and it is the community itself who manages them. Transitional initiatives represent the application of the principles of degrowth, in that they constitute a specific social-political attempt at a local level directed at experimental innovations with a practical application.

Slow tourism, here, is best understood as a tool within this larger paradigm of sustainability or degrowth. Slow tourism – a form of tourism characterized as being ethical and responsible, offering a field of endeavor which is capable of activating new political parameters for consumerism in a territory in which, according to some researchers (Costanza et al., 1991; Daly, 1996), would be able to create real sustainability. In these territories, slow tourism, rather than simply acting as a tool toward this model of development, actually reflects that model by embracing a multidimensional conceptualization of development that includes cultural, ethical and social aspects that bring with them a general betterment of the quality of life, both for the local community and for the tourists themselves.

Well-being – slow tourism – quality of life

The last paradigm analyzes the relationship between slow tourism and individualized well-being. This is distinctive from the previous section in that here the focus is on individual lifestyles rather than the health and status of communities or territories. Here, an intense debate has developed on the theme of well-being and the quality of life, which, apart from creating a new branch of the economics field ("happiness economics"), has also seen the participation of sociologists (Baumann, 2002; Veenhoven, 1991) and psychologists (Argyle, 1987; Kahneman & Tversky, 2000). Early on, the measurement of well-being and of quality of life were established by principally assessing objective indicators, including income, health and social status. More recently, numerous studies have demonstrated the importance of also identifying and quantifying *subjective* indicators of well-being and above all *perceived* well-being.

In fact, in recent years, the number of studies addressing life quality and the subjective perception of well-being has produced two different theoretical approaches. The first, attributable to the hedonic perspective, analyzes the dimension of pleasure, intended as personal well-being (Diener & Schwarz, 1999) and makes reference principally to emotional aspects and life satisfaction. The second, eudaimonic approach (Ryan & Deci, 2001), includes not only individual satisfaction but also the realization of development towards an integration with the surrounding environment. The term is often considered to be similar to "happiness," but the semantic field of reference is much broader, suggesting an interrelationship between individual and collective well-being, where individual happiness is realized in the realm of a social setting. In the definition of well-being, Sen (1992) emphasizes agency, indicating that the action is intended as intentional, conscious, self determined and responsible. Agency follows objectives that are relevant and significant for the individual, but in a wider perspective privilege the relationship between the individual and the social context, and the individual's values and the needs of other individuals. In this eudaimonic approach, well-being does not necessarily coincide with pleasure, but underlines the importance of the human capacity to achieve objectives relevant for the single entity and society at large.

The principal difficulty with research on well-being is the absence or weak connection between the subjective and the objective constraints (Kahn & Juster, 2002, p. 629). In particular, the aim to define subjective measurements has led research in different directions. Subjective well-being has often been rendered operative by an individual evaluation of satisfaction with reference to the quality of life overall or in some of its various aspects. Veenhoven (1991) uses the term "happiness" in the sense of life satisfaction, describing it as the degree in which an individual evaluates positively the overall quality of his or her life as a whole and furthermore underlines two aspects of happiness, the emotional and the cognitive. Nevertheless, concepts such as happiness, well-being and life satisfaction are often used interchangeably (Easterlin, 2004). Another synonym is the quality of life (QoL), which is a function of a person's life conditions. The QoL includes an economic dimension, aspects concerning social relationships, and health and environmental aspects. In the last 30 years, the observations and the description of the concept of QoL is generally attributed either to a perspective with reference to environmental or social or to a perspective of individual well-being. Initially, this perspective included personal values and the measurement of satisfaction, while more recently it become evident that the concept of QoL implies an integration of subjective and objective variables. As a result, researchers consider mainly objective indicators that take account of life events and broader life circumstances.

Some studies have examined the effects of touristic experiences on the psychological state of the tourist as well as considering the motivations and satisfactions investigated in earlier studies in this broader field (Pearce & Lee, 2005). New research has attempted to relate the behavior of the tourist to other spheres of life and to individual experiences and to explore in greater depth the consequences of touristic activity on the other people's lives (Uysal, Perdue, & Sirgy, 2012). While the personal advantages derived from tourism might be contestable, until recently few studies had examined the possible relationship between tourism and happiness, between subjective well-being and QoL and the factors that influence the relationship between tourism and QoL (Dolnicar et al., 2012). Studies on the positive effects of the activities carried out in one's leisure time have been widely documented (Godbey, 2009). The taking of a vacation correlates significantly to a rise in subjective well-being (Gilbert & Abdullah, 2004; McCabe et al., 2010), and is considered as an overall experience of long term relevance which determines positive attitudes towards life.

In view of these conclusions, stimulating and supporting slow tourism represents a possibility to improve people's well-being, coherent also with the recommendations that emerge from the Stigliz-Sen-Fitoussi report where, in the attempt to understand the various dimensions of social well-being, an evident relationship with leisure time emerges. In this way, slow tourism may be interpreted as a possibility for creating relational benefits, where the importance given to the factor of time is pertinent to the aim of creating interrelationships, giving attention to the issue of quality of life and promoting relationships based on respect for oneself and for others.

Conclusion

Slow living summons a sense of hospitality, ethical intercourse and social relationships that sustain the community and require a commitment of time (Parkins & Craig, 2006). In this context, Clancy (2014, p. 57) when comparing slow tourism with traditional tourism maintains that "slow tourism constitutes the antithesis of this system, valuing slowness of pace, enjoying the journey itself, and making connections with local practices and cultures." Applying the three paradigms proposed shows how slow tourism is not simply a touristic product analyzed in the premise of marketing or a momentary fashionable trend. For the researchers it is, in fact, a critical consumerist behavior attributable to an ethical tourism which, through various forms of responsibility, contributes on the one hand to a general slow living philosophy, and on the other to the acquisition of touristic consumption as having a central role in political and social participation. Individual responsibility and community sustainability come together in search for an innovative equilibrium between producer and the consumer and between territory and the tourist.

References

Argyle, M. (1987). *The psychology of happiness*. London, UK and New York, NY: Methuen.

Babou, I., & Callot, P. (2009), Slow tourism, slow (r)evolution? Nouvelles mobilities touristiques, *Cahier Espaces*, *100*(56), 48–54.

Baumann, Z. (2002). *La solitudine del cittadino globale*. Milan: Feltrinelli.

Bayon, D., Flipo F., & Schneider F. (2010). *La Décroissance. 10 questions pour comprendre et en de débatre*. Paris: La Découvert.

Beeton, S. (2006). *Community development through tourism*. Collingwood: Landlinks Press.

Bissell D., & Fuller, G. (2011). *Stillness in a mobile world*. New York, NY: Taylor and Francis.

Björk, P., & Kauppinen-Räisänen, H. (2014). Exploring the multi-dimensionality of travellers' culinary-gastronomic experiences. *Current Issues in Tourism*, *19*(2), 1260–1280. doi:10.1080/13683500.2013.868412

Björk, P., & Sfandla, C. (2009). A tripartite model of tourist experience. *Finnish Journal of Tourism Research*, *2*(5), 5–18.

Blanco, A. (2011). Una aproximacion al turismo slow. El turismo slow en las Cittaslow de Espana. *Investigaciones Turísticas*, *1*, 122–133.

Calzati, V. (2011). Territori lenti: Nuove traiettorie di sviluppo. In E. Nocifora, P. de Salvo, & V. Calzati, (Eds.), *Territori lenti e turismo di qualità, prospettive innovative per lo sviluppo di un turismo sostenibile* (pp. 62–72). Milan: FrancoAngeli.

Campbell, S. (1996). Green cities, growing cities, just cities? Urban planning and the contradictions of sustainable development. *Journal of the American Planning Association*, *62*(3), 296–312.

Clancy, M. (2014). Slow tourism: Ethics, aesthetics and consumptive values. In C. Weeden, and C. Boluk (Eds.), *Managing ethical consumption in tourism* (pp. 56–69). Abingdon: Routledge.

Codeluppi V., & Paltrinieri R. (a cura di) (2007). Il consumo come produzione. *Sociologia del lavoro e dei consumi*, n. 108. Milan: FrancoAngeli.

Cohen E. (1979). A phenomenology of tourist experiences. *Sociology*, *13*(2), 179–201.

Conway, D., & Timms, B. F. (2010). Re-branding alternative tourism in the Caribbean: The case for "slow tourism." *Tourism and Hospitality Research*, *10*(4), 329–344.

Conway, D., & Timms, B. F. (2012). Slow Tourism at the Caribbean's geographical margins, *Tourism Geographies*, *14*(3), 396–418.

Costanza, R., Daly H. E., & Bartholomew J. A. (1991). Goals, agenda and policy recommendations for ecological economics. In R. Costanza (Ed.), *Ecological economics: The science and management of sustainability* (pp. 1–20). New York, NY: Columbia University Press.

Daly, H. (1996). *Beyond growth: The economics of sustainable development*. Boston, MA: Beacon Press.

de Salvo, P. (2011). Cittàslow: Modello alternativo di sviluppo lento e sostenibile. In E. Nocifora, P. de Salvo, & V. Calzati (a cura di), *Territori lenti e turismo di qualità, prospettive innovative per lo sviluppo di un turismo sostenibile*. Milan: FrancoAngeli.

Dickinson, J. E., & Lumsdon, L. M. (2010). *Slow travel and tourism*. London: Earthscan.

Dickinson, J. E., Lumsdon, L. M., & Robbins D. (2011). Slow travel: Issues for tourism and climate change. *Journal of Sustainable Tourism*, *19*(3), 281–300.

Dickinson, J. E., Robbins, D., & Lumsdon, L. M. (2010). Holiday travel: Discourses and climate change. *Journal of Transport Geography*, *18*(3), 482–489.

Dolnicar, S., Yanamandram, V., & Cliff, K. (2012). The contribution of vacations to quality of life. *Annals of Tourism Research*, *39*(1), 59–83.

Easterlin, R. A. (2004). The economics of happiness. *Daedalus*, *133*(2), 26–33.

Fennel, D. (2003). *Ecotourism*. London: Routledge.

Forni, E. (2013). La città sostenibile. Oltre gli slogan. *Nuvole*, *46*, 1–13.

Fournier, V. (2008). Escaping from economy: The politics of degrowth. *International Journal of Sociology and Social Policy*, *28*(11–12), 528–545.

Gardner, N. (2009). A manifesto for slow travel. *Hidden Europe Magazine*, *25*, 10–14.

Gilbert, D., & Abdullah, J. (2004). Holidaytaking and the sense of well-being. *Annals of Tourism Research*, *31*(1), 103–121.

Godbey, G. C. (2009). Outdoor recreation and health: Understanding and enhancing the relationship. *Resources for the Future*, April.

Hall, C. M. (2009). Degrowing tourism: Descroissance, sustainable consumption and steady state tourism. *Anatolia*, *20*(1), 46–61.

Hall, C. M. (2010). Changing paradigms and global change: From sustainable to steady-state tourism. *Tourism Recreation Research*, *35*(2), 131–145.

Hamilton, C. (2004). *Growth Fetish*. Sydney: Allen and Unwin.

Harrison, C., & Donnelly, I. A. (2011). A theory of smart cities. *Proceedings of the 55th Annual Meeting of the ISSS*. Hull, UK.

Heitmann, S., Robsinson, P., & Povey, G. (2011). Slow Food, slow cities and slow tourism. In P. Robinson, S. Heitmann, & P. Dieke (Eds.), *Research themes for tourism* (pp. 114–127). Oxford: CABI.

Holbrook, M. B., & Hirschman, E. C. (1982). The Experiential aspects of consumption: Consumer fantasies, feelings, and fun. *Journal of Consumer Research*, *9*(2), 132–140.

Honoré, C. (2004). *In praise of slowness: Challenging the cult of speed*. New York, NY: HarperOne.

Hopkins, R. (2008). *The transition handbook: From oil dependency to local resilience*. Cambridge, UK: Green Book UIT Cambridge Ltd.

Inskeep, E. (1991). *Tourism planning: An integrated and sustainable development approach*. New York, NY: Van Nostrand Reinhold.

Kahn, R. L., & Juster, F. T. (2002). Well-being: Concepts and measures. *Journal of Social Issues*, *58*, 627–644.

Kahneman D., & Tversky, A. (2000). *Choices, values and frames*. New York, NY: Cambridge University Press and Russel Sage Foundation.

Kahneman, D., Diener, E., & Schwarz, N. (Eds.). (1999). *Well-being: The foundations of hedonic psychology.* New York, NY: Russell Sage Foundation.

Kallis, G. (2011). In defence of degrowth. *Ecological Economics, 70*, 873–880.

Lanzani, A. (2005). Geografie, paesaggi, pratiche dell'abitare e progetti di sviluppo. *Territorion, 34*, 19–36.

Latouche, S. (2011). *Décoloniser l'imaginaire. La Pensée créative contre l'économie de l'absurde.* Lyon: L'Aventurine.

Layard, R. (2005). *Happiness: Lessons from a new science.* London: Penguin.

Leonini L., & Sassatelli R. (a cura di). (2008). *Il consumo critico. Significati, pratiche, reti.* Roma-Bari: Laterza.

Lindholm, C., & Lie, S. B. (2013). You eat what you are: Cultivated taste and the pursuit of authenticity in the Slow Food movement. In N. Osbaldiston (Ed.), *Culture of the slow: Social deceleration in an accelerated world.* London: Palgrave Macmillan.

Lumsdon, L. M., & McGrath, P. (2011). Developing a conceptual framework for slow travel: A grounded theory approach. *Journal of Sustainable Tourism, 19*(3), 265–279.

Matos, R. (2004). Can "slow tourism" bring new life to Alpine regions? In K. Weimar & C. Mathies (Eds.), *The tourism and leisure industry: Shaping the future* (pp. 93–104). New York, NY: Routledge.

Mayer, H., & Knox, P. L. (2006). Slow cities: Sustainable places in a fast world. *Journal of Urban Affairs, 28*(4), 321–334.

McCabe, S., Joldersma, T., & Li, C. (2010). Understanding the benefits of social tourism: Linking participation to subjective well-being and quality of life. *International Journal of Tourism Research, 12*(6), 761–773.

Nocifora, E. (2011). La costruzione sociale della qualità territoriale. Il turismo della lentezza come conquista del turista esperto. In E. Nocifora, P. de Salvo P e V. Calzati (a cura di), *Territori lenti e turismo di qualità, prospettive innovative per lo sviluppo di un turismo sostenibile.* Milan: FrancoAngeli.

Osbaldiston, N. (2013). *Culture of the slow. Social deceleration in an accelerated world.* London: Palgrave Macmillan.

Paltrinieri, R. (2008). Consumi e etica in prospettiva sociologica, per una teoria del consumo responsabile. *Sociologia del lavoro, 111*, 101–109.

Parkins, W., & Craig G. (2006). *Slow living.* Oxford: Berg.

Pearce, P. L., & Lee, U. -I. (2005). Developing the travel career approach to tourist motivation. *Journal of Travel Research, 43*, 226–237.

Pine, J., & Gilmore, J. (1999). *The experience economy.* Boston, MA: Harvard Business School Press.

Pink, S. (2008). Sense and sustainability: The case of the slow city movement. *Local Environment, 13*(2), 95–106.

Ritchie, J. R., Wing Sun Tung, V., & Ritchie, R. (2011). Tourism experience management research emergence, evolution and future directions. *International Journal of Contemporary Hospitality Management, 23*(4), 419–438.

Ryan, R. M., Deci, E. L. (2001). On happiness and human potentials: A review of research on hedonic and eudaimonic well-being. *Annual Review of Psychology, 52*, 141–166.

Sassatelli, R. (2008). Pratiche di consumo e politica del quotidiano. In L. Leonini & R. Sassatelli (Eds.), *Il consumo critico* (pp. 113–119). Roma-Bari: Laterza.

Savoja, L. (2009). La Stakeholder Responsability nel turismo. I turisti oltre il confine della Sostenibilità. *Politeia, xxv*(93), 239–246.

Savoja, L. (2011). Turismo lento e turisti responsabili. Verso una nuova concezione di consumo. In E. Nocifora, P. de Salvo, & V. Calzati (Eds.), *Territori lenti e turismo diqualità, prospettive innovative per lo sviluppo di un turismo sostenibile.* Milan: FrancoAngeli.

Schneider, F., Kallis, G., & Martinez-Alier, J. (2010). Crisis or opportunity? Economic degrowth for social equity and ecological sustainability. Introduction to this special issue. *Journal of Cleaner Production, 18*, 511–518.

Sen, A. (1999). *Development as freedom*. Oxford: Oxford University Press.

Sen, A. K. (1992). *Inequality re-examined*. Cambridge, MA: Harvard University Press.

Sharpley, R. (2000). *Tourism and Sustainable Development: Exploring the Theoretical Divide. Journal of Sustainable Tourism, 8*, 1–19.

Stiglitz, J., Sen, A., & Fitoussi, J. (2009). *Report by the Commission on the Measurement of Economic Performance and Social Progress*, Paris.

UNWTO. (2012). Asia-Pacific Newsletter, Issue 27.

Urry, J. (1990). *The tourist gaze*. London: Sage.

Uysal, M., Perdue, R. R., & Sirgy, J. M. (Eds.). (2012). *The handbook of tourism and quality of life research*. Dordrecht: Springer.

Van den Bergh, J. C., & Kallis, G. (2012). Growth, a-growth or degrowth to stay within planetary boundaries? *Journal of Economic Issues, XLVI*(4), 909–919.

Vannini, (2014). Slowness and deceleration. In P. Adey, D. Bissell, K. Hannan, P. Merriman, & M. Sheller (Eds.), *The Routledge handbook of mobilities* (pp. 116–124). London: Routledge.

Veenhoven, R. (1991). Is happiness relative? *Social Indicators Research, 24*, 1–34.

Weaver, D. B. (2000). A broad context model of destination development scenarios. *Tourism Management, 21*(3), 217–224.

Westwood, S., Morgan, N., & Pritchard, A. (2006). Situation, participation and reflexivity in tourism research: Furthering interpretative approaches to tourism enquiry. *Tourism Recreation Research, 31*(2), 33–44.

Zago, M. (2012). Definire e operativizzare lo slow tourism: il modello Castle. In V. Calzati V. e P. de Salvo (Eds.), *Le strategie per una valorizzazione sostenibile del territorio*. Milan: FrancoAngeli.

4   Slow travel and tourism

New concept or new label?

Peter McGrath and Richard Sharpley

Introduction

Fast and *slow* are physical attributes but, as explained in previous chapters, are also adjectives that convey societal values. We live in an age where a "faster pace of existence, and an increasing 'busy-ness' in the time we have, is a central feature of global culture" (Parkins & Craig, 2006, p. 1). Moreover, in some societies, fast has until recently been considered synonymous with success, as in "fast learner" or "fast-track career," whereas slow has often been associated with failure or at least lack of achievement. Other societies, however, may be defined by or thought to embrace slowness. That is, slowness or, more precisely, a slower pace of life, whether actual or perceived, may be practiced and indeed celebrated by those societies and, perhaps, viewed with envy by other societies entrapped in "fastness." For example, it has been found that a causal relationship exists between the pace of life and cultural characteristics of societies (Levine & Norenzayan, 1999). Specifically, fast-paced (typically Western) societies tend to be more economically dynamic, encouraging individualism and a focus on wealth creation as the basis of well-being, but suffer the associated social costs, from diminishing social capital to a greater incidence of health problems. Conversely, slower-paced societies, though less economically productive, may demonstrate a greater (non-wealth related) sense of well-being.

It is with the inherent fast nature of many Western cultures that "leisure-ness," "unhurriedness" and "slowness" are becoming increasingly attractive concepts. That is, the costs of fast (economically successful) life are increasingly considered to outweigh the (non-economic) benefits of a slower pace of life. This apparent shift in cultural values can be aligned to the earlier work of Virilio (1991) who contended that speed is a major destructive force changing societies at a pace that is difficult to reverse, and it is this destructive nature of speed that, for example, lies at the very heart of the Slow Food Manifesto: "We are all enslaved by speed and have all succumbed to the same insidious virus: fast life, which disrupts our habits, invades the privacy of our homes, and forces us to eat fast foods" (Slow Food, 1989). Honoré (2004) concurs with these sentiments, explaining that slow has become a countercultural perspective that rails against the structures in Western society that encourage fast consumption. He suggests that the quest for fast brings about poorer diet, health, relationships, communities and environment. Thus, to live slowly is to engage in "mindful" rather than "mindless" practices (Parkins, 2004, p. 264), which can only benefit modern living. Meredith and Storm (2011, p. 1) further clarify the meaning of living slowly, describing it as:

> [S]tructuring your life around meaning and fulfillment. Similar to "voluntary simplicity" and "downshifting," it emphasizes a less-is more approach, focusing upon the quality of your life ... Slow Living addresses the desire to lead a more balanced life and to pursue a more holistic sense of well-being in the fullest sense of the word.

It can be argued that the global success of the Slow Food and Cittáslow movements that are discussed within this book has underpinned an increasing societal recognition of the benefits of adopting slowness, or being slow, in at least one or more aspects of daily life. This has, in turn, stimulated a shift in the meaning of slowness, it now being considered a metaphor for "stepping off the treadmill," seeking a more balanced life and refusing the dominance of speed inherent in modern Western society (Honoré, 2004). Thus, slowness may be regarded as particularly attractive notion in *faster* nations, acting as a countercultural response to the stresses and strains of daily life. Such an understanding is certainly far removed from once derogative interpretations of "slow" and is seen by some as a mechanism for signaling an alternative set of values that counter the dominant contemporary value systems.

It is in the context of this broad shift in cultural values that this chapter explores more recent additions to the Slow Movement in particular, namely, Slow Travel and Slow Tourism. The distinction between "travel" and "tourism" in this context is discussed shortly but, generally, the dominant value system of the modern tourism offering has long been called into question (Croall, 1995; de Kadt, 1979; Turner & Ash, 1975). As consequence, since the 1980s there has been a continued search for *new* and *alternative* types of tourism, such as eco-tourism, pro-poor tourism, responsible tourism and sustainable tourism. (Fennell, 2007; Goodwin, 2011; Holden, 2013; Mowforth & Munt, 2009; Sharpley, 2009). Given that the rise of the Slow Movement has taken place in parallel, it is unsurprising that the concept of "slow" has now come to be associated with the tourism sector.

Nevertheless, it is unclear when the prefix *Slow* was first added to *Travel* or *Tourism*. Lumsdon and McGrath (2011) and Markwell, Fullagar, and Wilson (2012) are in agreement that an early advocate of the movement was Jost Krippendorf. In his seminal text *The Holiday Makers*, Krippendorf (1987) expressed his doubts about the sustainability of the mass tourism product. More specifically, he questioned people's acceptance of the prevailing tourism value system and called for a re-balancing of both the production and consumption of tourism. This, according to Krippendorf (1987), would allow for a more relaxing, satisfying and environmentally friendly holiday experience for the tourist and would bring greater benefits (or fewer negative consequences) to the host, a philosophy closely related to that of the Slow Movement. Indeed, an explicit indication of Krippendorf's (1987, p. 10) advocacy for slowness is revealed in his "credo for a new harmony," in which he posed the questions: "Must we in the future, in order to get on, run twice as fast as before ...? Shouldn't we instead take the foot off the accelerator if we want to win the race? Should we not go one step back to view the thing from a distance and consider where the forces of circumstances are taking us?"

Unlike Slow Food and Cittáslow, however, there is almost no evidence to suggest that the concepts of slow travel and/or slow tourism are firmly rooted in modern Western society or are a tangible reaction to or rejection of fast culture in general, or fast travel and tourism in particular. That is to say, it cannot be claimed unequivocally that they are the manifestation of a Western counter travel-tourism culture. This may be explained in part by a continued lack of understanding and interpretation of the concepts of slow travel and slow tourism, perhaps characterized by a lack of organizational foundation/structure and no agreed manifestos, such as those of Slow Food and Cittáslow. In other words, slow travel and slow tourism arguably remain concepts or idealized approaches to travel and tourism, whereas Slow Food and Cittáslow are practical movements that can cross cultural boundaries as long as the hosts can relate to and follow some if not all of the policies in their clearly stated manifestos. Indeed, slow travel and slow tourism have some way to progress in terms of establishing a new "manifesto" for travel and tourism, particularly given the fact that, certainly in the Western world, it has become culturally acceptable (and desirable) that we should travel further, faster and more frequently than in any other era. At the same time, it can be argued that even in the modern era of fast international travel, "slow" travel and tourism has always existed, whether in the form of extended overland travel (backpacking) or related to particular travel modes (for example, cycling holidays, cruising on canal boats, and so on). Hence, not only does the slow-fast paradox becomes problematic in the context of travel and tourism, but also attaching the "slow" label to travel and tourism might be considered inappropriate or even misleading.

In this chapter, therefore, we critically appraise the concept(s) of slow travel and tourism, considering whether it is a valid appropriation of the cultural concept of "slowness" and, in particular, exploring whether in fact slowness can be a viable characteristic of tourism in "fast" countries and societies. This, in turn, points to an additional question requiring further research: In the absence of prescribed policies, are slow travel and slow tourism culturally defined and, hence, more easily adopted in some (culturally "slow") countries than in other (culturally "fast") countries, or is the "speed" of travel and tourism determined by other factors?

Before engaging in such discussions, however, it is first important to highlight the lack of consensus as to what "slow" actually means in the context of travel and tourism and how it should be practiced or conceptualized. More specifically, in recent years the two terms, *slow travel* and *slow tourism*, have become used in both academic and industry circles either as one (that is, slow travel and tourism) or interchangeably (see, for instance, Dickinson & Lumsdon, 2010; Fullagar, Markwell, & Wilson, 2012) to refer to what is commonly perceived to be a single concept. Yet "travel" and "tourism," whether as economic sectors or social practices, are distinct, travel being a fundamental characteristic of, but more narrowly defined, than tourism. Hence, this chapter commences by addressing this issue through a review of the conceptual terms that have emerged over the past decade.

Slow travel and slow tourism: towards a definition

As noted above, the Slow Movement was born in the 1980s, around the same time that Jost Krippendorf (1987) was developing his ideas with regards to an alternative approach to developing, practicing and understanding tourism in contemporary society. However, it was not until more than a decade later that the terminology *slow travel* was first used (predating *slow tourism*) through the launch of the slowtrav.com website in 2000. The website, founded by Pauline Kenny, along with the majority of the travel companies that it markets, is based in North America and specifically promotes slow travel as a style of travel for visiting Europe. This is an important point, the significance of which will become clearer later in this chapter. On the website, slow travel is defined as embracing two components: (i) "spend one week in one place" and (ii) "see what is near to you" (Slowtrav, 2015). The concept of slow travel is further explained as follows: "Spend a week in a vacation rental ... slow down, immerse yourself in the local culture and avoid the fast pace of rushing from one guidebook 'must-see' to the next" (Slowtrav, 2015). It is this, according to the website, that transforms and enhances the quality of the travel experience and in promoting this approach to travel, slowtravel.com espouses, in all likelihood accidently, the very philosophy underpinning Jost Krippendorf's ideas.

A plethora of websites soon followed the lead of slowtravel.com and, perhaps inevitably, academics then turned their attention to the concept, considering the fundamental ingredients of a slow travel (and later, a slow tourism) experience. Notably, two identifiable terms have subsequently emerged in the relevant literature, the first of which, most usually referred to as slow travel, focuses specifically upon the tourist. It considers the notion that tourists are seeking greater authenticity in their holidaying and require a different experience whilst also having a moral conscience of the impacts they bring to a destination. Typically, however, commentators focus on the journey element of the tourist experience – that is, travel to and from the destination – although some extend their analysis to include experiences within and around the destination.

The second term, more commonly referred to as slow tourism, centers upon supply side considerations within the tourism system, with commentators applying the principles of "slow" to destination management, business operations and consumer behavior in order to create a "change of status quo to oppose existing tourism ontologies" (Heitmann, Robinson, & Povey, 2011, p. 126). The principal consideration is the extent to which such a different type of tourism would benefit a host destination whilst, as a secondary factor, provide an enhanced experience for the tourist. Both slow travel and slow tourism are now reviewed in more detail.

Slow travel

The term *slow travel* has become synonymous with modes of transport that have lower environmental impact (Hall, 2006) and, in particular, characterized by an aspiration to reduce the significant contribution of greenhouse gas emissions produced by the tourism industry (Dickinson, Lumsdon, & Robbins, 2011). Slow travel has, therefore, been defined as "a trip made using non-aviation methods for departure" (Mintel, 2009, p. 1) and, hence, forms of transport that are also physically slower than aircraft. Dickinson and Lumsdon (2010) categorize slow travel as travelling on foot, by train, bicycle, bus or boat and, in addition, they advocate that less distance should be travelled. This definitional stance restricts the reach of slow travel geographically and perhaps also by time and wealth because, as Cresswell (2006) cited in Molz (2009, p. 281) points out, only certain people, namely the middle and elite classes have the "time and space to be slow by choice." Conway and Timms (2012, p. 367) contend that slow travel is "highly selective of geographical context and degree of infrastructure sophistication." They align the existence of slow travel to affluent regions such as Britain and Europe, the populations of which live in close geographical proximity to destinations with well-developed slow travel infrastructure. Such limitations in the scope of slow travel raise significant issues for tourists who wish to visit nationally or internationally distant tourist destinations, such as North American tourists seeking to travel to far flung regions of their country or alternatively to Europe or even further afield. Immediately, then this consequently raises questions with regards to the "slow" credentials of organizations such as slowtrav.com.

This initial misunderstanding or at least misinterpretation of slow travel, along with the increased media interest in the concept, provided Nicky Gardner (2009, p. 11), the editor of the Hidden Europe Magazine, with a platform to compile a "Manifesto for Slow Travel." In this, she offers a philosophical perspective on slow travel, as follows:

> Slow travel is about making conscious choices. It is about deceleration rather than speed. The journey becomes a moment to relax, rather than a stressful interlude imposed between home and destination. Slow travel re-engineers time, transforming it into a commodity of abundance rather than scarcity. And slow travel also reshapes our relationship with places, encouraging and allowing us to engage more intimately with the communities through which we travel.

In her rather all-encompassing definition, Gardner continues by outlining the guiding principles that slow tourists (or travellers) should follow, principles that may be considered stringent and perhaps somewhat elitist (McGrath, 2014, p. 24). Nevertheless, she provides further clarification of the concept of Slow Travel:

- Start at home. The key to travel is a state of mind. That can be developed at home.
- Travel slowly. Avoid planes if at all possible, and instead enjoy ferries, local buses and slow trains. Speed destroys the connection with landscape. Slow travel restores it.
- You may eagerly look forward to the arrival at your chosen destination, but don't let that anticipation eclipse the pleasure of the journey.
- Check out local markets and shops.
- Savor café culture. Sitting in a café, you become part of the cityscape and not merely a passing observer.
- Take time to get a feel for the languages and dialects of the areas you visit. Learn a few phrases, use a dictionary and buy a local newspaper.
- Engage with communities at the right level. Choose accommodation and eating options that are appropriate to the area where you are travelling.
- Do what the locals do, not only what guidebooks say.
- Savor the unexpected. Delayed trains or missed bus connections create new opportunities.
- Think what you can give back to the communities you visit. (Gardner, 2009)

Though Gardner does allude to the benefits of avoiding travelling by plane, she is in no way dictatorial about this. Other key commentators, however, take a more journey-centric stance in conjunction with a shift away from the airplane, though it is interesting to note that they tend to be based mainly but not exclusively in Europe. Dubois and Ceron (2003) were amongst the first academics to offer a narrative on the concept, though they refer to it as slow tourism. They suggest that by changing modal preferences to slower and more environmentally benign types of transportation (boat transport, biking and walking), a low-impact tourism utopia can be achieved. In a later study (Dubois & Ceron, 2007, p. 11), they review the additional positive intrinsic benefits of slow tourism for the tourist by describing the journey between home and the destination as not just "slower (more trains and buses), but considered as pleasant and interesting."

Other key commentators on Slow Travel are Dickinson and Lumsdon (2010, p. 75) who explicitly state that:

[T]he challenge for tourism in the 21st Century is seemingly how to reshape itself so that people can continue to enjoy their leisure time while, at the same time, the supply sector manages to avoid the worst scenarios of climate change.

They contented that slow travel (categorized as train, walking, cycling, bus and boat travel) has a central role in the process of change and, in a separate work, define the concept as "an emerging conceptual framework which offers an alternative to air and car travel, where people travel to destinations more slowly overland, stay longer and travel less" (Dickinson, Robbins, & Lumsdon, 2010, p. 482).

In an attempt to address the mass tourism market that, in recent years, has reaped the benefits of low cost carriers, the slow travel narrative focused on the lost "art of travel," to borrow the title of De Botton's (2003) influential work. From this perspective, it is argued that one outcome of modernity is that we have lost the "art" of travel – of traditional, authentic, real travel – and that slow travel can restore people's relationship with it so that they are no longer to be "sent" as parcels (to borrow the instrumental metaphor by Ruskin) but rather, through travel, become not detached from but at one with the landscape. Building this theme, Lumsdon and McGrath (2011, p. 12) add to the very few definitions of the concept of slow travel, as follows:

> Slow travel is a sociocultural phenomenon, focusing on holidaymaking but also on day leisure visits, where use of personal time is appreciated differently. Slowness is valued, and the journey is integral to the whole experience. The mode of transport and the activities undertaken at a destination enhance the richness of the experience through slowness. Whilst the journey is the thing and can be the destination in its own right, the experience of locality counts for much, as does reduced duration or distance of travel.

Gillespie (2007), one of the earliest champions of slow travel, expands on this in his writing of a year-long Slow Travel column for *The Observer* newspaper, explaining that in his view,

> Slow travel is all about appreciating the subtleties of the journey, the nuanced changes in the food served, the music played, the quirks of regional dialects and customs and, of course, the ever-changing scenery rolling by. This is what we are seeking and are excited about – the experience of genuine travel, not an abrupt series of disjointed holidays in different parts of the world interspersed by soulless airport departure lounges and hours in the air only to be dumped, disorientated, in a new destination.

To this end, the mode of transport facilitates "a visual 'cinematic' experience of moving landscape images" (Larsen, 2001, p. 80). Gillespie describes an appealing notion and although his writings have paved the way for a surge of self-defined slow tourists who comment upon their experiences through the medium of online blogs, there is no substantial research as to the demographic profile or motivational factors of the slow tourist.

Nonetheless there is a clear, albeit niche market that has developed over the past decade and this has been noted and responded to by an increasing number of Tour Operators (see for instance InnTravel, 2015), Tourism Authorities (see, e.g., the Austrian Tourism Authority) and travel writers (see, e.g., Sawday, 2015) who specialize in packaging Slow Travel experiences. With an emphasis on conscious enjoyment over hurried consumption and the encouragement to truly understand the host culture, *slow travel* is becoming a more recognizable term. For instance, the Thailand Tourism Authority (2015) encourages visitors to "take time to enjoy what travel offers." Urging tourists to "escape modern speed and … experience the real Thailand, the land of smiles," they suggest, "Slow travel tunes the time of human action and the ecology with the rhythm of nature where eco-resorts and local homestays play a major role." The recurrent theme of exploring beyond the superficial and instead "getting under the skin" of a local culture, a common means of promoting "authentic" destinations, can be achieved by switching to a slower mode of transport, in the case of Thailand, an elephant or bamboo raft. Similar sentiments are extolled by Milesworth Travel (2015), who offer slow travel tours in Delhi that swap the motorcar tour for organized walking or cycling tours which ensures "the real Delhi will not pass in a flash whilst visiting the fast paced cultural capital of India." Although perhaps a somewhat contradiction in terms, it adds weight to the earlier suggestion that slowness is not necessarily only practical in *slower* nations but can also be an attractive notion in *faster* nations, acting as a countercultural response to the stresses and strains of fast-paced societies.

As a concept however, it can be argued that slow travel as conceptualized by most commentators is nothing new. That is, until the twentieth century the majority of travel was slow by its very nature, with travellers exploring the world on foot, by horse and sailing boat and latterly, by train (Towner, 2002). Indeed, analogies can be drawn between the ideals of slow travel and many early travel experiences, such as religious pilgrimages, scientific investigation, anthropological studies, cultural excursions (Krantz et al., 2009), with the Grand Tour in particular being often identified as an antecedent to the slow travel concept. Hence, slow travel might be considered a nostalgic yearning for a bygone era of "real" travel or, more pragmatically, a response to the challenge of climate change dressed up in attractive clothing. Moreover, students of tourism will automatically draw parallels between the philosophy of slow travel and that of the so-called new tourist (Poon, 1993), the alternative tourist (Smith & Eadington, 1992) or, most recently, the responsible tourist (Goodwin, 2011).

Slow tourism

The second term that establishes a link between slow and tourism is, of course, *slow tourism*. Similar to the concept of slow travel, commonality can be found between slow tourism and Krippendorf's vision or desire for a "better" tourism experience offering. Those who use the term place significant emphasis upon the supply side of the tourism system as opposed to the tourist and the consumption of tourism experiences, arguing that offering slow tourism as a developmental approach at the destination level will revolutionize tourism (Matos, 2004, p. 95) and offer a "viable alternative to mass tourism" (Conway & Timms, 2010, p. 332). Hence, within the slow tourism concept the focus shifts away from the mode of transportation used and distance travelled to the "product" being supplied and consumed, because it is considered rather ironic that the objective of slow travel is to minimize the negative consequences of tourism by advocating a different type of travel. This would restrict such travel to local areas, hence denying the benefits of tourism development to destinations in rural and peripheral regions that are outside the day-trip zones of metropolitan areas (Hall, 2006) and, indeed, to international destinations.

Matos (2004, p. 100), one as the earliest contributors to the academic discourse on slow tourism, considers it a form of "soft" tourism that can help protect the natural environment. Recognizing that there is a *new* tourist segment that seeks to give up "fast, stressful tourism, in favor of an interlude of quiet serenity to recollect energies and genuinely enjoy the holiday," a deceleration of tourism is, he suggests, highly marketable. If managed correctly it can offer the required benefits at a destination level while also being a catalyst to reinvigorate the tourism offering. He draws particular attention to how this has the potential to protect the most sensitive regions from the detrimental impacts caused by traditional mass tourism. Once tourists are encouraged to change their pace they would "look rather than see and experience an area rather than endure it"; it would "allow for a more authentic discovery of a locality, of its people, and of its culture." He suggests that to be genuine, Slow Tourism must follow two essential principles: (i) "taking time" and (ii) attachment to a particular place. Taking time means modification of the daily time relationship, specifically a different perception of nature and living in harmony with a place, its inhabitants, and their culture. The environment is not merely perceived by sight, but by using all five senses.

More recently, Conway and Timms (2012, p. 368) have proposed slow tourism as a "development-from-below" initiative that has ecological sensitivity as well as human, capacity-building potential for peripheral regions of the world that have been overlooked, or undeveloped as local, authentic, tourism destinations. Premised on the need for slow growth (adopted by Daly, 1996) they highlight the need, as does Matos, to focus upon the three "Es" of sustainable development – environment, economy and equity. They propose that doing so will:

> [E]ncourage new ideas about how to grow locales in a more conscious and measured ways so that alternative, more inclusive, community centered and regional regimes are formed from the existing cultural hearths of local practice and communal/familial knowledge that have always existed in the many overlooked, marginal and out-of-the-way locales. (Timms & Conway, 2011, p. 333)

The Slow Tourism Association, based in Italy, encourages these ideals and works to "safeguard and promote the growth of territories, even those poorly known, to make them valuable tourism destinations" (Slow Tourism Association, 2015). The network develops links between travellers, tourism entrepreneurs and local communities to improve the quality of tourism offered whilst also aiming to "enhance the authenticity, history and culture of a place." Facilitating the positive slow growth proposed by Timms and Conway, the Slow Tourism Association is a member-supported association with a clear set of values, missions and objectives providing a framework for developing slow tourism as a development-from-below initiative. With offices in Italy and France and the imminent launch in the UK and Spain the trajectory is similar to Slow Food and Cittáslow, it is with this that it is plausible that, in time, the network will spread to other countries and shift from a idealized approach to tourism to a practical movement. Again, however, it is difficult to identify a distinction between slow tourism and more recognized alternative (to mass) approaches to tourism development, such as ecotourism and, more generally, sustainable tourism. That is, the outcome is the same; it is only the label that is different.

Overall, then, though ambiguous, the conceptual foundations and parameters of slow travel and slow tourism are becoming established in the literature and could be considered as a group of associated ideas rather than having a watertight definition. As the concepts evolve, so too will the debate, which will help unravel the complexity of how "slow" should be practiced in relation to travel and tourism. Appropriately, trying to rush this process is perhaps unnecessary, as highlighted in an earlier paper by Lumsdon and McGrath (2011, p. 9), who question the need to offer a definitive approach as they report on an interview conducted surrounding the definitional issues:

> [Y]ou can kill the thing you love by trying to define it. You've got to set ideas free and let things evolve. It's got to evolve; it's got to change, and in order to do that you can't put a conceptual or academic straightjacket around it; you need to let it breathe, let it stumble and make mistakes, let people argue about it and hammer away at it; you need to let it become what it becomes. I think there's always a danger [that] if you fix something, you suffocate it.

Conclusion

It is evident that slow travel is positioned as a demand-driven concept whilst slow tourism concentrates upon supply-side issues. Although we agree with these sentiments in part, we take objection with the current understanding of slow travel as critiqued in this chapter. The reason for our objection is that slow travel thus far has been conceptualized and proposed by a variety of commentators as a plea to fight the climate change battle by encouraging slower modes of transportation and restricting travel by geographical location which, as we already contend, is ironic in nature. If slow travel is to be considered and developed in this manner, then it is to be no more than a buzzword and a repackaging of sustainable transport, which could in turn be viewed as a nascent and somewhat eclectic movement.

It is our view that slow travel is a *mind-set* of how a tourist approaches a travel experience and, as such, acts as an extension to their already slow life-style based upon a pushback from a fast lifestyle, ideology and the practice of mass consumerism rather than, as others contend, as a response to an inherent motivation for sustainability and an alternative to mass tourism. The slow tourist may choose a physically slower mode of transport to facilitate this necessary deceleration or, alternatively, may take solace in a flight that detaches them from the stresses and strains of daily life and instead offers an opportunity to become reconnected with their thoughts. Speed becomes irrelevant and the focus shifts to doing things at the "right" speed for the individual in order to achieve *slowness*. This philosophical stance is a continuation of McGrath's (2014, p. 25) consideration that slow travel represents a "dual journey," the literal and the journey within, that encompasses engaging with local cultures at the "right" level which, in turn, facilitates a more sustainable approach and enables the tourist and the host to have a "better" tourism experience, just as Krippendorf envisaged. This can be facilitated through slow tourism, which can be agreed as a "development from below" initiative that acts as an extension to the already existing sustainable tourism notion or perhaps a new form of sustainable tourism development (Lowry & Lee, 2011).

Returning to the principle question addressed by this chapter, namely, whether slowness can be a viable characteristic of tourism in "fast" countries and societies, the answer must be yes, at least for those tourists seeking or receptive to the concept of "slowness." If indeed Slow Travel is a mind-set as opposed a tangible product as we suggest, then the broader social pace of life becomes irrelevant to the tourism experience. The (slow) tourist will live in either fast or slow societies and, equally, will seek out slow experiences in either slow or fast paced environments by, for example, sitting in a busy local café in the market square to "live like a local" in order to truly be immersed in the hosts' culture.

Similarly, if slow tourism is an ethos of supplying a tourism experience for those who engage in slow travel then this too can be achieved in a society or pace of life, which is fast or slow. Slow travel and slow tourism are not inter-linking concepts and therefore can be practiced in parallel or independently from one another. Nevertheless, slow tourism certainly lends itself to regions that are already actively engaged in the Slow Movement given the large stakeholder network and backing that is needed in order to be effective.

From the discussion thus far, slow travel and slow tourism are, clearly, rather ambiguous terms and there is a lack of evidence to support knowledge and understanding of the demographic profile of slow tourists or to quantify the size of the market. Indeed, as noted in the introduction, further research is necessary to "unpack" the concepts of slow travel and slow tourism and, in particular, to explore their relationship with the culture of slowness. Nonetheless slow travel and slow tourism are practiced by a group of travel writers, small-scale entrepreneurs, a growing number of academics and a small number of independent tourists (Lumsdon & McGrath, 2011). In the UK for instance, the supply of slow in relation to both travel and tourism is minimal with the greatest, albeit modest, success witnessed by Bradt publishers (see Bradt Travel Guides, 2015) who have developed a series of Slow Guides for a variety of UK destinations (sixteen in total) and one core tour operator (InnTravel, 2015) specializing in Slow Holidays (both in the UK and across Europe). This lack of supply may be equated to a lack of demand, at least from a UK perspective, or it may reflect the fact that, as we contend in this chapter, as slow travel is an approach to travel on the part of the individual tourist, then the market is thus unquantifiable. Conversely, slow tourism, as an approach to tourism supply, may be more tangible. In either case however, it remains uncertain to what extent slow travel and slow tourism differ from existing tourism concepts, philosophies and practices. Irrespective of their home sociocultural environment (fast or slow), tourists have always sought individual meanings and benefits from engaging in tourism and, hence, attaching the concept of slowness to travel and tourism may, at best, attract a receptive niche market and, at worst, become a meaningless marketing exercise.

References

Bradt Travel Guides. (2015). *Slow guides*. Retrieved from www.bradtguides.com/shop/series/slow-guides.html

Conway, D., & Timms, B. F. (2010). Re-branding alternative tourism in the Caribbean: The case for "slow tourism." *Tourism and Hospitality Research, 10*(4), 329–344.

Conway, D., & Timms, B. F. (2012). Are slow travel and slow tourism misfits, compadres or different genres? In T. V. Singh (Ed.), *Critical debates in tourism* (pp. 365–373). Bristol: Channel View Publications.

Cresswell, T. (2006). *On the move. Mobility in the modern western world.* Abingdon: Routledge.

Croall, J. (1995). *Preserve or destroy: Tourism and the environment.* London: Calouste Gulbenkian Foundation.

De Botton, A. (2003). *The art of travel.* London: Penguin.

de Kadt, E. (1979). *Tourism: Passport to development?* New York, NY: OUP.

Daly, H. E. (1996). *Beyond growth: The economics of sustainable development.* Boston, MA: Beacon Press.

Dickinson, J., & Lumsdon, L. (2010). *Slow travel and tourism.* London: Earthscan.

Dickinson, J., Lumsdon, L., & Robbins, D. (2011). Slow travel: Issues for tourism and climate change. *Journal of Sustainable Tourism, 19*(3), 281–300.

Dickinson, J., Robbins, D., & Lumsdon, L. (2010). Holiday travel discourses and climate change. *Journal of Transport Geography, 18*(3), 482–489.

Dubois, G., & Ceron, J. (2003). The interactions between climate change and tourism. In *Climate Change, the Environment and Tourism: The Interactions, European Science Foundation – LESC Exploratory Workshop, Foundazione Eni Enrico Mattei,* 4–6 June 2003 in Milan, Italy.

Dubois, G., & Ceron, J. (2007). Limits to tourism? A backcasting scenario for sustainable tourism mobility in 2050. *Tourism and Hospitality Planning and Development,* *4*(3), 189–208.

Fennell, D. (2007). *Ecotourism* (3rd ed.). Abingdon: Routledge.

Fullagar, S., Markwell, K., & Wilson, E. (Eds.). (2012). *Slow tourism: Experiences and mobilities.* Bristol: Channel View Publications.

Gardner, N. (2009). A manifesto for slow travel. *Hidden Europe Magazine, 25,* 104–119.

Gillespie, E. (2007). The Slow Traveller. Retrieved from www.theguardian.com/travel/2007/mar/18/green.ethicalholidays.escape

Goodwin, H. (2011). *Taking responsibility for tourism.* Oxford: Goodfellow Publishers Ltd.

Hall, C. M. (2006). Tourism, biodiversity and global environment change. In S. Gössling & C. M. Hall (Eds.), *Tourism and global environmental change: Ecological, economic, social and political interrelationships* (pp. 211–226). London: Routledge.

Heitmann, S., Robinson, P., & Povey, G. (2011). Slow Food, slow cities and slow tourism. In P. Robinson, S. Robinson, & P. U. C. Dieke (Eds.), *Research themes for tourism* (pp. 114–127). Oxford: CAB International.

Holden, A. (2013). *Tourism, poverty and development.* Abingdon: Routledge.

Honoré, C. (2004). *In praise of slowness: How a worldwide movement is challenging the cult of speed.* San Francisco, CA: Harper.

InnTravel. (2015). *InnTravel: The slow holiday people.* Retrieved from www.inntravel.co.uk/

Krantz, D., Chong, G., Contreras, J., Durham, W., Espeso, P., Honey, M., & Salters, R. (2009). *The market for responsible tourism,* SNV Netherlands Development Organization, The Netherlands: Author.

Krippendorf, J. (1987). *The holiday makers.* London: Heinemann.

Larsen, J. (2001). Tourism mobilities and the travel glance: Experiences of being on the move. *Scandinavian Journal of Hospitality and Tourism, 1,* 80–98.

Levine, R., & Norenzayan, A. (1999). The pace of life in 31 countries. *Journal of Cross-Cultural Psychology, 30*(2), 178–205.

Lowry, L. L., & Lee, M. (2011). CittaSlow, slow cities, slow food: Searching for a model for the development of slow tourism. *Travel & Tourism Research Association, 42nd Annual Conference Proceedings: Seeing the Forest and the Trees – Big Picture Research in a Detail-Driven World,* London, Ontario, Canada, June 19–21.

Lumsdon, L., & McGrath, P. (2011). Developing a conceptual framework for slow travel: A grounded theory approach. *Journal of Sustainable Tourism, 19*(3), 265–279.

Markwell, K., Fullagar, S., & Wilson, E. (2012). Reflecting upon slow travel and tourism experiences. In S. Fullagar, K. Markwell, & E. Wilson (Eds.), *Slow tourism: Experiences and mobilities* (pp. 227–233). Bristol: Channel View Publications.

Matos, R. (2004). Can slow tourism bring new life to Apline Regions? In K. Weiermair & C. Mathies (Eds.), *The tourism and leisure industry: Shaping the future.* New York, NY: Haworth Press.

McGrath, P. (2014). Escape from time: Experience the travel within. In S. Elkington & S. J. Gammon (Eds.), *Contemporary perspectives in leisure: Meanings, motives and lifelong learning* (pp. 18–27). Oxon: Routledge.

Meredith, B., & Storm, E. (2011). *Slow living.* Retrieved from www.create-the-good-life.com/slow_living.html

Milesworth Travel. (2015). *Slow travel in Delhi.* Retrieved from http://ashish.moonfruit.com/golden-triangle-slow-travel/4575985716

Mintel. (2009). *Slow travel special report.* London: Author.

Molz, J. (2009). Representing pace in tourism mobilities: Staycations, slow travel and The Amazing Race. *Journal of Tourism and Cultural Change, 7*(4), 270–286.

Mowforth, M., & Munt, I. (2009). *Tourism and sustainability: Development, globalisation and new tourism in the third world*. Abingdon: Routledge.

Parkins, W. (2004). At home in Tuscany: Slow living and the cosmopolitan subject. *Home Cultures, 1*(3), 257–274.

Parkins, W., & Craig, G. (2006). *Slow living*. New York, NY: Berg.

Poon, A. (1993). *Tourism, technology and competitive strategies*. Wallinford: CABI.

Sawday, A. (2015). *Go slow guides*. Retrieved from www.sawdays.co.uk/bookshop/go_slow/

Sharpley, R. (2009). *Tourism, development and the environment: Beyond sustainability*. London: Earthscan.

Slow Food. (1989). *The slow food manifesto*. Retrieved from www.slowfood.com/about_us/eng/manifesto.lasso

Slow Tourism Association. (2015). *Slow tourism asssociation*. Retrieved from www.slowtourism-italia.org/

SlowTrav. (2015). *Slow travel: Travel slowly, staying in vacation rentals (villas, farms, cottages and apartments)*. Retrieved from www.slowtrav.com/

Smith, V., & Eadington, W. (Eds.). (1992). *Tourism alternative: Potentials and problems in the development of tourism*. Philadelphia, PA: University of Pennsylvania Press.

Thailand Tourism Authority. (2015). *Slow travel Thailand: Taking time to enjoy what travel offers*. Retrieved from www.thailand.org.il/sites/thailand/UserContent/files/pdf/special-slow-travel.pdf

Timms, B. F., & Conway, D. (2011). Slow Tourism at the Caribbean's geographic margins. *Tourism Geographies, 14*(3), 1–23.

Towner, J. (2002). Literature, tourism and the grand tour. In M. Robinson & H.-L. Anderson (Eds.), *Literature and tourism: Essays in the reading and writing of tourism* (pp. 226–238). London: Thompson.

Turner, L., & Ash, J. (1975). *The golden hordes: International tourism and the pleasure periphery*. London. Constable.

Virilio, P. (1991). *La vitesse*. Paris: Flammarion.

5 Practicing Slow

Political and ethical implications

Michael Clancy

Introduction

Recent scholarship has devoted increasing attention to the individual and everyday practice, both in terms of consumption and in embodied practice as a way of knowing and making the world (Coleman & Crang, 2002; Crouch, 2001, 2007; Pink, 2012). Haenfler, Johnson, and Jones (2012) suggest that life-style movements, in fact, should be thought of as a continuation of new social movements in that they intend to change the world. What is at stake here and where do slow food, tourism and cities fit in? Is Slow simply a new, fashionable hedonism or is it a new form of local and global activism? This chapter examines the politics of practice within the Slow movement.

Slow consumption as ethical consumption

Beginning with the Slow Food movement, the language of Slow has consistently made ethical claims. At least part of that language involves rethinking the good life and directly contradicts its purported connection with speed and modernity. As such it is part of the larger process of reflexive modernization (Beck et al., 1997), a second modernity that confronts the undesired side effects produced by initial consequences of modernity (Holzer & Sørenson, 2003, p. 81). Everyday aspects of life, formerly non-political in nature, become politicized. Food, of course, has long been political, but one promise of modernity, the promise of abundance, meant to depoliticize it. As mentioned in the opening chapter, the original impetus for Slow Food was the opening of a MacDonald's restaurant in central Rome. As not only the embodiment of fast food but also of neoliberal globalization, MacDonald's symbolizes key aspects of modernity – speed, rationalization, routinization, and standardization (Ritzer, 1993).

Food also holds a special place at the center of seeking the good life because of its multifaceted nature, involving the political, the economic, the cultural and the agricultural. In addition it frequently involves family and community and is connected to larger values such as care, love, wealth and tradition just to name a few. As such, it is not surprising Slow Food adherents argue that food "is far more than a simple product to be consumed: it is happiness, identity, culture, pleasure, conviviality, nutrition, local economy, survival" (Petrini, 2007, p. 166). Schneider (2008) contends that Slow Food is first and foremost a rhetorical and educational movement. This education works on several levels, from the scientific to chronicling and working to protect species but also to the social, gastronomic and economic aspects of food. Ultimately, the goal is to "promote gastronomy as a democratically and socially engaged process" (Schneider, 2008, p. 391).

Slow Food's motto, "Good, Clean, Fair," reveals its central moral claims. Good centers on the virtue ethic of living the good life. If the promise of modernity is one of happiness and the good life as expressed by abundance and quantity, Slow Food emphasizes quality as expressed by diversity and locality of food products. The preservationist aspect through the formation of the "Ark of Taste" in 1996 was done not just to protect endangered food and ingredients for being overwhelmed by standardization but also for the sake of pure pleasure. In fact, a big emphasis in the SF movement is that of educating the palate in order to better appreciate quality food. This training becomes "an act of resistance against the destruction of taste and against the annihilation of knowledge" (Petrini, 2006, pp. 80–81). The Clean in "Good, Clean, Fair" directly refers to the ecological orientation of Slow Food. Slow Food directly challenges the dominant organization of global food chains as unsustainable. It is no accident that the movement started in 1986, the year of the Chernobyl nuclear disaster. That same year wine produced in Austria, Germany, and Italy was found to contain diethylene glycol, and wine produced in the Langhe region of Italy was contaminated by methanol, resulting in several deaths. Sassatelli and Davolio (2010) contend that over time the movement has made a shift from being primarily gastro-oriented to more eco-oriented in nature. They argue founder Carlo Petrini solidified this change in a 2004 speech, when he claimed, "a gastronome who is not an environmentalist is an idiot" (p. 215). Finally, Slow Food claims to be Fair in a market sense and makes a claim of solidarity between producer and consumer. The Biennial Salone del Gusto takes place in a former Fiat automobile factory in Turin and by 2002 became the single largest convention of its kind, bringing together 138,000 small producers and consumers (Schneider, 2008). Fair food is food that is produced sustainably, with an emphasis on social justice through fair wages and prices (Petrini, 2005, p. 135).

Although arising much more organically shortly after the turn of the century, the slow tourism movement has adopted similar rhetoric. Slow tourism also arose as a reaction to mass tourism where the emphasis has been not only on volume but also on quantity over quality. In fact much of the so-called ethical turn in tourism (Butcher, 2002; Caton, 2012; Mostafanezhad & Hannam, 2014; Smith & Duffy, 2003; Weeden & Bulok 2014; WTO, 1999), has been inspired by similar concerns with mass tourism and perceptions of its negative impacts on local destinations.

Parallel to slow food, slow tourism also makes multiple claims. One is that slow tourism is a superior commodity to traditional tourism. Because the tourism product is largely experiential, this argument has several components. The first is with regard to destination mobility. Slow tourism urges tourists to travel to the destination more slowly and sustainably. Here the trip itself is reintegrated into the valued touristic experience. While much of mass tourism demarcates the holiday itself from the travel to get to the destination, slow tourism returns destination mobility to the centrality of the tourist product itself (Lumsdon & McGrath, 2011). As Gardner (2009, p. 25) puts it, "the journey becomes a moment to relax, rather than a stressful interlude imposed between home and destination." Next, because tourism often involves knowledge – knowledge of place, of self, of history, of nature or culture – proponents argue slow tourism is superior because the more time spent in in the destination allows for greater depth of knowing. Finally, quality is asserted in the social and relational aspect of tourism. Although the tourist product itself is in actuality several products put together (transport, accommodation, activities, food and drink, entertainment), tourism is mainly an experience good. The host-guest relationship is central here. Tourists often report on the value of their holiday as depending on their perceived quality in the host-guest relationship. In most cases perceptions of "friendly, genuine, welcoming" hosts are crucial to the tourism product. The additional promise of slow tourism commodity is that of higher quality through more genuine human interactions. Much of this depends on the tourist him/herself. Slow tourists are urged to "engage the [host] community at the right level," "do what locals do" and "think what you can give back to the communities you visit" (Gardner, 2009, p. 25).

In addition to the quality claim, proponents of slow tourism also make an equal consequentialist claim: Done right, this form of tourism is more environmentally sound and provides more economic and social benefits for destination communities than more traditional forms of tourism. Travelling more slowly and sustainably helps the globe by reducing greenhouse gas emissions (Dickinson & Lumsdon, 2010; Dickinson, Lumsdon, & Robbins, 2011). Staying in one locale for longer periods of time, tourists inject more resources into the local economy, thereby encouraging more meaningful "slow growth" (Conway & Timms, 2012; Daly, 1996) or sustainable development as opposed to simply growth alone. By engaging "rightly" with the local community the promise is to maximize the economic and social benefits promised by tourism while minimizing negative impacts. Ultimately, by respecting local cultures, spaces and environments, slow tourism "values social responsibility while celebrating diversity and connecting people" (Heitmann, Robinson, and Povey, 2011, p. 117).

In sum, slow food and tourism, and for that matter the broader slow movement is central to a broader "life politics" (Parkins & Craig, 2006; Rojek, 2010) that emerges in reaction to late modernity and the conditions noted by Beck's (1992) risk society and resulting individuation (also see Giddens, 1991). This leaves questions of "what is the good life" and "how to live a just life" to individuals rather than the state or traditional institutions of authority and support. Parkins and Craig (2006) suggest slow living is more than a slow-motion version of the same post-modern life but rather living in such a way that creates meaning and pleasure while simultaneously being other-oriented. Both are central to life politics and to broader theorizing regarding ethical consumption. De Geus (2009) refers to this as the "art of living." It involves alternative ideas of pleasure and happiness but also of morality and responsibility to others.

The broader practices of ethical consumption are based on the idea of individuals as consumers in an increasingly deregulated and global marketplace. Neoliberalism posits consumer identity as both sovereign and by its very nature good. As long as we are making choices based on self interest (desires mediated by supply and demand) and markets are operating as they should, then we are ethical beings. Yet the realities of those markets challenge this imagining. Neoliberalism, seemingly impersonal and yet benign, now *implicates* individual consumers in actively participating in what they witness as bad or unjust outcomes through their self-interested consumer practices. This realization challenges the foundational identity of neoliberal citizens to the extent that their actions, as long as voluntaristic and self-serving, should not be questioned. The point of neoliberal globalization for residents of Northern post-industrialized societies is that by consuming, they are active participants in the outcomes that the system produces. Moreover, as globalization widens and deepens, more and more of that consumption involves complicated global production networks that tend to reproduce and exacerbate inequality. Lastly, because of communications technology, consumers know more about these processes. They come across more stories of sweatshop fires in Bangladesh, factory suicides in China, and children performing slave labor in cocoa fields in Cote d'Ivoire. Invariably these stories note that the unfortunate workers are producing consumer goods for export, mainly to the Global North. In sum, neoliberalism doesn't simply happen to us; we are complicit. We are implicated in the system through our very consumerism and often we see the resulting human suffering.

Borrowing from Bourdieu (1980), Bennett et al. (2013) argue that many contemporary political activists practice political "disavowing," where individuals who care about politics separate themselves from formal politics in order to still strive for the democratic ideals they care about. In other words, they share this antipathy toward modern politics and in some cases even eschew traditional political civic practices such as voting and party membership. Yet while disavowing they system they simultaneously take part through practices such as community organizing. Similarly, ethical consumerism is a form of economic disavowal. The promise of ethical consumerism is the promise of momentary escape from that participation. Yet we can do this through buycotting rather than boycotting (Micheletti, 2003). If products we consume involve exploitation and other bad social outcomes, rather than not buying them at all we can simply create alternative markets that exist adjacent to the exploitative markets in question. By participating in these alternative markets – buying sweat-free clothing, a fair-trade banana or an ethical holiday trip – we avoid contributing to suffering through our consumption. In fact, the promise of ethical consumption is ironically the same promise of neoliberalism: by participating in this alternative marketplace we are not only satisfying our needs and wants; we are doing good! Aside from the very real issue of whether the reality of ethical consumption meets its promise (Devinney, Auger, & Eckehardt, 2010; Lyon & Moberg, 2010), there are at least two additional problems here. One is the nature of our obligation and the other is the scope.

The ethics of slow and alternative consumption

As I suggest above, all ethical consumption practices are based on implicit or explicit criticisms of neoliberal markets and yet they rely on markets as a corrective. The Fair Trade coffee movement, for instance, arose largely as a result of the breakdown of the International Coffee Agreement in 1989 and the precipitous decline in global coffee prices that followed. The immediate result was the farmers participating in newly deregulated global commodity coffee markets could no longer make a living wage. Fair Trade coffee, by promising a floor in pricing going to farmers' cooperatives for their product, along with a small premium for local social development, creates a moral economy that exists along side the liberalized global coffee markets. Most fair trade schemes over similar products such as tea, cocoa, water and bananas operate similarly (Devinney et al., 2010; Lewis & Potter, 2011; Lyon & Moberg, 2010).

What does all of this have to do with the Slow movement? First it is important to reiterate that Slow Food and slow tourism are lifestyle movements but more specifically alternative consumption movements. They are ultimately about how and what we buy in the marketplace. As discussed above, both make dual claims: first their form of consumption is more satisfying and meaningful *for the* consumer. This is the hedonistic component. Second is the simultaneous claim that Slow is preferable to the more dominant form of consumption (fast food, mass tourism) because of their respective consequences. In short, they make ethical claims that are other-oriented. While holding much in common with other ethical consumption practices, there are also important differences. Many fair trade schemes utilize identity marketing in order to eliminate distance, break down class difference and create symbolic bonds between buyer and seller (Brown, 2013). This identity marketing typically involves narratives of producers as well as information about how the market transaction in question directly benefits this specific producer and their families. Slow food often follows this model by providing genealogies of specific food products themselves, often accompanied by stories of producers – farmers, artisan cheese makers or bakers. This is supplemented by creating alternatives to traditional mass food chains through such institutions as farmer's markets and farm-to-table restaurants. In some cases the market transactions are direct and consumers are able to ask questions and gain additional information regarding the food in question from the producers themselves.

Rather than certification and creation of a social premium in order to assure the market price is "fair," however, price is left to the market. Put differently, producers of slow food may face higher production costs but they are left to attempt to recoup them through utilizing slow food as a brand in order to charge a social premium. This is one reason why some who study social movements don't take slow food as a serious transformational movement. Instead they see it as a niche consumption market that largely caters to those who can afford that premium. Slow tourism, though less institutionalized, faces similar critiques as well-off consumers can be accused of pursuing niche consumption as a form of Bourdieu's distinction. As a niche form of tourism, the activity likely breaks down production chains by so far leaving large providers out of the market. Tourism already brings hosts (producer) and guests (consumer) physically together, leaving out large hotel chains and tour operators helps make this relationship more direct. To the extent that slow tourism possesses an other orientation, however, much like slow food the benefits are left to the market. Providers may charge a built-in premium, but whether this makes the transactions "fair" is unclear.

Creating cosmopolitan (neoliberal) citizens through consumption

Behind these initiatives are civic imaginings that contain several ideas: First is the shifting of responsibilities for identifiable global problems, especially those associated with suboptimal market outcomes. In the absence of national or international regulation, adjudication in courts or the establishment of minimal industry standards by leading firms, consumers have started to take on ethical obligations themselves to ensure fairness in their market transactions (Barnett et al., 2011; Soper, Ryle, & Thomas, 2009; Stolle & Micheletti, 2013). Ethical consumers reimagine themselves as consumer citizens, repairing the world through their purchases (Micheletti, 2003; Sassatelli, 2006; Soper, 2009; Stolle & Micheletti, 2013).

Cosmopolitan notions of citizenship argue that global society is based on a mutual set of obligations rooted in the well-being of all persons based on their status as human beings (Appiah, 2006; Kant, 1970; Sypnowich, 2005). Obligation to strangers, then, is universal and based on what Kant refers to as every individual's status as "citizens of a universal state of humanity" (cited in Linklater, 1998, p. 26). Parekh (2003, p. 6) outlines what these obligations entail. First, all human beings have equal claims to pursue their well-being. All human beings also possess negative and positive duties to others. The central negative duty is not to inflict evils on others and prevent them from pursuing their well-being. Positively we all have an obligation to alleviate suffering and render such help as needed within the limits of our own abilities of resources. Finally, such assistance is obligatory and a matter of justice, not charity. Unlike global communitarianism, however, the obligations lie not only with a society of nation-states but also with individuals.

We can think about why we have an obligation to others in very different ways and from different ethical traditions. Kant's deontology emphasizes duty toward others based on their status as humans; Singer's (2002) cosmopolitanism is predicated on utilitarianism – maximizing happiness while minimizing human suffering. Some virtue ethicists (Appiah, 2006; Hamington, 2008; Popke, 2006; Smith, 2000; Tronto, 1993) emphasize the ethic of care on a global scope. Writing on ethical consumption, Dolan (2010), citing Smith (2000), suggests that much cosmopolitanism is based on "the ethics of impartiality" or a sort of Golden Rule. My contention is that Slow ethics, along with other forms of market-based ethical consumption, are very different from any of these notions. As such they amount to a sort of false cosmopolitanism in that our obligation is not to all humans. Moreover the reason for our obligation is not connected to any of the above but rather is mandated by ethic of reducing harm within neoliberal markets.

Consumer citizens face partial obligations and only to others in the market, even if others in the market are distant. Their ethical obligation, then is to sellers –providers of their consumer products.[1] The basis is not their status as humans but rather as market participants *with whom we have an economic relationship*. Additionally, ethical consumption practices and codes are most prevalent in consumer products that are commonly the result of globalized production, usually involving Northern consumers buying products sourced in the Global South. This should come as no surprise. Neoliberalism promises individual freedom that produces voluntarist, individualized markets where buyers and sellers come together to their mutual benefit. Alternative ethical markets are most likely to arise under conditions of knowledge of the extreme inequality that exists globally between these buyers and sellers as well as information that suggests the poor are gaining very few of the benefits that these markets produce.

It should not be surprising that ethical tourism contains much of the same rhetoric and assumptions as the larger ethical consumption movement. Much of it contains language of "fairness," "equity," "rights," "empowerment," "democracy," and "sustainable development," all emerging out of ethical tourism initiatives. Again this envisions the tourist as either the provider or key partner in these initiatives. As such it re-envisions the role of tourist as citizen. Writing separately, Castañeda (2012) and Bianchi and Stephenson (2013) have addressed global tourism and traditional notions of citizenship that have accompanied the phenomenon, arguing the "rights" of tourists have traditionally been conceived of in neoliberal terms. Certainly efforts by the U.S. government and the UNWTO to formalize the fundamental "right to travel" as part of human rights discourse during the midst of the Cold War was strategic, propagandistic and yet rooted in classical liberal thought.

Bianchi and Stephenson (2013) emphasize the resource-based "right" to international mobility as global tourists – that is, we have the right to global tourism but only to the extent that we command the resources to do so. This works both financially and bureaucratically through the processing of passports, visas and border controls. Ultimately, they argue, tourism is a right, but only for an elite transnational class that can pay for it. This is wholly consistent with neoliberal notions of citizenship (Hindess, 2002).

Castañeda (2012) concurs with this view, but goes further. Asserting rights for one party also confers obligations for another. In analyzing the UNWTO's conception of a global code of ethics on tourism, he points out that most of the obligations outlined by the organization are obligations for the "makers" of tourism. These are the providers, suppliers, planners and policymakers. When tourists themselves are addressed at all, the language changes abruptly to discuss rights as claims on others. Consistent with Bianchi and Stephenson's claims of neoliberal citizenship, the UNWTO's Global Code of Tourism Ethics not only reiterates the universal *right* to tourism but also makes the claim, "The prospect of direct and personal access to the discovery and enjoyment of the planet's resources constitutes a right equally open to all the world's inhabitants" (UNWTO, 1999, quoted in Castañeda, 2012, p. 49). This not only claims a right for tourists, but also tacitly asserts an obligation for hosts: Host providers, wherever they are, should commodify and make available to the marketplace their share of the planet's desired resources for tourist consumption. Finally, implicit in this conceptualization is that marketizing tourist-related products will lead to optimal outcomes for all involved.

Of course these claims of the globe as little more than a tourist product available for purchase have undergone considerable criticism in recent years, but most criticism is consequentialist in nature. It questions the impact that the marketization of tourism actually *has* had socially, economically, environmentally. Discussion of the moralization of tourism or responsible tourist behavior is motivated either on the belief that tourism has failed to deliver the positive benefits promised by tourism markets and/or the perceptions of negative externalities that have accompanied whatever benefits that have accrued. Some ethical tourism initiatives are market-based while others add social activities to tourism. Many ecotourism initiatives, for example, contain an additional price premium that is earmarked for some kind of conservation. Some pro-poor tourism schemes attempt to alter existing or create new markets in order to create additional material benefits that go directly to the poor in the underdeveloped world (Ashley, Boyd, & Goodwin, 2000; Bennett, Roe, & Ashley, 1999). Alternatively, volunteer tourism combines tourism with the provision of tourist volunteer labor in local destination community projects. Little judgment is made regarding the merits of the economic consequences of the tourism itself here, though implicitly it is considered at worse benign and more likely beneficial. Certainly critics have questioned 1) how beneficial the volunteer projects actually are and/or who really benefits here, host or guest (Koleth, 2014; Lyons et al., 2012; Wearing, 2001).

What these activities and initiatives also demonstrate is that different forms of ethical tourism contain different conceptions of ethics and, related, citizenship. One could argue, for instance, that volunteer tourism is motivated by notions of cosmopolitan neoliberal citizenship that operates (slightly) outside of the formal marketplace as well as an area neglected by the state. In other words, when markets fail to lead to optimal outcomes, responsibility is neither that of the state or firms but instead is privatized to individual volunteer action. By its very nature, that participation is optional. This is consistent with Muehlebach's (2012) findings in Italy. As the welfare state withdraws, solving social problems is left to volunteers –neoliberal republican subjects, in this case – who through their volunteer acts gain a sense of social solidarity. International volunteerism simply takes this to the global level. This conception of ethical obligation and citizenship is very different from most ecotourism, which may involve traditional ethics of conservation or alternatively deeper ideas of ecology. The point is that ethical tourism in general, and slow tourism in particular, re-envisions tourists as citizens by making new claims regarding tourist's obligations. Abstinence is not the answer to the perceived negative impact of tourist practices. Instead, by selecting alternative products they can enjoy their holiday while protecting the planet and helping others.

Again, at issue here is who we are obliged to help and why? Whether the subject is specifically slow tourism or food, ethical tourism, or even more broadly ethical consumption, the answers are the same. Obligation is not universal but rather confined only to those participating within the market in question. Moreover, the primary reason for that obligation is *our* participation in the market. This amounts to a *partial* or false cosmopolitanism. The relationship of obligation lies between consumer and producer, not human being and human being. This is an important distinction for several reasons. First, it implicitly posits that the reasons why we have responsibilities to others in the world is because we are complicit in their suffering when we consume incorrectly. This not only ignores the other reasons for suffering in the world, from historical injustice to noneconomic sources of suffering. Second, it also narrows our responsibility. It tacitly absolves people of suffering in the world when they are not taking part in its perceived source (e.g., "I don't buy chocolate; therefore conditions for cocoa workers are not my concern"). True cosmopolitanism argues for an obligation to others even when we are not the cause to their suffering. In other words, our obligation is the product of shared humanity, not the result of a shared market transaction.

To the extent that the Slow movement emphasizes ethics beyond the self, the primary ethical values it reflects are those of neoliberalism. It does so in several ways. One, it creates markets for doing good. Like other ethical consumption movements, these activities commercialize social justice work on a global scale. Like many neoliberal initiatives, they create market solutions to market-caused problems. Two, it isolates those who deserve our ethical attention from those who do not. To be suffering injustice is not enough; it is through the symbolic and real ties of market transactions that create our obligation and specify to whom it is owed. What this effectively does is contribute to the long history of distinguishing between the deserving and non-deserving poor. Those who deserve our help are those who enter into this alternative market in good faith, in other words as willing neoliberal subjects. Others are either unable or unwilling to do so are owed nothing, at least not from us. This is consistent with other neoliberal initiatives to manage the poor, such as promoting social entrepreneurship or micro-credit in development or welfare to workfare schemes (Dolan, 2010).

Finally, by doing good through markets, these initiatives embrace the fundamental neoliberal ethic of choice. A central ethic of markets is that of the consumer as sovereign. Further, markets cherish choice on the part of that consumer. The sovereign consumer is sovereign *because* of choice. They may buy or not buy, and if they decide to buy a central virtue associated with market consumption is that we should have wide choice in what we buy. In part this emerges from additional virtue ethics such as realization of self and family interest (a care ethic) (Micheletti, 2003) or that of frugality. Shaw (2010) points out that the modern virtue of frugality in the marketplace (getting good value for money) has long historical roots within the politics of gender and the household. Today ethical consumers must weigh "doing good" in the world through their purchases with the ethic of searching for value. Consumers may value the ethical holiday or fair trade coffee, but if the price premium conflicts with this ethic of frugality, often the consumer will (rightly) choose the discounted product. Or, they may go on an ethical holiday one year, but not the next. Helping others becomes completely optional and an independent function of each purchasing act. This is highly problematic for virtually all other forms of normative ethics because for them obligation is just that: obligatory. As Amstutz (2013) points out, cosmopolitan ethics prioritizes global bonds among citizens of the world. When this conflicts with other virtues or interests, priority must go to global society.

Conclusion

The purpose of this chapter has been to discuss Slow Food and slow tourism, two consumer markets that make up significant parts of the larger Slow movement, within the larger context of ethics and citizenship. To the extent they focus on others, particularly in the consequences of that consumption, they make up a subset of the larger ethical tourism and ethical consumption markets. Placing them there allows us to examine the specific ethical claims made as well as the imaginations and conceptions of citizenship. These involve questions of to whom we have obligations and why.

In the conclusion of her 2003 book, leading scholar of political and ethical consumption Michele Micheletti argues, "democratic political consumerism is a virtue-practicing activity" (p. 150). These virtues include empathy, moderation, patience, wisdom (knowledge), honesty and fair-mindedness. The problem is the assumption that these are the only virtue ethics at work here. Ultimately while many of the fairness claims made by slow food and tourism – much like other ethical consumption markets – purport to reflect a new cosmopolitanism by creating alternative markets that reposition consumers, in reality they operate side by side with existing ethical values inherent in neoliberalism. Most important among these are placing social justice issues within a market setting where consumerism itself is treated as unproblematic. In addition, a distant geography of care differentiates among those who are deserving from those who are not while simultaneously preserving the ultimate power of choice inherent in consumerism on whether and how often we are obliged to help at all.

Note

1 Of course one of the most fascinating aspects of the fair trade movement is the particular items of consumption that are identified as fair trade worthy. Most are non-necessity food items or items often bought as gifts. We seldom hear of fair trade washing machines or steel, for example.

References

Amstutz, M. (2013). *International ethics: Concepts, theories, and cases in global politics* (4th ed.). Lanham, MD: Rowman & Littlefield.

Appiah, K. A. (2006). *Cosmopolitanism: Ethics in a world of strangers*. New York, NY: Norton.

Ashley, C., Boyd, C., & Goodwin, H. (2000). Pro-poor tourism: Putting poverty at the heart of the tourism agenda. *ODI Natural Resources Perspectives, 51*(March).

Barnett, C., Cloke, P., Clarke, N., & Malpass, A. (2011). *Globalizing responsibility: The political rationalities of ethical consumption*. Chinchester: Wiley-Blackwell.

Beck, U. (1992). *Risk society: Toward a new modernity*. London: Sage.

Beck, U., Giddens, A., & Lash, S. (1997). *Reflexive modernization: Politics, tradition and aesthetics in the modern social order*. Cambridge, MA: Polity Press.

Bennett, E. A., Cordner, A., Taylor Klein, P., Savell, S., & Baiocchi, G. (2013). Disavowing politics: Civic engagement in an era of political skepticism. *American Journal of Sociology, 119*(2), 518–548.

Bennett, O., Roe, D., & Ashley, C. (1999). Sustainable tourism and poverty elimination: A report for the department of International Development. London. DFID, London CNTR, 98, 6845.

Bennett, W. L. (1998). The un-civic culture. Communication, identity and the rise of lifestyle politics. *PS: Political Science and Politics, 31*(4), 740–761.

Bianchi, R., & Stephenson, M. (2013). Deciphering tourism and citizenship in a globalized world. *Tourism Management, 39*, 10–20.

Bourdieu, P. (1980). The production of belief: Contribution to an economy of symbolic goods. *Media, Culture and Society, 1980*(2), 261–293.

Brown, K. (2013). *Buying into fair trade: Culture, morality, consumption*. New York, NY: New York University Press.

Butcher, J. (2002). *The moralisation of tourism: Sun, sand and saving the world?* London: Routledge.

Castañeda, Q. (2012). The neo-liberal imperative of tourism: Rights and legitimation in the UNWTO global code of ethics. *Practicing Anthropology, 34*(3), 47–51.

Caton, K. (2012). Taking the moral turn in tourism studies. *Annals of Tourism Research, 39*(4), 1906–1928.

74   *Michael Clancy*

Coleman, S., & Crang, M.(Eds.). (2002). *Tourism: Between place and performance.* New York, NY: Berghahn.
Conway, D., & Timms, B. F. (2012). Are slow travel and slow tourism misfits, compadres, or different genres? In T. V. Singh (Ed.), *Critical debates in tourism* (pp. 365–373). Bristol: Channel View Publications.
Crouch, D. (2007). The power of the tourist encounter. In A. Church & T. Coles (Eds.), *Tourism, power and space* (pp. 45–62). London: Routledge.
Crouch. (2001). *Leisure/tourism geographies: Practices and geographical knowledge.* London: Routledge.
Daly, H. E. (1996). *Beyond growth: The economics of sustainable development.* Boston, MA: Beacon Press.
De Geus, M. (2009). Sustainable hedonism: The pleasures of living within environmental limits. In K. Soper, M. Ryle, & L. Thomas (Eds.), *The politics and pleasures of consuming differently* (pp. 113–129). London: Palgrave.
Devinney, T., Auger, P., & Eckehardt, G. (2010). *The myth of the ethical consumer.* Cambridge: Cambridge University Press.
Dickinson, J. E., & Lumsdon, L. (2010). *Slow travel and tourism.* London: Earthscan.
Dickinson, J. E., Lumsdon, L., & Robbins, D. K. (2011). Slow travel: Issues for tourism and climate change. *Journal of Sustainable Tourism, 19*(3), 281–300.
Dolan, C. (2010). Fractured ties: The business of development in Kenyan fair trade tea. In S. Lyon & M. Moberg (Eds.), *Fair trade and social justice: Global ethnographies* (pp. 147–177). New York, NY: NYU Press.
Gardner, N. (2009). A manifesto for slow travel. *Hidden Europe Magazine, 25,* 10–14.
Giddens, A. (1991). *Modernity and self-identity: Self and society in the late modern age.* Stanford, CA: Stanford University Press.
Haenfler, R., Johnson, B., & Jones, E. (2012). Lifestyle movements: Exploring the intersection of lifestyle and social movements. *Social Movement Studies, 12*(1), 1–20.
Hamington, M. (2008). Care ethics and international justice: The cosmopolitanism of Jane Addams and Kwame Anthony Appiah. *Social Philosophy Today, 23,* 149–160.
Heitmann, S., Robinson, P., & Povey, G. (2011). Slow food, slow cities and slow tourism. In P. Robinson, S. Heitmann, & P. J. C. Dickey (Eds.), *Research themes for tourism* (pp. 114–127). London: CAB International.
Hindess, B. (2002). Neoliberal citizenship. *Citizenship Studies, 6*(2), 127–143.
Holzer, B., & Sørenson, M. P. (2003). Rethinking subpolitics: Beyond the 'iron cage'of modern politics? *Theory, Culture and Society, 20*(2), 79–102.
Kant, I. (1970). *Political writings.* Cambridge texts in the history of political thought. H. S. Reiss (Ed.). Cambridge: Cambridge University Press.
Koleth, M. (2014). Travelling goods: Global (self) development on sale. In C. Weeden & K. Bulok (Eds.), *Managing ethical consumption in tourism* (pp. 123–133). London: Routledge.
Lewis, T., & Potter, E. (Eds.). (2011). *Ethical consumption: A critical introduction.* London: Routledge.
Linklater, A. (1998). Cosmopolitan citizenship. *Citizenship Studies, 2*(1), 23–41.
Lumsdon, L. M., & McGrath, P. (2011). Developing a conceptual framework for slow travel: A grounded theory approach. *Journal of Sustainable Tourism, 19*(3), 265–279.
Lyon, S., & Moberg, M. (Eds.). (2010). *Fair trade and social justice: Global ethnographies.* New York, NY: NYU Press.
Lyons, K., Hanley, J., Wearing, S., & Neil, J. (2012). Gap year volunteer tourism: Myths of global citizenship? *Annals of Tourism Research, 39*(1), 361–378.
Micheletti, M. (2003). *Political virtue and shopping: Individuals, consumerism, and collective action.* London: Palgrave MacMillan.

Mostafanezhad, M., & Hannam, K. (Eds). (2014). *Moral encounters in tourism.* London: Ashgate.

Muehlebach, A. (2012). *The moral neoliberal: Welfare and citizenship in Italy.* Chicago, IL: University of Chicago Press.

Parekh, B. (2003). Cosmopolitanism and global citizenship. *Review of International Studies, 29*(1), 3–17.

Parkins, W., & Craig, G. (2006). *Slow living.* Oxford: Berg.

Petrini, C. (2007). *Slow food nation: Why our food should be good, clean and fair.* New York, NY: Rizzoli Ex Libris.

Petrini. (2006). *Slow food revolution: A new culture for eating and living.* New York, NY: Rizzoli.

Pink, S. (2012). *Situating everyday life: Practices and places.* London: Sage.

Popke, J. 2006. Geography and ethics: everyday mediations through care and consumption. *Progress in Human Geography* 30: 4, 504–512.

Ritzer, G. (1993). *The MacDonaldlization of society.* Thousand Oaks, CA: Pine Forge Press.

Rojek, C. (2010). *The labour of leisure.* London: Sage.

Sassatelli, R. (2006). Virtue, responsibility and consumer choice: Framing critical consumerism. In J. Brewer, & F. Trentmann (Eds.), *Consuming cultures, global perspectives: Historical trajectories, transnational exchanges* (pp. 219–250). Oxford: Berg.

Sassatelli, R., & Davolio, F. (2010). Consumption, pleasure and politics: Slow food and the politico-aesthetic problematization of food. *Journal of Consumer Culture, 10*(2), 202–232.

Schneider, S. (2008). Good, clean, fair: The rhetoric of the slow food movement. *College English, 70*(4), 384–402.

Shaw, J. (2010). *Shopping: Social and cultural perspectives.* Cambridge: Polity.

Singer, P. (2002). *One world: The ethics of globalization.* New Haven, CT: Yale University Press.

Smith, D. (2000). *Moral geographies in a world of difference.* Edinburgh: Edinburgh University Press.

Smith, M., & Duffy, R. (2003). *The ethics of tourism development.* London: Routledge.

Soper, K. (2009). Introduction: The mainstreaming of counter-consumerist concern. In K. Soper, M. Ryle, & L. Thomas (Eds.), *The politics and pleasures of consuming differently* (pp. 1–21). Basingstoke: Palgrave MacMillan.

Soper, K., Ryle, M., & Thomas, L. (Eds.). (2009). *The politics and pleasures of consuming differently.* Basingstoke: Palgrave MacMillan.

Stolle, D., & Micheletti, M. (2013). *Political consumerism: Global responsibility in action.* Cambridge: Cambridge University Press.

Sypnowich, C. (2005). Cosmopolitans, cosmopolitanism and human flourishing. In G. Brock & H. Brighouse (Eds.), *The political philosophy of cosmopolitanism* (pp. 55–74). Cambridge: Cambridge University Press.

Tronto, J. (1993). *Moral boundaries: A political argument for an ethic of care.* New York, NY: Routledge.

UNWTO. (1999). *Approval for global code of ethics for tourism.* UNWTO General Assembly Resolution. Retrieved from http://ethics.unwto.org/sites/all/files/docpdf/unwtoresolutiona-res-406xiii1999.pdf

Wearing, S. (2001). *Volunteer tourism: Experiences that make a difference.* New York, NY: CABI.

Weeden, C., & Boluk, K. (Eds). (2014). *Managing ethical consumption in tourism.* Abingdon: Routledge.

Part II
Places and practices of slow

6 Creative tourism as slow tourism

Roberto Lavarini and Rosantonietta Scramaglia

Introduction

This paper aims to address two different types of tourism widely spoken of today: slow tourism and creative tourism. We will begin by defining these two concepts and outlining the link between them. We will thereby try to identify the motivations that lead people to practice or seek this kind of tourism. We will than analyze the types of travel that are closest to these two models; those that are rooted in the past, such as pilgrimages, ethnical tourism and cultural tourism, leading up to today in the aim to analyze the offer through both the different forms of hospitality that are best suited to promote slow and creative tourism, and through the initiatives and activities that place the tourist in contact with the territories, cultures and local populations. Finally, we will provide a few examples of the offer put forth by creative cities and territories.

Slowness and creativity: The needs of today's travellers

Slow travel

One of the characteristics of slow travel is essentially taking the time not only to observe, but also to live the territory being crossed. But what does "live a territory" actually mean? When planning the ideal journey, Eric Leed (1992) breaks it down into three stages. The first is *the departure*. The stage of abandonment of what we know and cherish to face the unknown. The second is *the passage*, meaning the path that serves as a link between the act of departing and the act of arriving. The third is, precisely, *the arrival*, or, in other words, when we try to integrate with the place of destination. It is a time for new encounters and for gaining knowledge of others, of those who are remote and different from us. It is the moment in which each individual puts itself to the test to be accepted by the residents.

Nonetheless, according to Leeds the cornerstone of the travel experience is the "passage," towards which less and less interest is shown nowadays, gradually reducing itself to a merely symbolic aspect of many journeys. We arrive at a shelter, which we call airport. We get on a plane and find ourselves on the other side of the world without any awareness of what lies between the point of departure and the point we call arrival. This is how slow travelling can allow us to rediscover the "passage" phase of a journey, to "live" the territory being crossed and to engage with the local culture made up of numerous activities. Slow travel is becoming one of the few traveling solutions capable of leaving the traveller with a lasting impression of the experience made during the passage. This is how, therefore, the slowness of the travel is supplemented by the activities offered by the territory in a creative tourism perspective.

Creative tourism

While slow tourism emphasizes on the "passage" phase and thereby on the importance of taking the time to interact with the cultures being met during the journey, creative tourism does not necessarily take place only during the passage but also at the destination, since, likewise, the traveller takes the time it needs to perform local – and not strictly tourist – activities, in contact with the residents. Throughout the journey and upon arrival, travellers feel the growing desire to discover the local culture by taking part in local activities, as shown by a number of research projects conducted on the Italian and French territories. Travellers seek unique experiences, which in time they can link back to their memory of a specific place. In a "hectic" type of tourism, everything is muddled. In its memories, the traveller is unable to distinguish between all the places visited that did not leave a lasting impression, and often such places merely generate great dissatisfaction as well as the desire, upon returning home, to leave once again in search of that experience and the particular gratification the traveller was unable to find the first time.

Essentially, creative tourism is:

> [L]earning a skill or engaging in a practice that is part of the culture of the country or community being visited. Creative tourists develop their creative potential, and get closer to local people, through informal participation in interactive workshops and learning experiences that draw on the culture of their holiday destinations. (Laliberté, 2006)

This active engagement induces to a more profound knowledge of the local community's lifestyle, and goes beyond commonplace, stereotypes and superficial information.

Many tourists believe that travel is a real opportunity to learn and be spiritually and culturally enriched. A "vacation," which from an etymological point of view means "freedom" from duties and suspension of daily activities, becomes an opportunity for an authentic educational experience. A vacation – which has come a long way from its original meaning of rest and suspension of one's identity – is turning into a strong moment of search and assertion of oneself, of one's values and passions. Cultural tourism therefore may develop into experiential tourism, which, in turn, takes on the connotation of creative tourism when it involves the user's active participation and engagement by immersion and assimilation (Mercury & Becheri, 2009).

In any case, creative tourists love doing, participating and creating. These would be the kinds of tourist that take part in pottery classes during which they chat with teachers and classmates. Tourists could take cooking classes to learn the quality of local products, their history and use. They explore new flavors and tastes and turn them into their own. Creative tourists are the ones that learn by doing, and often they develop skills they didn't even know they had. This is how they integrate in the local culture, appreciate local products and get to know those who live on the territory. And only by knowing the territory, can one truly grow to respect and accept it. In this context, the symbolic dimension of the typical souvenir object gains increasing importance when the travel takes on experiential value. The gift can no longer be considered a merely standard souvenir object bought in a small gift shop or at a stand on the street. On the contrary, the souvenir is now filled with meaning because it is the memory of a specific personal experience – perhaps the tourist built it at an arts and crafts workshop (Rossi & Goetz, 2011).

From speed to experience

Our history is made up of constant fascination for speed. The greatest invention, acknowledged by all, that drove us to the future as we know it is the wheel; an invention that progressively freed man from the physical effort of doing and moving. Even Newcomen's steam engine marked a leap forward, since it gave way to the combustion engine, father of modern means of transport such as cars and, in particular, trains, which quickly took on a key role in medium-to-long-distance travels. Of particular interest is the account of the train travel organized by Thomas Cook, the English Baptist minister who invented package holidays. On July 5, 1841, the birth of organized tourism, he arranged to convey 570 people, at the price of one shilling, from Leicester to Loughborough – 11 miles away – where an important town fair was taking place. Cook chartered a train with open carriages in which people had to travel standing. Passengers crossed the English countryside and later reported how the train had terrorized the herds along their path with all the noise, the smoke from the locomotive and the astonishing speed of approximately 20 km/h! A large crowd greeted the travellers upon their arrival, including reporters who narrated of how white their smiles were compared to their faces turned black from the smoke of the engine.

Since then, we have moved on to modern-day trains, capable of achieving impressive speeds of 400 km/h, or the Maglevs (Magnetic Levitation trains) such as the Shangai Transrapid, which connects the city to its airport at an average speed of 250 km/h with peaks up to 501 km/h. (Monorail Society, 2015). A parallel escalation exists in air transport. Today, after a little over a century of adventurous progress made by air pioneers, it is normal for a constantly increasing number of people to travel within a few hours to remote places – perhaps even in the other hemisphere – and to experience a rapid change in time zone or season. Nonetheless, alongside such trend, there is another tendency that is more and more taking hold and leading us to slow down and come closer together. Today, the dissatisfaction characterizing many modern travellers who, in little time, want to experience everything, raises a doubt: Is it really necessary to cross the world in order to discover new realities and cultures we are not familiar with?

Up until a few years ago this was essential in order to gather documentary evidence of those realities. Today, all we need is an Internet connection. Even before leaving, tourists already know everything about their destination: the weather, the monuments, the physical and social environment, its history and current affairs. Therefore, once they arrive they will search for what they can see, and often what they have already seen, but also for what they can do and perhaps do it with someone else. A tourist seeks for an exclusive experience, an unexpected sensation and an excitement that will justify the transfer. And, ironically, they may often find this new experience and thrill more easily in places that are closer to them and which they have heard less about, rather than in more remote places that are shown on TV or in movies or described in novels. Places close to home, whose customs, knowledge or inhabitants' tastes or skills tourists know nothing about, because everything is buried under the standardized and globalized urban civilization (Scramaglia, 2008).

To experience a pleasant journey means owning your own time and being able to manage it freely. It means discovering breathtaking and unexplored corners of the world and tasting forgotten flavors. The journey takes on new meanings, leads to new motivations and curiosities. By traveling slowly on new, yet equally ancient, paths – marked by the traces left by wayfarers from earlier centuries – spirit and mind open to new perspectives that allow to discover the people in their own land with its history, art, crafts and with the marks of a past faith that gives purpose to and guides the lives of many still to this day. According to Ejarque (2004, pp. 20–25), there has always been a traditional dichotomy at the heart of tourism. On one hand, we have the highly standardized tourists that are a part of the four S's (sea, sun, sand and sex), where the form may change by the substance stays the same. On the other, we have a model of tourism that can be defined as the "Three L's," landscape, leisure and learning, which is very similar to the "Three D's" defined by Dumazedier (1962): *Delassement* (relaxation), *Divertissement* (leisure), *Developpement* (development). It is this second area we wish to address.

A new tourist

The model of tourism composed of the famous 4 S's mentioned in the previous paragraph was extremely popular in the 1950s, and it became quickly widespread. While this type of tourism will unlikely disappear in the near future, it is bound to be joined and perhaps surpassed by other forms of tourism. This is due to a number of considerations. There has been an increase in the so-called fragmented holidays – vacations that have multiplied in terms of frequency per year but that have been greatly downsized in terms of duration. There are holidays that merely last a weekend or a few days over the Christmas or Easter break. The advantage is that these holidays in "bits and pieces" allow people to create many different experiences in several destinations, during varied time periods and, perhaps, even with separate travel companions each time.

Travel is also going through different kinds of segmentation. One category that is taking hold is that of elder travel. Older people often seek holidays that are less hectic, more relaxed, moving at a slower pace and mainly revolving around wellness and cultural activities. This type of traveller is often well educated and loves to experiment new things rather than spend its days basking in the sun on a beach. Many travellers are interested in cultural tourism. Those who visit another country usually wish to learn about its culture. For the time being, this type of tourism is rather passive, but it is already gradually taking more innovative and interactive directions. Other segments also proliferate demographically: gay and lesbian tourism, gap years and other student-age tourism are some examples.

It must be added that today tourism is rapidly evolving, perhaps also due to the widespread economic crisis in Europe and elsewhere, which pushes it, on one hand, towards choices that are more modest and closer to home. Perhaps tourists are more cultured and know what they want, or perhaps they are rediscovering old-time values and give greater importance to the originality of craft as opposed to industrial artificiality; to genuine culinary products as opposed to prepackaged foods. It is this same framework that has inspired the choices made by Expo 2015 Milan: the desire to shift the attention from modern-day, technological progress and urban culture towards traditional agriculture; from industrial goods to earth products – food and water.

Other forms of tourism

Despite today's tendency to depict slow tourism and creative tourism as a new form of travel since its satisfies the need of modern-day tourists, such models are actually rooted in other forms of tourism and travel practiced long before tourism was even born. After all, travelling in itself implies the desire to put oneself to the test, to engage with new realities and new people, and it requires patience, flexibility and creativity in order to come up with solutions to unexpected situations or problems. Nonetheless, in past decades the tendency has been to minimize all of these aspects thanks to safe, fast and detached means of transport; large hotel chains and tourist resorts where one can feel at home; and package tours that schedule every moment of the day, leaving no space to setbacks but neither to improvisation, discoveries and spontaneous contacts. Only a small niche of travellers decided to overcome the obstacles associated with language barriers, cultural and currency differences, in the desire to embark on an adventure in a foreign country. Historically, pilgrims of all times and places necessarily practiced slow tourism, nearly always by foot by necessity and inevitably coming into contact with the local communities that hosted them during the different stages of their journey. We then had and still have the travellers – usually emigrants – who return to their home countries where they relearn their customs thanks to the regained contact with their relatives and fellow countrymen and women; they learn things they had forgotten just like in creative tourism. Then there is cultural tourism, maybe one of the first forms of tourism known as the Grand Tour, the traditional trip to Italy or Greece undertaken by young upper-class men of northern European countries, not only to study the remains of a glorious past but also to become men, by gathering meaningful experiences through the contact with different populations and customs. Finally, there are also other forms of tourism that contain elements that overlap with slow tourism and creative tourism, including educational and nature tourism.

An "ancient" slow tourism: pilgrimage

One of the oldest and most widespread forms of slow tourism, worldwide, is pilgrimage, an experience for singles, families, groups, children, young people, elderly people, disabled and sick people who wish to discover and share through this journey an experience of joy and hope. This experience can open up life perspectives to new horizons, to find one is a pilgrim of the world on a journey with the Church (Lavarini, 1997). The destinations for pilgrimages are many throughout the world. In Italy alone the shrines, according to the SPI (*Segretariato Pelligrinaggi Italiani* – Italian Pilgrimages Secretariat) add up to 225. These include the internationally renowned destinations of Assisi, Loreto, Padova or San Giovanni Rotondo and those – many – that attract the faithful of a limited adjacent area. Moving slowly and gradually, and performing the devotions, is essential for this type kind of journey.

Among the few initiatives undertaken at a European level, is PER VIAM, a European project for slow tourism along historical routes. *Per Viam, Pilgrims' Routes in Action* is the title of the European project coordinated by the European Association of the Vie Francigene, the ancient pilgrim road and route between France and Rome. The project is financed by the European Union within the framework of the preliminary action "Sustainable Tourism." The aim of this project is to strengthen cooperation at the European level between the public and private actors involved in the promotion of the tourist-cultural routes of the vie Francigene. The project concerns the Via Francigena and other transnational pilgrimage routes recognized by the Council of Europe that are regarded as a catalyst of cultural and sustainable tourism development and as an instrument of EC participation in the promotion of European cultural diversity. The project partners will cooperate in the form of a consortium in order to promote a responsible and sustainable approach to cultural tourism along the European pilgrimage routes. The aim of this concerted action is to improve visibility, communication, awareness and the accessibility to such routes. Thanks to the work of institutions, European networks and local organizations, the project is aimed at creating a European network of pilgrimage routes officially recognized by the Council of Europe, which includes the Via Francigena, the Santiago de Compostela Pilgrim's Routes, the St. Olav's Ways and the Saint Martin of Tours Route (www.viefrancigene.org; www.sloways.eu).

Roots tourism

Generally, roots tourism is more developed in territories closer to one's hometown, but may also include visits to more remote places, which are, nevertheless, in some way connected to one's life or heritage. For instance, a tourist may live with its family in the U.S.A., where many Europeans emigrated over the past centuries, and feel the desire to visit a little village in the mountains in Italy, where its grandparents used to live, to trace back the history of a past existence of which it has heard so many stories. This is what happens:

John, the Californian tourist, arrives at Malpensa airport in Milan, rents a car and drives through the small roads of Genoa's inland. He stays at a small boarding house and tries to adopt the locals' lifestyle. He goes to the local pub and entertains conversations with the elderly population about his grandparents. Someone remembers them and points to an old abandoned house. They then talk about life in California but especially of life here in the mountains. They talk about food, of the few cows left, of how beautiful the fields and woods used to be back then. Carrying on our imaginary tale, someone may even invite him over for dinner to taste simple homemade food. He, too, would love to cook or go down to the cellar with new friends to pick out a good bottle of wine. Meanwhile, he chats and helps out in the kitchen. The neighbors come over as well; someone mentions an old-time song and they get swept away by the memories. How relaxing to sit down in company and how fun to listen to stories of the past. Surely John will take those stories back home with him and share them with his friends and family. On his journey, John experienced both slow and creative tourism, bringing back home with him something very different than his fellow countryman who, unlike John, opted for a package tour in Italy that same week, getting a chance to merely skim over the main cities. The "three D's" and the "three S's" have marked his journey.

From cultural to creative tourism

The approach adopted by the ATLAS Cultural Tourism Research Project in 1991 aimed to encompass process and product-based approaches. The project, supported by the European Commission, sought to increase cultural tourism in the European Union. The current ATLAS definitions are conceptual definitions: "The movement of persons to cultural attractions away from their normal place of residence, with the intention to gather new information and experiences to satisfy their cultural needs" and a technical definition: "All movements of persons to specific cultural attractions, such as heritage sites, artistic and cultural manifestations, arts and drama outside their normal place of residence" (Richards, 1996). Greg Richards defines creative tourism as an extension of cultural tourism: "a form of tourism which offers visitors the opportunity to develop their creative potential through active participation in courses and learning experiences which are characteristic of the holiday destination where they are undertaken" (Richards & Wilson, 2007, p. 125).

If we compare creative tourism to cultural tourism, the former strips the cultural tourist of that typical passive approach. This includes those who sit back and watch the creations of artists who have left traces of their genius, the masterpieces of extraordinary beauty displayed in museums and cathedrals, or the buildings designed by renowned architects and the visible remains of a fascinating past. Even musical acts playing in theatres or during music festivals are a result of genius. This is not to imply that this admiration must cease but rather that it could be supported through the creativity of the observer; for example, by taking part in painting or sculpture classes that draw on the masterpieces admired, or by participating in music workshops to reproduce folk tunes heard during the journey. In other words, tourists experience the atmosphere, the light, the warmth of a place, take it in fully and slowly. Even needlework, carving or cooking classes can help to embrace a mood of thorough participation that will turn the journey into an authentic and fruitful experience. Culture is also all of this; a culture that physically and spiritually penetrates the mind and soul of the visitor, and the two become one. This is the aim of cultural tourism, even though it often remains implicit.

The ATLAS research indicates that the experiences that are more highly appreciated by cultural tourists are the ones offered by less visited places that give a taste of the "local" or "authentic culture." Tourists increasingly wish to learn about the local culture, mingle with the local community and discover the real identity of the places they're visiting (Richards, 2009). Over the past few decades, cultural tourism has grown massively but perhaps due to the unstoppable process of globalization, it has done nothing more than reshuffle the cards in the competition among cities around the world. The differences between cultural offerings, in terms of services, have become smaller and smaller. Large cities copy the successful initiatives of their rivals, with offers that thereby all look alike, and the less shrewd visitors get the feeling of a déjà vu. This may be one of the reasons why creative tourism has developed so rapidly, as a way to physiologically and mentally strengthen the experience gained during the visit of a city where the peculiarity of the cultural offer is supplemented by the learning experience gained in "doing."

Today creativity attracts, and it does this in parallel with other similar forms of tourism to a number of cultural icons, such as museums like the Guggenheim of Bilbao or particularly popular events like the World Cup, the Olympic Games, world Expos, or the UNESCO human heritage sites.

The concept of creative tourism was re-elaborated in 2006 by the United Nations Educational, Scientifics and Cultural Organization (UNESCO, 2006), which provides its own definition: "Creative tourism is travel directed toward an engaged and authentic experience, with participative learning in the arts, heritage, or special character of a place, and it provides a connection with those who reside in this place and create this living culture" (UNESCO, 2006, p. 3).

Slow traveling promotes and integrates cultural tourism, bringing it closer to creative tourism. In brief, if we were to make a comparison between the different types of tourism we could say that the "typical" cultural tourist seeks traces of both the past and the present, but remains a mere passive observer. In contrast, the creative tourist is interested not only in the past and the present but also in the future. Moreover, they take on an active approach because learning and experience come from participating rather than watching.

The supply of slow and creative tourism

It appears that tour operators have come to realize that nowadays the tourism product must have a strong participatory element, because travellers are no longer willing to sit back and watch as passive spectators. In any case, this is where the organizational ability of the offer stands, because it should give the user the chance to undergo a complete and complex experience in line with the three E's: education, entertainment, excitement (Mercury & Becheri, 2009, p. 612). Many countries around the world would gain considerable advantage from the model of slow travel becoming a new widespread travelling trend. Its implementation is rather simple because it does not require any significant means of transport. One may travel by car, by bus or by train – making a few stops – or even by foot, bicycle or horse. Any "slow" means of transport will be sufficient to be able to carefully observe the surroundings and interact with those met during the journey.

If local governments were to promote the maintenance of slow routes by putting up signs and building rest areas, this would provide major benefits to this type of tourism, as well as generate economic activity along the way. Rest areas positioned strategically along the more popular and charming routes, equipped with bike grills and Internet points; interesting services managed by young people – following the example of the Trentino region in Italy – and connections with the local railway stations. There are a number of other interesting projects that struggle to move forward such as the itinerary by horse or carriage from Sicily to Alto Adige, or the cycle lane that crosses from East to West, from Venice to Turin.

The creative supply

Those who operate in the tourism industry are constantly seeking for something unusual or new to offer prospect customers. The important thing is to differentiate offerings from mass tourism. They can attract visitors by stimulating them to explore their creativity and their inclination to "doing." Often, as we have seen, an invitation to creativity combines itself with the discovery of a territory's culture together with nature, built environment and the features of the people who reside in it. This active engagement induces to a more profound knowledge of the local people's lifestyle and goes beyond commonplace, stereotypes and superficial information. Furthermore, the creative tourist does not merely learn, replicate objects or local know-how; doing gives free rein to the personal dimension, bringing one's own culture and balancing it with the local one.

Analyzing the issue from the viewpoint of the hosting communities, creativity is a vital "pull factor" capable of driving, on one hand, an increasing number of people from the local community to permanently settle in the territory and continue their traditional craft businesses, and, on the other, tourists to visit. Whether it is a city or an entire nation, creative choices make a place pleasant for both those who live in it and those who visit. Therefore, as we well know, a successful destination benefits not only tourists and those who are staying there temporarily, but it especially gives great pride to those who live there permanently. Greg Richards stresses the fact that the experience of creative tourism must necessarily go hand in hand with the context, through key words such as *participation, immersion, diversity*: a sophisticated management and an organization that has nothing to do with traditional mass tourism. Creative tourism does not apply only to travellers but also to entrepreneurs. In order to evolve in competition and be successful nowadays it is important to be creative, to innovate products and methods without forgetting quality. A winning formula that is not always easy to apply; too often the tendency is to copy the successful initiatives of someone else to the point of saturating the market where a growing number of tourists seek creative experiences (Richards & Wilson, 2006).

New ways to stay

Over the past year, the number of listings on the Airbnb website – the Californian company specialized in short-term rentals between private homeowners and travellers in 190 countries across the world – has more than doubled. And Airbnb is only one example of many companies that have proliferated during the past decades. Now even real estate agency websites are equipped with this method of hospitality. The most common guests are tourists, managers and students. Such contracts provide that homeowners can offer guests not only their house but also customized services upon request, advice and recommendations, useful information on how to discover the most characteristic aspects of a location, particularly those usually hidden to tourists, or even engage in activities together. Add to this home swappers, whose top motivation is the opportunity to gain an authentic cultural experience (36.5 percent), rather than merely economic savings (14.7 percent) (Ruisi, 2011, p. 60). Another way to connect tourists with the local life, as well as make new encounters and get to know different cultures, is couch-surfing, where homeowners host guests on their couch for free.

Another model that has developed in Italy and other European countries is that of farm holidays, especially thanks to the proliferation of environmental and heritage assets and family-owned agricultural businesses. In 2013, these *agriturismi* in Italy amounted to 20,897, showing a 60.5 percent increase compared to 2003: from 13,019 to 20,897 (ISTAT, 2014), and initially it was the foreigners, especially the British and Germans, who practiced this new model, as lovers of the Italian countryside and local products. Bear in mind that Italy obtained world leadership in the wine and food tourism, thanks to 4,886 local products recognized and recorded by the Regional governments, 272 PDO/PGI specialties recognized at the EU level, 415 DOC (Controlled Designation of Origin)/DOCG (Controlled and Guaranteed Designation of Origin) wines, and over 6,600 farms where you can buy products directly from the farmers.

At first, the *agriturismi* started out by offering restaurant services, then accommodations and in a few cases even the possibility to take part in the daily activities and work of the farm. Since then, 1,176 farms have turned into proper "educational farms," hosting schools and groups interested in actual workshops on the growing and processing of agricultural products. Out of the 22,738 *agriturismi* registered in 2015, over half of them (55.8 percent) – meaning 12,416 businesses (+2.3 percent compared to 2014) – are authorized to carry out other agritouristic activities (horseback riding, hiking, wildlife watching, trekking, mountain biking, educational farms, cooking classes, craft and farming workshops, sports and others) (ISTAT, 2016).

Another concept of hospitality launched in Italy in the early 1980s: the *Albergo Diffuso*, with the purpose to restore abandoned houses in the historic centres and medieval hamlets (or *borghi*) of depopulated villages, which are very common in Italy and widely spread out across the country, although at the current state the specific number is unknown. In today's emerging experience economy, the *albergo diffuso* not only offers a wide range of services, but it also becomes an actual industry of memories. It looks to create a narrative world, turn a service into a story, offer the chance to live the territory, provide memorable experiences, establish positive relationships with guests even after their stay and thereby encourage them to return and become active endorsers of the destination. Thanks to the *Albergo Diffuso*, guests become temporary residents of the *borghi*, (Dall'Ara, 2010) which, in July 2015, were included in the *Rapporto sul Patrimonio Culturale* (Cultural heritage report), entitled "*Patrimonio Culturale: identità del Paese e inestimabile opportunità di crescita*" (Cultural Heritage: Country identity and inestimable growth opportunity). The report underlines how diversity and landscape are indispensable assets of Italy and how investments in cultural heritage are essential to change and development. The report examined in depth the extent to which factors such as natural and artistic heritage, history, culture, local tradition and the quality of life represent "effective opportunities" for the territories;

and whether or not physical resources and economic activities reflect the "cultural and attraction vocation" of the territories (where such definition also includes the resources of the cultural, creative, wine and food, and artistic crafts industries).

Even B&Bs, which traditionally have not had a well-rooted tradition in Italy compared to other European countries, are experiencing significant growth. In 2016, their number grew to approximately 25,000, a 5.8 percent increase compared to 2012 And this success owes to the demand for a new concept of tourism (relational tourism rather than mass tourism). Among the motivations: a direct relationship with the host, the feeling of being at "home" and the chance to experience the daily life of a place, and closely connect with the local reality. Above all, the aspect guests appreciate the most (74 percent) is the hospitality of the local population (Bed-and-Breakfast.it, 2016).

Creative cities

The growth of creative tourism today is visible in numerous forms. A tour package can include painting, drawing and cooking classes. Decently successful was a package that offered a grape harvesting experience in Tuscany, with activities such as grape pressing, wine tasting and bottling. There are large cities like Paris or small villages in Tuscany where the classes and workshops offered are combined with the hospitality of a charming hotel and day trips to old craft shops in pursuit of those products that have now become industrialized – and perhaps more perfect than they used to be but without those small imperfections that once made them unique. Tourists are not only attracted to the countryside; offers in cities have become creative as well. There are areas that are well known for fashion, design, technology, architecture, music and dance. The evolution of many museums is a rather significant sign. Cathedrals of culture, keepers of the fruits of Man's genius – where the visitor was often considered a necessary evil to put up with and forced into obliged pathways – have now transformed; some museums offer themed workshops for both children and adults, play music in the background and diffuse home fragrances. Visiting a museum has become more stimulating, especially with regards to the "new" ones, where the works displayed are recent and represent a specific theme and where the notices put up read "touch me, please," rather than "please do not touch."

Currently, more than half of the global population lives in cities Many urban dwellers have managed to carve out an image of "creative city" for themselves – under the assumption that creativity can play an important role – not only, for instance, by renovating their structure, by building new paths and opening social spaces, but also by encouraging and educating users, whether residents or guests, to take the time to truly enjoy these spaces, through an active and participatory approach, and by putting forward an offer that is varied yet at the same time characteristic of the territory. In October 2004, UNESCO launched the *Creative Cities Network*, to promote cultural diversity throughout the world in the aim to unlock the creative, social and economic potential of cultural industries, bringing together public and private partners and increasing the awareness among civil societies in order to encourage the development of the creative industries and generate new forms of international cooperation. The network is built around seven themes: literature, cinema, music, crafts and folk art, design, media art and gastronomy, which can be chosen by the cities according to their preferences for a specific sector of creative industry to which to devote their talent and energy. Once a city becomes part of the network, it can share experiences and create new opportunities for itself and for others on a global platform.

Cities that have become a part of the network are spread out across the entire world, testimony to the fact that creative tourism, and consequently cultural tourism and slow tourism, constitute a new opportunity (UNESCO, 2006). In 2012, Beijing joined the UNESCO Creative Cities Network (CCN) as "City of Design." Among the 116 cities from 54 different countries identified by UNESCO in 2017 are Barcelona, Spain; Dunedin, New Zealand; Aswan, Egypt; Santa Fe, Detroit, U.S.A.; Berlin, Germany; Buenos Aires, Argentina; Montreal, Canada; Popayan, Colombia; Edinburgh and Glasgow, Scotland; Melbourne, Australia; Bologna, Italy; and Lyon, France. Over the years creative tourism projects have evolved and generally tend to vary. This is obviously due to the fact that each one is intimately tied to its territory and to the experiences it can offer. In particular, all around Europe we see offers that seem like a direct response to the creative potential of new tourists. In 2009 three major cities – Rome, Barcelona and Paris – decided to create a first network of creative tourist cities. The joint goal was to encourage the exchange of best practices, promote creative destinations and spur partnerships and agreements between cities. First in Barcelona and then in Paris, international conferences were held with the purpose to discuss the different prospects for creative tourism. At the conference in Paris, "Creative: the new tourist attitude, Developing & enhancing creative tourism" in December 2012, Jean Bernard Bros, *Adjoint au tourisme* for the Paris local government, stated that Paris – top tourist destination in the world – has long been offering visitors the opportunity to carry out creative activities during their stay. Further, he indicated that it is a priority of the Paris municipality to "accompany, encourage and promote" a more quality-and-conviviality-oriented tourism.

Bros continued confirming his intent to continue investment in tourist practices for a long time because a client base who has already visited the city will not go back if we fail to offer them:

[A]n intense and original personal experience. This is why we launched the "Créative Paris" initiative in February 2012. We are proud to say that after only 10 months, 200 art centres and 1000 creative activities have registered. I believe it is a world record! (Bros, 2012)

Creativity across territories

It is not just cities that are creative; vast territories such as Tuscany or even entire nations also take on these qualities. New Zealand is a perfect example. The country is overshadowed by the major tourist destination Australia, but offers a unique destination that combines both ethnic and cultural diversity. One of the key actors in the transformation of this nation into a "creative nation" is Raymond Crispin (2003). Crispin worked alongside Richards to define in 2000 the concept of "creative tourism" and contributed to its establishment since the very beginning. When he moved to New Zealand in 2003, Crispin launched "Creative Tourism New Zealand." Since then, there has been a constant improvement in the experiences and initiatives, with economic benefits for the communities and great satisfaction for the residents participating and the visitors enjoying them. Creative Tourism New Zealand promotes exploring the land while taking part in workshops and seminars – lasting from two hours to four days – on handicrafts, the customs of the Maori culture, or the uses of vegetable fiber or wool, or – highly popular – in regional cooking classes.

In addition to projects launched in New Zealand, where the supply of creative tourism is built around workshops and seminars, a number of creative strategies have been applied in traditional tourist destinations, such as the region of Algarve in Portugal (Ferreira & Costa, 2006) or creative programs such as the "Creative Austria" project. Singapore, with its rich rainforests, stunning beaches, luxury residences, numerous museums, national parks, botanical gardens and nature reserves, is the creative cornerstone of Asia, making tourism an effective vehicle for creative development (Richards, 2011). Italy is also experimenting new paths for its tourism offerings. Many operators and promoters are trying to make the country's inland areas more and more appealing to tourists. As pointed out by Andrea Rossi and Maurizio Goetz (2011), the concept of experience becomes of central importance in the approach to consumer markets, in which even traditional products are marketed, thereby putting increasing emphasis on their experiential content. Experiences are prepared, lived, remembered and shared with others. At the forefront of this is the promotion of culinary tourism. An influential Italian daily newspaper, when reporting the results of a survey in 2014, wrote: "They call them culinary travellers and they are the joy of travel agencies and cooking schools. Nearly 800 thousand foreigners in 2013 attended cooking classes for a turnover of 134 million euros" (Scalise, 2014).

If, on one hand, rural areas and holiday farmhouses manage to greatly satisfy culinary travellers, on the other, even large cities have set out to respond to their needs. In Rome for instance, "A cooking day in Rome" was recently launched with the purpose of serving as both a historic and cultural experience in the streets of the capital. The chef meets with the tourists-students at the Pantheon for a coffee; together they select the products at the market at *Campo dei Fiori* and then head back to the workshop where the chef teaches them how to prepare a complete meal, from first course to desert. At the end of the class, they have lunch altogether. And, depending on the successful abilities of the organizer, it is these small experiences that drive tourists to come back for more and perhaps even to attend professional cooking classes.

Conclusion

Within an ever-increasing competitive global tourism market, the question different tourist destinations frequently ask themselves is, How can they provide tourists with an experience of value, one that will allow them to differentiate from the competition, while attracting new clients and retaining existing ones? Rossi and Goetz (2011, p. 63), who direct their attention to that specific share of the market that is interested in developing the tourist experience and that is in need of innovation, give one possible response. The basic starting point is the presence of different actors playing a key role in the creation of the tourist experience: the tourist, other travellers, tourism operators, hosting communities and other actors such as stakeholders and opinion leaders (Rossi & Goetz, 2011, p. 22). Tourists have changed. They are more aware in their expectations, they know their rights and, in particular, they have gained considerable experience in past travels. However, we still find tour operators that consider themselves mere merchants of sleeping accommodations and package tours. Until now it has worked, there has never been a lack of clients and earnings have been decent. Nonetheless, it is more and more evident that this kind of operator, anchored to an outdated logic, is bound to face a number of difficulties in the creation of a tourist product in the form of experience.

It is no surprise then that growing numbers of tourists have developed a discerning approach, highly aware of what they desire and of what they are being offered. They entirely bypass the old-school tour operator with its standardized offers. Instead travellers prefer building their travel creatively, by assembling the different pieces that compose their journey on the basis of what they wish to see, when they wish to see and how much they are willing to spend for it. These experiences are usually oriented towards engaging with a local culture, rather than the global culture (Richards, 2009). As Mercury and Becheri (2009, p. 611) point out, experiential tourism fully fits into the idea of experiential economy, according to which growing competition forces producers to differentiate their products by adding values, features or services that can be transformed into experiences; likewise, destinations modify their offer systems in an experiential perspective to satisfy a cultural demand that is increasingly diversified and complex.

References

Bed-and-Breakfast.it. (2016). *Rapporto sul B&B Italia 2014* (Report on Italian Bed & Breakfasts 2016). Retrieved from www.bed-and-braekfast.it 2016

Bros, J. B. (2012). Allocution d'Ouverture. In J. Sicsic (Ed.), *Le tourisme à l'heure du touriste créatif* (p. 4). Retrieved from www.tourisme-creatif.org/wp-content/uploads/2013/01/ Synthese_tourisme_creatif_6_7_ dec_2012.pdf

Crispin, R. (2003). *Creative tourism New Zealand and Australia*, Council for the Arts. Retrieved from www.fuel4arts.com

Dall'Ara, G. (2010). *Manuale dell'albergo diffuso: l'idea, la gestione, il marketing dell'ospitalità diffusa.* Milan: FrancoAngeli.

Dumazedier, J. (1962). *Vers une civilisation du loisir?* Paris: Seuil.

Ejarque, J. (2004). *La destinazione turistica di successo, marketing e management.* Milan: Hoepli.

Ferreira, A., & Costa, C. (2006). «Novos turistas» no centro histórico de Faro. *Análise Social, 41*(180), 767–799.

ISTAT. (2016, October 13). *Le aziende agrituristiche in Italia, 2015*, Report.

Laliberté, M. (2006). *Le tourisme créatif à trois volets.* Retrieved from http://veilletourisme .ca/2006/12/11/le-tourisme-creatif-a-trois-volets/

Lavarini, R. (1977). *Il pellegrinaggio Cristiano.* Genova: Marietti.

Leed, E. J. (1992). *La mente del viaggiatore. Dall'Odissea al turismo globale.* Bologna: Il Mulino.

Mercury & Becheri, E. (Ed.). (2009). *Rapporto sul turismo italiano 2008–2009* (16th Ed.). Milan: FrancoAngeli.

Monorail Society. (2015). *Shanghai maglev train.* Retrieved from www.monorails.org/ tmspages/magshang.html

Richards, G. (Ed.). (1996). *Cultural tourism in Europe.* Wallingford: CABI.

Richards, G. (2009). *Tourism development trajectories-from culture to creativity? Tourism research and marketing.* Paper presented to the Asia-Pacific Creativity Forum on Culture and Tourism, Jeju island, Republic of Korea.

Richards, G. (2011). Creativity and tourism: The state of the art. *Annals of Tourism Research, 38*(4), 1225–1253.

Richards, G., & Wilson, J. (2006). Developing creativity in tourist experiences: A solution to the serial reproduction of culture? *Tourism Management, 27,* 1209–1223.

Richards, G., & Wilson, J. (2007). *Tourism, creativity and development.* London: Routledge.

Rossi, A., & Goetz, M. (2011). *Creare offerte turistiche vincenti con Tourist Experience Design.* Milan: Hoepli.

Ruisi M. (2011). *Prospettive relazionali intra- e inter- aziendali nelle nuove tendenze della ricettività turistica. Fattorie didattiche, hotels, home swappers, couchsurfing, residenze per artisti.* Milan: Aracne.

Scalise, I. M. (2014, February 26). I turisti a lezione dagli chef italiani 'Svelateci i segreti dei vostri sapori.' *La Repubblica.* Retrieved from http://ricerca.repubblica .it/repubblica/archivio/repubblica/2014/02/26/turisti-lezione-dagli-chef-italiani-svelateci.html

Scramaglia, R. (2008). Valori, modi e mezzi del viaggiar lento. In R. Lavarini (Ed.), *Viaggiar lento. Andare adagio alla scoperta di luoghi e persone* (pp. 1–30). Milan: Hoepli.

UNESCO Creative Cities Network. (2006, October 25–27). *Towards sustainable strategies for creative tourism.* Discussion Report of the Planning Meeting for 2008 International Conference on Creative Tourism Santa Fe, New Mexico, U.S.A., p. 3. Retrieved from http://unesdoc.unesco.org

7 Slow food in slow tourism

Paolo Corvo and Raffaele Matacena

Introduction

In this chapter, we intend to propose a reflection about the pivotal role food and gastronomy play in the slow tourism discourse. Given its societal and cultural relevance, gastronomy directly interfaces with tourism, and holds the potential to become a *medium* of cultural tourism. Yet, to promote successful slow touristic projects, host societies must not only acknowledge and preserve the deep cultural value of local gastronomy, but also acquire the ability to share original food- and life-styles with the visitors, aiming at the ultimate purpose of satisfying the experiential needs of tourists while maintaining authenticity of relations and daily practices. Slow Food principles, it is argued, can guide this process, and foster the fertile exchange between hosts and visitors while safeguarding traditional knowledge and moving towards in the sustainability agenda. The sections of this chapter follow these lines of argumentation, aiming at setting the basis for furthering the comprehension of the interconnections between food, society, culture and tourism.

Food, society, culture

The meanings food take on within different cultures are multiple and varied in nature. According to the UCLA Center for Human Nutrition (2010), the search for food has exerted a forging operation on our society. The rush to obtain the means of livelihood influenced the growth of populations and urban expansion, stimulated economic and political theories, and instigated wars. Science and religion have often focused on food as well. As is well known, many religions follow strict dietary rules; at the same time, some of the first discoveries in the world of chemistry resulted from the preparation and cooking of food. Even technology progressed through attempts toward satisfying dietary needs: the water wheel, one of the main instrumental innovations that allowed for the Industrial Revolution, was originally developed for grain milling purposes. In some societies, class distinction is still underlined by the foods that are brought to the table (*ibid.*).

Eating is an intensely personal act. It has the power to communicate to our peers our beliefs, our experiences and our sociocultural backgrounds. As Appadurai (1981) argues, food is a highly condensed social fact, playing a key role in the construction of our identities. Sociological, anthropological, psychological and semiotic thought deals with investigating the ways through which food consumption meanings are expressed. Food is a universal experience that constitutes a shared ground. It is an activity that brings together all human beings and is daily employed in order to meet basic needs, and yet its meaning does not relate exclusively to simple nutritional circumstances. Following a semiotic approach, the social and cultural use of food can be compared to a language. Synthetizing Roland Barthes's thought (1961), when a food item is bought, served or consumed, it is able to resume and transmit a situation, it constitutes information, it signifies. For the author, a meal represents a dominant character that is complex and helps to define a general system of tastes and habits. A similar conceptualization is also proposed by Lévi-Strauss (1958), for whom food constitutes a language that expresses social structures and cultural systems. Preparing a meal means setting up a communication system, a body of images, and a protocol of uses, situations and behaviors (Barthes, 1961). As a cultural artifact, then, the meal possesses a prosodic value that transcends the physical combination of the foods on the plate (Scarpato, 2002), and such prosody allows individuals to participate every day in the past of their own nation (Barthes, 1961), and, as Scarpato adds (2002), in its present as well.

Mary Douglas (1972) detects in the act of eating a capacity to incorporate a series of nutritional codes, useful to define the place of individuals within society and to actively keep the social order. The English anthropologist believes that every society needs to manage a set of common meanings to make sense of things and allow for communication and comprehension among individuals. The construction of this whole of meanings is remitted (also) to consumer goods and to the rituals which are linked to them, as a visible part of culture (Douglas & Isherwood, 1979). The goods are object of a continuous exchange between implicit and explicit meanings: the first are the outcome of symbolically relevant rituals, whose sense is not wholly perceived by the individual, yet are commonly felt as important for the social life of the community. Their meaning is removed from the conscious world to avoid incongruities within the system of thought or conflicts with other bodies of knowledge, but they play a fundamental role in creating a shared ground of communication (*ibid.*). In this way, they provide people with the possibility to manifest community membership without constantly renegotiating common concepts. Thus, food rituals, to varying degrees of consciousness, produce the effect of reaffirming one's own participation in a sociocultural collectivity.

Food rituals also vary with socioeconomic development. Ethnographic research, for instance, shows that in the food practices of less social-stratified societies, the emphasis is put on the quantity of food and on the elaboration of base ingredients, such as cereals, while greater attention toward the quality and style of the ingredients is detectable in those societies characterized by institutionalized forms of social hierarchy (Van der Veen, 2003). In the first context, the consumption of "special" dishes (on occasions such as celebrations or rites of passage) is primarily aimed at creating or strengthening social ties, while in the latter the main objective is to increment exclusivity and distance (*ibid.*). Following a similar path, Jack Goody (1982) found that in societies described by a relative homogeneity of members' lifestyle, special occasions are celebrated by consuming great quantities of food. In contrast, in hierarchical societies, where many different subcultures coexist, the quality or the exoticism of the food consumed takes on the role of status marker. Body image, as related to food, is another strong means of social signification, as Brown and Konner (1987) suggest. For these scholars, in those societies where food is abundant, and the idea of a quantity-based meal as a social level marker is fading, thinness has come to be associated with privilege and status. Conversely, in many societies that suffer from food scarcity, being overweight continues to mean being healthy and/or rich.

Food, thus, is highly polyvalent in its communicative aspect. As Appadurai (1981) argues, it is able to establish and highlight relations of equality, intimacy and solidarity; at the same time, it can sustain relations pointed at marking rank, distance or segmentation. Throughout the Renaissance, as the historian Emanuela Scarpellini (2012) reminds us, in Italy the necessity of social differentiation was so strong that its evidence was observable even among the guests of a meal or a banquet: there were different seats (thrones, tall chairs, stools) and even different foods served, according to social rank. Nowadays, the relevance of food as a holder of symbologies, as a powerful tool of signification and communication, is by no means weaker. A vivid example is provided by the social perception of globally spread fast food chains: in many poor countries they represent a symbol of status, thus attracting large strata of population, while in most wealthy countries they are seen as just the opposite and refused by those willing to consume (and able to afford) fresh and quality food.

On a more universal level, food choices have marked the evolution of our species. Our being omnivores is seen by Claude Fischler (1988) as a sort of paradox: in being able to digest almost everything, we are physiologically attracted by novelty and variety and thus motivated to explore new foods, though we are simultaneously reluctant to taste unknown foods, because we fear they could represent a danger for our health. These two contradictory imperatives, in the opinion of the French socio-anthropologist, generate anxiety in the relationship of man with food; a tension centered on the act of *incorporation*, which is the action with which we send a food beyond the boundary that divides the world from the self, separating the "external" from the "internal" of our body. The principle of incorporation operates both in real and imaginary terms, serving as a fundamental element of identity: the eaters does not only incorporate some or all the properties of food, becoming what they eat, but are themselves incorporated into a culinary system and, as a consequence, integrated into a specific group of practices, that would otherwise irremediably exclude them.

From this short excursus it is easy to grasp the consensus around the attribution to food of an importance that lies way beyond the physiology of nutrition. Food contributes substantially to construct and sustain our identities, to impose or shatter social bonds and to cultivate or distinguish our cultures. Food characterizes us as individuals, as a community, as a people, as mankind (also, see Lupton, 1996). It is due to these features that it becomes the keystone (also) of a touristic project. The process of knowing the Other-from-Self, the visited community, and the desire to experience its concrete manifestations and lifestyles find in the gastronomy a *passepartout*, a privileged standpoint from which to observe the world. Sharing the view of Ulderico Bernardi, it is:

> [P]recisely from food that the examination of the contents of a specific culture can start. It is in the production and collection of food, in the times of consumption and in the relation to places that aspects of material and non-material knowledge come together, so as to portray a scenario which is complex and significant and, in its own way, *exemplary*. (1997, p. 100, emphasis added)

It is upon this awareness that slow tourism finds its basis.

Food as a medium of cultural tourism

The juxtaposition of the concept of *slow* with touristic practice mirrors the growing interest of individuals to devote a *fair* amount of time to the discovery and in-depth exploration of territories. This means encountering the people that inhabit them, the culture the land is imbued with and the ways through which it is expressed, exhibiting a prior interest towards gastronomic customs. The tourist's will to travel to unknown localities is motivated by a variety of reasons, among them the possibility of experiencing new cultures. Food has always been one of the assets of a touristic destination, even if, in general terms, eating local specialties has often fulfilled the role of a marginal experience, far from representing the core of the touristic demand (Blakey, 2012). Nevertheless, a new "culinary tourist" has currently emerged in the form of someone that rediscovers the value of authenticity. In addition, enogastronomic tourism has rapidly expanded from being a small market niche to becoming a model of territorial development to which many policy makers aspire, especially in western countries, for its ability to revitalize the local economic and productive fabric. In Italy, for example, in 2011, 4.2 percent of domestic tourists and 6.9 percent of foreign tourists chose a vacation themed on gastronomy (Rossato, 2013).

For slow tourists, the search for good food and good wine does not merely answer a purely hedonistic aspiration, but rather constitutes part of a more complex cultural approach to knowledge, in which food, geography, place and identity are intertwined in a symbolic perspective. Slow tourists are interested in the discovery of the territory, understood as an inextricable whole of local resources and distinctive "signs" of production places, and of typicality, seen as the incorporation of culture and identity into products whose nature is anchored to history and traditions (Corvo, 2007). Such actors are aware that every gastronomic culture is the expression of a specific capacity of a community to cope with its nutritional needs through time, within a peculiar environment. Following the definition of Malinowski (1931), culture is that vast apparatus, partly human and partly spiritual, with which humans can solve concrete problems – among which, we would add, is that of ensuring nutrition (and concurrently enjoying food). A cultural approach to travel, then, cannot leave aside the gastronomic issues, and the taste of food from being an end becomes a means or, as Gaia De Pascale argues,

> [O]ne of the most pleasant and recommended means to get in touch with the alterity of a place never visited before. But also, more generally, [it becomes] taste for life, for comprehension, for communication: for savoring reality with eagerness and patience. (2008, p. 58)

An authentic meal is able to produce a communion, a proximity, not only between individuals, but also between the individual and culture, between the human being and a variety of aspects of the natural world (Symons, 1999). In a touristic context, consuming what is considered to be an "authentic" meal is not just a way to have a window into local life but also to share that life, if only momentarily. Crucial to facilitate the process of breaking down the barriers between visitors and hosts, this element proves strategic for the "cultural success" of any slow tourism practice.

Indeed, as argued by Xu (2007), nutrition constitutes one of the ways to meet, and comprehend other cultures. For the author, food operates as a fundamental cultural sign that structures people's identity and the way they conceptualize the Other. For Lévi-Strauss (1968), the cuisine of a society forms a language in which every society consciously translates its own structure, or even unwittingly reveals its contradictions. A nutritional system is, thus, a practical response to existential and universal needs of specific cultures within determined circumstances of time and space: a direct expression of the interaction of nature and culture in a specific environment.

The slow tourist is commonly therefore a gastronome-tourist, in which gastronomy embeds a spirit of reflexivity that drives the search for the best food and drinks, becoming culture itself and undoubtedly a *medium* of cultural tourism (Scarpato & Daniele, 2003). The nutritional needs a society expresses underscore the relationship with its own system of traditional values (Bernardi, 1997); the interest in deeply analyzing the cuisine therefore lies in its being the focal point of the culture of every people: on the cuisine a whole set of both material and nonmaterial elements converge, such as environmental resources, experiences, techniques and collective rituals.

Through the generations, humans have learned to transform, control, cook, preserve, share, establish values and hierarchies related to food, forbidding some while privileging others, up to the supreme religious transfiguration (*ibid.*). Slow tourism practitioners are then willing to plunge into a complex and truly meaningful experience, enabling analysis, experimentation, and exchange, not only eating and drinking local products, but also taking part in thematic events, getting in touch with producers, visiting production sites and artisan workshops, enjoying museums, exhibitions and artistic sites, and participating in the historical events and traditional rituals. It is the attempt to understand the working patterns of the sharing mechanism of existential meaning through generations, that consensus through time that for Edward Shils (1971) represents the very same concept of *tradition*. Food is celebrated as the concrete connection of material and immaterial culture, never lacking rituality, religiosity and peculiar symbols, historically determined and socially situated, able to act as a narrator of the experience of a people. The commitment of such gastronomy-oriented cultural tourism, to employ a neologism quoted by Scarpato and Daniele (2003), is to underline the *eatimologies*, the food etymologies of the visited locales, getting involved in the analysis of the origins and the development of specific products, of their diffusion through commerce, of their cultural expansion, adaptation and hybridization. The history of a nation's diet, in the view of Bell and Valentine (1997), *is* the history of the nation itself, made of fads, manias and passions, and it accounts for lived episodes of colonialism and migration, commerce and exploitation, cultural exchange and imposition of boundaries. Finally, reporting the words of Emanuela Scarpellini (2012, p. 10, author translation):

> [W]e can say that on the act of eating a whole world converges: a place's agricultural, industrial and commercial conditions, traditional habits, religious beliefs, social barriers, gender and age divisions, economic differences, culinary culture, tastes and esthetics, geographical characters, identity and sense of belonging, public policies and much more. By carefully observing a meal we are able to explain everything, or a great deal, about a certain people.

Slow food

At this point, we shall introduce a new aspect, which is *time*. The time dimension leads us to an antinomy we wish to highlight, related to the relevance attributed to the act of eating in everyday life, which stretches between *fast* and *slow food*. The fast/slow dichotomy is not limited to food. Instead it permeates every dimension of contemporary society: the prevailing lifestyle, especially in urbanized areas, is characterized by velocity, lack of time, a constant frenzy that often prevents people from enjoying and "tasting" encounters and situations. It seems hard to switch to another modality of daily living, as we often feel like slaves of a mechanism that regulates everything in the name of the myth of speed. Slow diverges from this usual practice, a way of thinking that detects in the slow life a chance to reach the desired well-being (Menétrey & Szerman, 2013).

In some circumstances, fast food seems to have no rivals; for example, at lunchtime in big cities, where people get lunch during a small break. One result is the tendency to favor speed over quality. In addition, fast food frequently associates with low cost, which makes it extremely desirable for a whole range of customers. When evaluating the quality of the food consumed, and relatedly health risks, though, problems start to rise. For these and other reasons slow food is gaining an ever increasing popularity, as a very different approach to food is diffusing, one that advocates a renewed attention to quality and freshness and relaxation while dining. For 25 years the Slow Food association has promoted "good, clean and fair" food (Petrini, 2007). Devoting more time to meals means giving value to the work of those who have produced the foods we find on our table, knowing the quality of every substance, verifying the sustainability of the supply chain, and ultimately underlining the socializing value of eating together.

For the theme of this book, the most interesting dimension is linked to people's desire to dedicate a greater amount of time to the meals not only of public holidays, as tradition suggests, but also wherever touristic practices take place. Here food itself becomes a tourist attraction, both as a site and a tourism consumption product, becoming a discriminant feature of the vacation. It is no accident that many hotels have improved the level of their cooking, which in the past seemed to have a lesser weight in clients' judgments. And this "quality turn" is also expressed in the "slow attitude" tourists adopt when going to restaurants in the touristic localities. One of the most important criteria of Slow Food is the transition from individual choices to social practices (Holm, 2013; Kjaernes, Harvey, & Warde, 2013), together with the increased valorization of local territory (Carolan, 2012; Counihan & Van Esterik, 2006). The consumer is charged with the key role of choosing the most sustainable products, despite the influences of advertising and marketing (Guptill, Copelton, & Lucal, 2013). Petrini's core concept of "good, clean and fair" takes into account both the esthetic-sensorial dimension and the sociopolitical aspect. *Good* is founded on the education of the senses, on the curiosity for the unknown, on the delightfulness of taste. *Clean* refers to agroecology, to the importance of the land, and to sustainability. *Fair* is based on coproduction and respect of farmers and fishers' rights, especially the right to earn a living wage (Perullo, 2008).

One of the aspects Slow Food–inspired associations and movements develop more carefully is nutritional education, from primary schools onwards. Their aim is to raise the awareness of a larger stratum of population about slow nutritional practices. The global economic crisis since 2008 surely does not help people privilege the quality of products over their cost, yet it is crucial to show consumers that the lower price of some food items with respect to others frequently depends on the exploitation or weak remuneration of producers. Ultimately, it is important to underline that slow does not simply imply a nostalgic return to the past, to the premodern, but rather it advocates a recovery of the natural dimension of agriculture and production. The use of technology undergoes criticisms only if it jeopardizes the quality or healthiness of food. In addition, the term "slow" has to be understood in a qualitative rather than quantitative sense, since it refers not to prolonging time to arrive *later*, yet to a remodeling of time to arrive *better*. It is a matter of grasping the depth of the time dimension, which in the global society finds itself strongly compressed.

Case study: the *pescestocco* (stockfish)

Below we consider the example of a typical product inhabiting the two sides of the Strait that divides Calabria from Sicily, in southern Italy: stockfish. In these lands, there is a custom to prepare a series of recipes employing, as the principal ingredient, the well-known Atlantic cod that takes the name of stockfish once it is air-dried by the cold winds of the Northern Sea. While the ingredient is not local, the recipes are a very localized tradition, not extended to other parts of the same regions (actually, the use of stockfish is disseminated in other small areas of Italy, like Veneto, Liguria or the Ancona region; yet they are isolated from each other and there is a strict differentiation in terms of recipes) (Birri and Coco, 1998). They assume an important symbolic value, since *pescestocco* dishes (as they are locally called) are representative of a popular and poor cuisine, even though they are also worthy of festive occasions (such as Christmas Eve supper, for instance). Moreover, this food is characterized by strong identity connotations, to the point where, due to traditional local rivalries, the people from Reggio Calabria are "offensively" called by their Sicilian neighbors *piscistoccari*, meaning stockfish eaters.

This has become a significant element of the local foodscape, then, even though the main ingredient has to be constantly imported from the opposite shore of Europe, mainly along Scandinavia. As we have said, this cod does not live in Mediterranean waters, and for its curing process requires the climatic condition of the Arctic islands. Why, then, does this product coming mainly from Norway end up in Calabria and Sicily? How would the consumption of such a culturally and geographically "distant" food spread in these localities?

Italy came to know stockfish thanks to a fifteenth-century report from a Venetian seafarer to the Senate of the *Serenissima*. After a shipwreck, the captain was saved by a community of fishermen of the Lofoten Islands, well beyond the Arctic Circle off the coast of Norway, that brought him to their village and nourished him with stockfish (ADN Kronos 2016). He appreciated the storability of such food and, as an expert merchant, decided to bring some to Venice, to propose it as a remedy for the lack of proteins long-range mariners suffered from in their diets during voyages. Venetians then began to import it, but it did not spread widely until the years that followed the Catholic reaction to the Lutheran protest, when it became a solution – a tasty but mainly economic solution – to the prohibition of eating meat, especially during the Lenten season, the Church imposed after the Council of Trent (1545–1563). Stockfish was cheap and transportable, and could be easily brought even to areas far from the sea – an important element in an era when the conservation of food was still a difficult business (Birri and Coco, 1998).

Ultimately sailing from the Bourbon port of Naples, stockfish began to reach the two cities overlooking the Strait of Messina; and from there was transported over mountains on mule's backs to get to the inland villages. The story linking this food to this territory, though, continued to evolve. Local elderly people recount that, during the rescue and rebuilding phases following a devastating earthquake of 1908 that nearly destroyed the two cities and killed half of the population, intense humanitarian activity followed, involving many countries' navies. In an effort to help, then, a Norwegian ship unloaded a large amount of stockfish (Gruppo Astrofili Hipparcos, 2016). For this reason, in a moment when every ordinary activity (such as fishing) was suspended and every collective effort was aimed at solving a condition of emergency, the multiple and varied recipes of *pescestocco* were developed. Clearly, they were all adapted to the local tastes, and so prepared coupling the "exotic" element with the most common ingredients of the Mediterranean cuisine: tomato, olives, capers, peppers, cauliflower and so on (Baccellieri, 1999; also see Balma Tivola, 2010).

This story exemplifies the spirit of slow food and slow tourism: "following the traces" of a culturally relevant food item aids us in understanding elements of continental history, religion, trade exchanges among peoples, wounds and fractures, natural disasters and responses, and ultimately habits and customs. These are large and small factors furthering the comprehension of the spirit of a place, the behavior and collective personalities of the people who live there.

To complete the illustration of our case study, we must reflect upon how the reported account relates to tourism. Even though the preparation of such dish is diffused in the whole area observed, one peculiar place has gained prominence and fame for the quality of the stockfish that can be consumed there. It is the small town of Mammola which, quietly lying on the hills facing the Jonic sea, is deemed as the place where the most delicate and tasty *pescestocco* is to be found. Gourmets argue that it is due to the peculiar nature of the freshwater that springs in the surroundings of the town, employed by the locals to "wash" the dried cod: to be eaten, indeed, this dried fish requires a long process of washing in running water, and the quality of the water therefore inevitably affects the organoleptic properties of the final product. This small town's economy is nowadays significantly shaped by the activities of selling and catering stockfish. Despite the reduced dimensions of this urban center, a host of stockfish-based restaurants and retailers welcome the great number of visitors that come from all over the region (often engaging in hours-long trips) with the purpose of eating the renowned *pescestocco*. Such gastronomic tourism, though, is limited to the act of eating, since no further link to other local touristic resources appears to exist, and by no means the stay of the visitors is extended and/or integrated into a broader touristic project. These and other shortcomings, that often hinder the development of a slow tourism strategy in many locales, are outlined and discussed in the following section.

Food and wine tourism

With the rise of slow food, enogastronomic tourism represents a growing niche within the overall global tourism market. The niche is of interest both from a sociocultural point of view since it correctly interprets tourists' new motivations, and from an economic perspective because it affects various productive and commercial supply chains. This requires the local industry and community to rethink and remodel services in order to meet new market requirements. We should remember that, particularly in Italy, the development of wine tourism has become a "testimonial" of the most peculiar features of many Italian locales: many national associations such as *Città del Vino* (Wine Cities) or *Movimento Turismo del Vino* (Wine Tourism Movement, since 1993) have arisen in response to the growing linkages between local products and tourism. Events such as *Cantine Aperte* (Open Wineries) and hundreds of fairs, exhibitions and food festivals are being organized throughout the country for the same reason. The *strade del vino* (wine routes) are particularly important because of the large number of tourists they attract. Reliable hard data on the activity, however, is still missing, mainly because most research institutes still do not consider the "enogastronomic tourist" as a specific entry in their surveys and reports (besides, we have to take into account that it is not easy to detect the exclusivity of motivation, following the definition we have proposed).

Despite anecdotal evidence of the widespread growth of food and wine tourism, we can identify more puzzling realities, such an inadequate ability to communicate the identity of a product and its values within a region. In many cases we continue to observe a lack of a clear territorial message underscoring the link between leisure, food and wine production and *terroir*. As a result, both the food and wine and the region lose an element of identity and relevance. In addition, agricultural businesses are not always able to properly welcome tourists, organize their visit and tasting sessions that generally are a prelude to the purchase. Finally, also lost are the specific relational and experiential aspects tourists commonly strive for.

Considering those difficulties, which are an expression of the complicated and delicate relationship between agriculture and tourism, it seems relevant to underline some basic elements of enogastronomic tourism:

1   There is the need for many operators to combine productive and touristic activities. These diverse spheres require very different cultural backgrounds and professional skills; as a consequence, the development of a double level of skills is needed: it is a process that produces the best results

when such competences succeed in integrating. The professionalization processes should not limit their scope to the companies' management, but also involve the human resources from the territory, those related to business management and customer satisfaction (Corvo, 2011). There is a need, then, for new professionals who are able to combine technical skills, organizational competences and professional culture. Education assumes a strategic value, for it is not only oriented to overcome the competence gap, but because it becomes a fundamental instrument for the cultural progress of the touristic-enogastronomic company.

2　Successful food and wine tourism requires coordination and cooperation. This forces operators to abandon a standpoint strictly limited to their own businesses. Instead they must coordinate with other actors. The formulation of a local tourist policy requires a profound knowledge of the relations between tourist consumption and the productive activities that compose the economy of the territory. Tourism is the only economic system that still presupposes the localization of companies and resources: it is important to let tourists know the typical products, and make their purchase available even in their home countries. This serves as a way of branding the territory for tourists. In addition, in order to develop such a touristic supply, the local network needs to share a common project: a strategic partnership between participants, the sharing of a set of development projects. These are some of the most relevant components of a touristic system. A touristic system demands from its operators an analysis of the territorial system to stimulate corporate collective intelligence, a definition of a clear and shared vision, and practical actions to bolster local society dynamism.

3　There is a need for the recognition of public institutions' specific functions, both referring to the institutional role of managing operators education and update processes, and regarding the activity of coordination of the different initiatives. They should be aimed at optimizing the services offered to the clients, while respecting the diversity and specificity of their demands. Another function that the public institutions should carry out relates to the promotion of a *sustainable* and *respectful* enogastronomic tourist, one that protects the landscape and the environment through the involvement of the local population in the decision making process, as well as introducing tourists to the social life of the visited communities (Hall et al., 2003). It is also important to consider that not every locality is fit for hosting enogastronomic tourism, and not every place can follow the same modalities. Some requirements are indeed inexorable: the product must feature a high organoleptic quality, it has to be perceived by the consumer as unique, original, rare and produced on a small scale, historically and culturally rooted in a definite place, where most of its sales take place (Corvo, 2015). Further elements to be considered are the perceived value of the typical products – which depends on the consumer's culture and on the peculiarity of the productive process – together with the circumstances of consumption and the degree of satisfaction it delivers.

Gastronomy and slow tourism as a cultural-touristic product

Conceived as a contemporary tourist resource, gastronomy satisfies all the conventional requirements of a cultural-touristic product (Scarpato, 2002). In accordance with current patterns of tourist consumption (or *post-tourist*, as Urry [1990] argues), which is oriented to the search of experiential products that deliver a high degree of satisfaction, gastronomy is generally associated with high-end tourism. Furthermore, it represents a reliable alternative for those locales not sufficiently equipped with "classic" touristic resources, such as sun, beaches or mountains (Scarpato, 2002). And, quite importantly, gastronomy is a tool that perfectly fits into a sustainable tourism and sustainable development framework. Centering tourism around food and drink serves as a stimulus for agricultural activity and the whole food production sector, while preserving cultural authenticity. It allows the community to be self-assertive, generating pride and sense of belonging and, at the same time, strengthening the touristic-commercial vocation of the destination (Telfer & Wall, 1996). Local gastronomic systems promote respect for the environment, social justice and fair trade. The creation of a market for local specialties, for gastronomic centers, for traditional agriculture and culinary systems, for wine routes or eco-museums, furthers local development and environmentally friendly infrastructures (Karakas & Yurtseven, 2013). Sustainable gastronomy gives communities an opportunity to thrive socially and economically, keeping an ecologic-nutritional commitment to the safeguarding of the environment and of the health of their members (*ibid.*), concurrently contributing to the conservation of essential values and lifestyles, along with traditional knowledge and tastes.

Gastronomy, then, can become an active force against *deculturation*, defined as the more or less traumatic dismissal of the original cultural premises of a society, due to cultural imperialism or homogenization processes (Bernardi, 1997; Ritzer, 1983). These operate through a slow deletion of non-material cultural traits (e.g., language, religiosity, rituality), or of elements of material culture, including those linked to nutrition. Once again, food turns out to be a resource. The cultural components tightly linked to food consumption show a stronger resistance to assimilation or eradication, as migrant communities' food habits, for instance, can testify: they tend to be perpetuated even by the new generations, whilst language or other customs are instead more easily dismissed (Bernardi, 1997).

In order to enable slow/enogastronomic tourism to produce its beneficial effects, local operators must know how to adequately meet the needs of the post-tourist, who – having become more discerning than his or her predecessor –is prone to spend more for desired experience (Hjalager and Richards, 2002). These tourists are frequently happy to pay a premium price because they are aware, as Urry (1990) suggests, that the authenticity they seek commands it. The territory must face this challenge developing the ability to share its heritage with visitors, welcoming them in the places of social life, like wine cellars, oil mills, laboratories, and making collective knowledge accessible, from recipes to plant properties or artisanal production techniques, letting them encounter traditional lifestyles (beekeepers, boat-builders and so on).

It is crucial, however, to underline that cultural openness requires both tourists and the host community to participate in such a predisposition, aimed at preparing the ground to meet the Other through the mediation of food. All the elements that synthetize the spirit of *slow food* (attention, knowledge and care of *one's own* food culture, together with a marked educational attitude, pointing to the transmission of its values) must be adopted. To prevent *deculturation*, then, and further *transculturation*, or the fertile exchange between different cultures and societies, a systematic processes of *inculturation* of society members needs to be implemented, so that individuals could receive and participate in their own cultural heritage (Balma Tivola, 2010). Joining that body of knowledge and value-based references, which is handed down from one generation to another, helps rejecting the fear of being overwhelmed by what is different, facilitates dialogue and makes the coming together of host and guest more fruitful.

Under this framework, slow tourism holds particular promise and fits in accordance with broader principles of slowness, meaning taking the just time to tune in to the rhythm of community life, synchronizing one's own biorhythm to the one of nature and of the activities that take place in it. This stands in opposition to the "rush-to-leave game" that often characterizes mass tourism, a sort of relay race from one interesting site to another, to phagocyte as fast as possible for then hastily pass on, leaving a small trace of disorder and waste, building a collection of background images on which, at most, to collocate one's presence with a souvenir snapshot. In this way, maybe, we would offer our small contribution to teaching respect between peoples, and dialogue between cultures (Leed, 1991).

References

ADN Kronos. (2016). *Una storia originale, da alimento base dei Vichinghi a delizia della cucina moderna.* Retrieved from http://www1.adnkronos.com/IGN/Speciali/Stoccafisso/Una-storia-originale-da-alimento-base-dei-Vichinghi-a-delizia-della-cucina-moderna_4021718871.html

Appadurai, A. (1981). Gastro-politics in Hindu South Asia. *American Ethnologist, 8*(3), 494–511.

Baccellieri, C. (1999). *La buona cucina di Calabria.* Reggio Calabria: Falzea.

Balma Tivola, C. (2010). *Il senso degli altri. Cibo, identità e metissage,* intervento per *Aspettando Terre 2011,* Rovereto.

Barthes, R. (1961). Pour une psychho-sociologie de l'alimentation moderne. *Annales: Economies, Sociétés, Civilisations, 5,* 977–986.

Bell, D., & Valentine, G. (1997). *Consuming geographies – We are where we eat.* London: Routledge.

Bernardi, U. (1997). *Del Viaggiare. Turismi, culture, cucine, musei open air.* Milan: FrancoAngeli.

Birri, F., & Coco, C. (1998). *Nel segno del Baccalà.* Venice: Marsilio.

Blakey, C. (2012). *Consuming place: Tourism's gastronomy connection.* University of Hawai'i at Hilo: Hawai'i College of HOHONU, 10, pp. 51–54.

Brown, P. J., & Konner, M. (1987). An anthropological perspective on obesity. *Annals of the New York Academy of Sciences, 499*, 29–46.

Carolan, M. (2012). *The sociology of food and agriculture*. Abingdon: Routledge.

Corvo, P. (2007). *Turisti e felici? Il turismo tra benessere e fragilità*. Milan: Vita & Pensiero.

Corvo, P. (2011). The pursuit of happiness and the globalized tourist. *Social Indicators Research, 102*(1), 93–97.

Corvo, P. (2015). *Food culture, consumption and society*. Basingstoke: Palgrave MacMillan.

Counihan, C. M., & Van Esterik, P. (2006). *Food and culture. A reader*. New York, NY: Routledge.

De Pascale, G. (2008). *Slow travel*. Milan: Ponte alle Grazie – Salani.

Douglas, M. (1972). Deciphering a meal. *Deadalus – Journal of the American Academy of Arts and Sciences, 101*(1), 61–81.

Douglas, M., & Isherwood, B. (1979). *The world of goods – Towards an anthropology of consumption*. New York, NY: Basic Books.

Fischler, C. (1988). Food, self and identity. *Social Science Information, 27*, 275–293.

Goody, J. (1982). *Cooking, cuisine and class*. Cambridge: Cambridge University Press.

Gruppo Astrofili Hipparcos – Università Roma 3. (2016). *Tra i più disastrosi terremoti della storia. Il disastroso terremoto e maremoto in Sicilia e in Calabria del 28 dicembre 1908 che devastò Messina e Reggio Calabria*. Retrieved from http://diamante.uniroma3.it/hipparcos/TerremotoSiciliaCalabria1908.htm

Guptill, A. E., Copelton, D. A., & Lucal, B. (2013). *Food & society. Principles and paradoxes*. Cambridge: Polity Press.

Hall, M., Sharples, L., Mitchell, R., Macionis, N., & Cambourne, B. (Eds.). (2003). *Food tourism around the world*. Oxford: Butterworth-Heinemann.

Hjalager, A. M., & Richards, G. (Eds.). (2002). *Tourism and gastronomy*. London-New York: Routledge.

Holm, L. (2013). Sociology of food consumption. In A. Murcott, W. Belasco, & P. Jackson (Eds.), *The handbook of food research* (pp. 324–337). London-New York: Bloomsbury.

Karakas, N., & Yurtseven, R. H. (2013). Creating a sustainable gastronomic destination: The case of Cittaslow Gokceada-Turkey. *American International Journal of Contemporary Research, 3*(3), 91–100.

Kjaernes, U., Harvey, M., & Warde, A. (2013). *Trust in food. A comparative and institutional Analysis*. New York, NY: Palgrave Macmillan.

Leed, E. J. (1991). *The mind of the traveler. From Gilgamesh to global tourism*. New York, NY: Basic Books.

Lévi-Strauss, C. (1958). *Anthropologie structurale*. Paris: Librairie Plon.

Lévi-Strauss, C. (1968). *Mythologiques. L'origine des manières de Table*. Paris: Librairie Plon.

Lupton, D. (1996). *Food, the body and the self*. London: Sage.

Malinowski, B. (1931). Culture. In *Encyclopaedia of the Social Science*. New York.

Ménétrey, S., & Szerman, S. (2013). *Slow attitude!* Paris: Armand-Colin.

Perullo, N. (2008). *L'altro gusto. Saggi di estetica gastronomica*. Pisa: Edizioni ETS.

Petrini, C. (2007). *Slow food nation: Why our food should be good, clean and fair*. Milan: Rizzoli.

Ritzer, G. (1983). The "McDonaldization" of society. *Journal of American culture, 6*(1), 100–107.

Rossato, M. (2013). La sostenibilità: Un percorso obbligato anche per le imprese turistiche. In E. Becheri & G. Maggiore (Eds.), *XVIII Rapporto sul turismo italiano* (pp. 231–237). Milan: Edizioni FrancoAngeli.

Scarpato, R. (2002). Gastronomy as a tourist product: The perspective of gastronomy studies. In A. M. Hjalager & G. Richards (Eds.), *Tourism and gastronomy* (pp. 51–69). London-New York: Routledge.

Scarpato, R., & Daniele, R. (2003). New global cuisine: Tourism, authenticity and sense of place in postmodern gastronomy. In M. Hall et al. (Eds.), *Food tourism around the world* (pp. 298–313). Oxford: Butterworth-Heinemann.

Scarpellini, E. (2012). *A tavola! Gli italiani in 7 pranzi*. Laterza: Roma-Bari.

Shils, E. (1971). Tradition. *Comparative Studies in Society and History, 13*(2), 122–159.

Symons, M. (1999). Gastronomic authenticity and sense of place. *Proceedings of the Ninth Australian Tourism and Hospitality Education Conference*, Adelaide, CAUTHE, 333–340.

Telfer, D., & Wall, G. (1996). Linkages between tourism and food production. *Annals of Tourism Research, 23*(3), 635–653.

UCLA Center for Human Nutrition, Nutritional Anthropology. (2010). *Why we eat what we eat*. Retrieved from www.learnnc.org/lp/media/uploads/2010/03/why_we_eat.pdf

Urry, J. (1990). *The Tourist Gaze*. London: Sage.

Van der Veen, M. (2003). When is food a luxury? *World Archaeology, 34*(3), 405–427.

Xu, W. (2007). *Eating identities: Reading food in Asian American literature*. Honolulu: University of Hawai'i Press.

8 Slow and intelligent cities

When slow is also smart

Giovanni Tocci

Introduction

Cities continue to be a matter of great interest, both in theory and in practice. Literature about cities is increasingly enriched by a variety of theoretical considerations concerning practical interventions and strategies that make the urban development more dynamic in terms of balance and sustainability. In particular, the study of urban economy has made enormous progress in recent decades due to the commonly recognized importance that cities play in relation to economic growth processes. The real driving forces for development are the local strategies put into practice in the cities and territories (Amendola, 2007; Amin & Thrift, 2002; Martinotti, 1993). In an ever more urbanized world, the city of the future will inevitably point to the management of resources according to sustainability criteria and the creation of an attractive economic and social context for citizens, businesses and governments. Therefore, cities will have to develop more intelligent strategies and management models.

Debates about the future of urban development, particularly in many Western countries, have been increasingly influenced by discussions of "smart cities" (Hollands, 2008; Komninos, 2011; Lindner, 2013; Nam & Pardo, 2011). "The concept of the smart city has recently been introduced as a strategic device to encompass modern urban production factors in a common framework and, in particular, to highlight the importance of Information and Communication Technologies for enhancing the competitive profile of a city" (Caragliu, Del Bo, & Nijkamp, 2011, p. 65). But what does intelligence for a city really mean? A critical dimension is that cities deliver services based on so-called smart technologies, aimed at integrating intelligence in the infrastructure of the city in order to extend the effectiveness of the services offered (Berthon & Guittat, 2011). The risk is that we focus too much on technology and infrastructure, losing sight of the meaning of intelligence, which is sometimes the most important concept. For purposes here, intelligence refers not simply to technology. Instead a city is considered to be smart when it manages to innovate and meet criteria of economic, environmental and social sustainability.

In this scenario the "slow city" emerges as an alternative model of urban development (Grzelak-Kostulska, Holowiecka, & Kwiatkowski, 2011; Knox, 2005; Mayer & Knox, 2010; Miele, 2008; Pink, 2008), or, better, as a new approach "to urban development that does not merely focus on community based economic development, but also on issues of sustainability and social equity" (Mayer & Knox, 2006, p. 321). According to the idea that being slow means being smart, the study highlights some points of convergence between the two urban models of smart city and slow city and supports the thesis that the concept of slow city can be adapted to large cities as well as the smaller ones where it has been applied. Framed in this manner, the smart city and the slow city tend to converge within a new specific model of sustainable city, or better, they are an important variation of it.

Urban transformations and contemporary city

In 2007 the world's urban population outnumbered the rural one for the first time (Véron, 2008). According to the United Nations population projections, by 2050 this figure will reach the threshold of 70 percent (United Nations, 2010). Another important fact, behind the process of population growth, is that the growth rate has increased at a faster pace in smaller cities than in metropolitan ones in the last decade. The second largest cities, or medium-sized cities[1] are ones that are able to emerge combining success and sustainability, offering greater services, a better quality of life and cultural vibrancy. At the socio-economic level, the change into the postindustrial city has now been completed, at least in advanced economies (Amin & Thrift, 2002; Le Galès, 2002). However, the remnants of the industrial city model has led to several issues related to the unequal distribution of resources, lack of core services, poor attention to natural resources and to the environment more generally. Other requests concerning environmental quality, culture, different lifestyles and social relations have been added to the other needs deriving from the "industrial" city (Amendola, 2007; Martinotti, 1993).

As a result, attempts at innovative policies at urban level, combined with an ability to anticipate problems through long-term strategies, are taking shape. In terms of sustainability, these policies aim at preventing problems rather than improving crisis situations. Sustainable strategies have become one of the main objectives of the political agenda of some cities (Haughton & Hunter, 2004; James, 2015), whether the concept of sustainability includes other priorities such as development, quality of life and citizens' well-being (Mayer & Knox, 2006, 2010; Pink, 2008; Polese & Stren, 2000). Urban quality directly depends on the level of effectiveness of the solutions that administrations are able to provide to these issues in terms of sustainability. Cities must necessarily promote development policies in order to guide their economy towards activities able to produce "sustainable" goods in relation to the environment (low energy consumption, protection and promotion of natural resources) as well as to social aspects (social equity and cohesion, well-being, enhancement of cultural diversity and social identity).

Sustainable urban models

In this scenario, in the last decade, several models of sustainability have been developed and among these smart cities and slow cities take a major role. The concept of slowness has become a basic criterion within urban eco-compatibility processes, that is sustainable strategies adopted by cities, as well as a political and economic issue, in the governance of both small and medium-sized city centers. The vast majority of studies on urban sustainability (Haughton & Hunter, 2004; James, 2015; Mayer & Knox, 2006, 2010; Polese & Stren, 2000) point out how the latest internationally adopted eco-compatible strategies praise the concept of slowness, not only combining cities of the slow network, but also urban centers of all sizes. The smart city context – current metaphor of an intelligent, efficient and green city – expresses this trend (Cittalia, 2012). At the same time, the adjective smart is more frequently used in different fields, including traditional and slow contexts. Efficiency and slowness are simultaneously mentioned in many eco-compatible models of urban governance. It is in this perspective that the idea of analyzing the points of convergence between smart city and slow city is worthy of discussion (Catalano & Tocci, 2012).

The smart city

The definition of smart city is not yet sufficiently built up in the culture of urban research, although a few aspects of its structure are now becoming more stable features. In the literature the term intelligent city is not used in a holistic way to describe a city with specific features, but it is used with reference to specific aspects. These range from the smart city as a technology district (Batty et al., 2012; Caragliu et al., 2011), to the smart city related to educational achievement or specific skill set on behalf of its population (Nam & Pardo, 2011). In other cases it refers to the relationship between the city governance and its citizens, particularly it focuses on innovative forms of e-governance and citizen participation (Eurocities, 2007; Van der Meer & Van Wilden, 2003). Furthermore, it has also been used in reference to issues of urban growth and social and environmental sustainability (Polese & Stren, 2000) and the aforementioned use of technology in providing the efficient delivery of government services or provision of infrastructure.

Because of the lack of clear and holistic criteria, several critiques have questioned the usefulness of the smart moniker. As Komninos (2011, p. 172) points out, the proliferation of cities that adopt intelligent city strategies, recorded since 2005, has often led to a simplistic use of the terms "smart" and "intelligent," which are easily assigned to any digital application associated with the cities – often just for marketing purposes – without making clear what intelligence is being improved and how.

Similarly, Holland (2008) accurately highlights that urban development in many countries has been increasingly influenced by "smart" concepts, but despite the wide use of this urban labeling phenomenon, we know little about so-called smart cities, particularly in terms of what the label both reveals and hides. Finally, as Lindner (2013, p. 14) notes,

> [I]n the race to bring technological and engineering innovations into the heart of urban planning, architecture, and design, we too often skip over more fundamental discussions about what values should underpin and steer the development of smart (and smarter) cities.

While the meaning of what it means for cities to be "smart" remains unspecified, this has not prevented an inflation of the concept of smart city, in a wider use, especially in reference to urban planning and development issues. Accordingly, in general, the term "smart city" refers to an innovative urban dimension, characterized by high efficiency and wise use of resources, both environmental and economic, and also supported by the use of green technologies in the management and planning of the territory (Catalano & Tocci, 2012), where the social and relational capital[2] play a fundamental role (Caragliu et al., 2011).

The term smart city also refers to the use of modern technologies in everyday urban life. This includes ICTs and, most of all, modern transportation technologies and "intelligent" systems for the improvement of urban traffic and inhabitants' mobility. The slogans associated with the idea of smart city recall concepts summarized in metaphors, such as having an urban center with sustainable development policies, a creative environment able to promote and accelerate innovative sociocultural models, a political context capable to provide shared tools of e-governance in order to broaden citizens' participation, a urban system with good management capability concerning mobility. Another factor that cannot be neglected is the development of community intending to revitalize common social practices and shape the identity and image of the place through creative projects and strategic interventions (Catalano & Tocci, 2012).

One study, carried out by the Polytechnic University of Vienna,[3] has identified the fundamental characteristics of a smart city. A sample of 70 medium-sized European cities has been evaluated on the basis of six specific features (cf. Table 8.1): Economy, People, Governance, Mobility, Environment, and Living. These dimensions connect with traditional, regional and neoclassical theories of urban growth and development. In particular, the six features are based respectively on theories of regional competitiveness, transport and

Table 8.1 Characteristics of a smart city

Smart economy (competitiveness)	Smart people (social & human capital)	Smart governance (participation)	Smart mobility (transport & ICT)	Smart environment (natural resources)	Smart living (quality of life)
Innovative spirit	Level of qualification	Participation in decision-making	Local accessibility	Attractivity of natural conditions	Cultural facilities
Entrepreneurship	Affinity to lifelong learning	Public and social services	(Inter-)national accessibility	Pollution	Health conditions
Economic image & trademarks	Social and ethnic plurality	Transparent governance	Availability of ICT-infrastructure	Environmental protection	Individual safety
Productivity	Flexibility	Political strategies & perspectives	Sustainable, innovative and safe transport systems	Sustainable resource management	Housing quality
Flexibility of labor market	Creativity				Education facilities
International embeddedness	Cosmopolitanism/ Open-mindedness				Touristic attractivity
Ability to transform	Participation in public life				Social cohesion

Source: Adapted from Centre of Regional Science (2007, p. 12).

ICT economics, natural resources, human and social capital, quality of life, and the participation of society members in cities (Caragliu et al., 2011). According to these characteristics, a smart city is referred to as a living space and economic platform.

The category of Smart Economy includes all factors of economic competitiveness concerning innovation, entrepreneurship, trademarks, productivity and flexibility of the labor market, as well as (inter)national market integration. The definition of Smart People not only refers to the level of qualification or education of citizens, but also to the quality of social interactions in the field of integration, public life, and interest in the world around them. Smart Governance includes open political participation and citizen services. In the matter of Mobility, local and international accessibility concerns important aspects, such as the availability of information and communication technologies and modern sustainable transportation systems. A Smart Environment expresses itself through fascinating natural conditions in respect to the climate and green spaces, pollution reduction, resource management and efforts to protect the environment. Finally, Smart Living covers various aspects of the quality of life, such as culture, health, safety, social cohesion, housing and tourism (Centre of Regional Science, 2007). In this perspective,

> [A] city is smart when investments in human and social capital, as well as in traditional (transport) and modern (ICT) communication infrastructure fuel sustainable economic growth and a high quality of life, with a wise management of natural resources, through participatory governance. (Caragliu et al., 2011, p. 70)

Framed in this way, the smart city serves as a model for a politically open, economically vibrant, livable and sustainable city.

The slow city

Promoted at the end of the 1990s and modeled after the Italian slow food movement, which arose a decade earlier in opposition to the "McDonaldization" phenomenon (Ritzer, 1997), slow cities have become a specific urban brand (Grzelak-Kostulska et al., 2011; Knox, 2005; Miele, 2008; Pink, 2008). Slow food initially started as a reverse trend against globalization, becoming the hallmark of changing pace, developing taste, and linking producer and consumer of food in a way that promotes local development processes. Indeed, the slow movement considers small towns as a privileged place to experiment with qualitatively different lifestyles including alternative consumption practices. Today, the slow cities network (Cittàslow) includes an increasing number of cities, not only in Europe but also on other continents. By early 2015 there was an international network of 192 members widespread in 30 countries around the world.[4] The Italian network is by far the largest.

The Cittàslow network includes small and medium-sized cities that are committed to improving the quality of life of their residents. The philosophy of slow city is based on the following cornerstones:

> [R]espect for local identity, memory and heritage of the community; respect for the environment, landscape and biodiversity; introduction of technologies for sustainability, conservation and reuse in the city as well as in the countryside; responsibility as an integral part of local development. (Rur, 2012, p. 9)

These parameters correspond to a set of criteria divided into six macro areas, including also other extraordinary and specific criteria related to activities and projects of the network as shown in Table 8.2.

In order to become a member of the network, cities must meet several criteria concerning environmental and infrastructural policies, urban planning, promotion and enhancement of local products, conviviality and hospitality:

> Environmental measures such as air-quality control, waste management, light pollution control, and alternative energy sources are aimed at protecting the town's environmental assets. Some of the criteria are also concerned with economic growth through the production and consumption of local products. (Mayer & Knox, 2006, pp. 327–328)

Also tourism, rather than being considered as an industry on the edge of carrying capacities[5] (McCool & Lime, 2001; O'Reilly, 1986), is treated as a central element, with model of hospitality emphasizing a "slow-pace." Within this perspective, tourism draws benefits from the "slow" strategies of slow cities (Thimothy & Boyd, 2003): the experience of a trip becomes more concrete in a urban environment where there is a stronger social cohesion, as well as a sufficient presence of relationships and more environmentally friendly spaces. Thus, the brand "slow" has gone beyond the mere meaning of "good food and good life" and it has become a recurrent mode to describe sustainable cities.

The Cittàslow movement, based on the culture of "slow living," is specifically known for the willingness to apply the philosophy of slowness to the entire urban system. In this perspective, the Cittaslow model becomes particularly important for two reasons. The first one is to reimagine the city in terms of pace. The dominant model of the twentieth and twenty-first centuries has seen cities characterized by fast rhythms, integrated in non-sustainable global industrial systems. In contrast, slow cities promote an alternative model of competition through pace and scale: a sustainable city based on small and medium-sized local business fostering local identity and diversity (economic sustainability), environment protection and the quality of the territory (environmental and territorial sustainability), plurality of interests, appreciation of local history and cultures (social sustainability).[6]

Table 8.2 Requirements for Cittàslow certification

Macro areas	Requirements
Energy and environmental policy	Air quality conservation Water quality conservation Urban solid separate waste collection Energy saving in buildings and public systems Conservation of biodiversity
Infrastructure policies	Efficient cycle paths connected to public buildings Bicycle parking in interchange zones Planning of eco-mobility as an alternative to private cars Removal of architectural barriers "Sustainable" distribution of merchandise in urban centers
Quality of urban life policies	Interventions of recovery and increasing the value of civic centers Recovery/creation of social green areas with productive plants and/or fruit trees Requalification and reuse of marginal areas Use of ICTs in the development of interactive services for citizens and tourists Service desk for sustainable architecture (bio-architecture, etc.) Cable network city (fiber optics, wireless) Monitoring and reduction of pollutants (noise, electromagnetism, etc.) Promotion of private sustainable urban planning (passive house, building materials, etc.) Creation of spaces for the commercialization of local products
Agricultural, touristic and artisan policies	Development of agro-ecology Protection of handmade and labeled artisan production (certified, museums of culture, etc.) Increasing the value of working techniques and traditional crafts Increasing the value of rural areas Use of local products in communal public restaurants (school canteens etc.) Conservation and increasing the value of local cultural events Prohibiting the use of GMO in agriculture
Policies for hospitality, awareness and training	Good welcome (training of people in charge, suitable infrastructure) Increasing awareness of operators and traders (transparency of practiced prices, clear visibility of tariffs) Availability of "slow" itineraries (printed, web, etc.) Adoption of active techniques suitable for launching bottom-up processes in the more important administrative decisions
Social cohesion	Integration of disable people Children care Multicultural integration Political participation The existence of youth activity areas and youth center

Source: Adapted from Cittaslow International Charter (2014). Retrieved from
www.cittaslow.org/download/DocumentiUfficiali/Charter_2014.pdf, pp. 27–29.

The second reason is the importance of places in citizens' everyday lives. Cities are not only a place of production, but also of social reproduction. The contemporary world is increasingly characterized by the proliferation of standardized and meaningless spaces, not considered as real places, in other words what Marc Augé (1992) calls "non-space." In this sense, the purpose of Cittaslow is to support the creation of a place considered as an essential human need for wellbeing, security and sense of direction, in the attempt to take control over alienation and estrangement phenomena.[7] In many definitions of place, orientation appears as a basic element – that is, a cognitive element that allows one to understand the position of others and act accordingly. Similarly Giddens (1985) talks about local areas as the settings of interaction, meant as a space where significant relationships take place and the players in the field share at least the meaning of the context in which they are interacting (cf. Osti, 2010). It is through the importance given to a place and to the urban fabric, that Cittaslow can operate in several areas promoting "slowness," including food, culture, urban planning, environment, energy, means of transport, and tourism (Rur, 2012).

When slow is also smart: common aspects

Discussion about smart cities also involves asking what kind of "intelligence" should be striven for, and above all what social, political and economic needs "smart" should serve. Considering the environmental excesses and precarious human and economic conditions that are now being faced by cities worldwide, sustainability becomes a crucial issue within smart city design. Therefore, smartness is best understood as the ability of a city to innovate and meet criteria of economic, environmental and social sustainability. According to Lindner (2013, p. 14):

> now is the right time to step back from the growing hype surrounding smart cities and ask whether smarter is indeed better, (and whether) perhaps we should also be talking about slowness alongside smartness. Smart and slow do not necessarily preclude one another, and indeed there are many ways in which the two can not only co-exist but also create the material and cultural conditions for supporting each other in urban contexts.

Comparing the main criteria of slow cities and the features of the smart city, it is possible to identify several aspects that both models have in common.

The interpretation of the shared characteristics reported in Figure 8.1 shows that many practices, central to the philosophy of slowness and intrinsic within slow cities (recovery and reuse of green spaces, eco-compatible practices, enhancement of identities, support of handicrafts and local products) represent the constant connections between the so-called slow cities and smart cities. For instance, from the mobility point of view, the smart city supports the availability of ICT-infrastructure; sustainable, innovative and safe transport

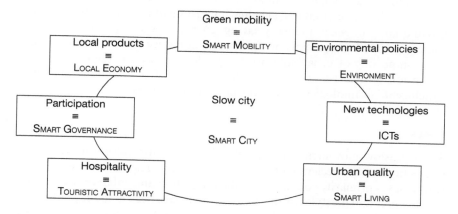

Figure 8.1 Shared aspects in slow and smart cities.

systems. Similarly, the slow city promotes efficient cycle paths connected to public buildings, bicycle parking in interchange zones, planning of eco-mobility as an alternative to private cars, and the removal of architectural barriers.

With regard to urban quality, the smart city promotes housing quality and general health conditions. Similarly, the slow city promotes the recovery/ creation of social green areas with productive plants and/or fruit trees, requalification and reuse of marginal areas; service desk for sustainable architecture (bio-architecture, etc.), promotion of private sustainable urban planning (passive house, building materials, etc.), and monitoring and reduction of pollutants (noise, electromagnetism, etc.). The environmental dimension certainly represents a further point of convergence between the two models. For instance, the smart city aims to limit pollution (air, noise, etc.), provide environmental protection, sustainable resource management. The prerogative of slow cities consists of air and water quality conservation, solid separate waste collection, energy savings in buildings and public systems, and conservation of biodiversity. Regarding the governance dimension, smart cities promote broad participation of all stakeholders, citizens included, in the decision-making process. Likewise, the slow city fosters political participation and the adoption of active techniques suitable for launching bottom-up processes in the more important administrative decisions.

In addition to eco-compatibility policies and inclusive governance, the introduction of new technologies represents a clear connection between the slow and smart models. In fact, as pointed out by Grzelak-Kostulska et al. (2011), the slow city also aims at encouraging the use of new technologies since they are considered as important tools to transform the city into "ideal" places to live. Slow cities promote innovation and the use of new technologies[8] aimed at improving the quality of the environment and of the urban fabric. Although much of the literature on smart technologies is actually about "fast technologies," what is common to the two city models is certainly the use of those technologies that aim at achieving sustainability and improvement of urban quality in general (energy saving, energy production from alternative sources, nonpolluting means of transport that reduce the use of motor vehicles, composting of urban solid waste). In this perspective, the technological dimension of smart and slow cities find a point of intersection concerning "intelligent" technologies such as the green technologies.

Cases

The Cittaslow movement can be defined as a counterculture movement in opposition to the accelerated pace of globalization. The alternative model of slow cities is primarily committed to the promotion and enhancement of specific features and lifestyles of those cities which have been at the edge of global circuits until now – and to which the slow philosophy is trying to give back a central position. But it is also committed to achieve higher ambitions through the "transfer" of specific features of slow living typical of suburbs and smaller towns, to large metropolitan cities (Rur, 2012). According to Mayer and Knox (2006, p. 332), "the concept of slow city can become a standard urban model adaptable to large cities, bigger than the ones where it has been applied." At the international level, there are several cases which help to explain the current progression of slow cities and, in particular, the transferability of many practices, part of the slow model, to large and medium-sized cities.

The city of Namyangju

In member cities of the slow network there are several examples of green spaces recovery in suburban areas, especially for agricultural purposes. Concern over food quality lies at the heart of this practice. The protection of soil, water and air, through the reduction of pollution emissions, are primary motivations. The city of Namyangju in the province of Gyeonggi in South Korea has worked to reach these goals. It is one of the satellite cities of Seoul, with a population of over 500,000, and it is one of nine certified cities of the Cittaslow network in Korea. Despite the proximity to the capital city Seoul, there is an area in Namyangju where the magnificent natural scenes with clean water and green trees are well preserved. The area is designated as a water conservation zone that meets perfectly the conditions that a slow city requires: harmony with humans and nature.

Initiatives in the city have focused on three main fronts. One is organic farming, cultivation and processing practices of natural products with recognized health benefits. Organic farming is meaningful because it represents not only the preservation of the biological diversity but also the fundamental system that improves healthy agriculture and organisms in the soil. In addition, it promotes healthy dietary practices. Namyangju is rapidly developing a reputation as a regional center of excellence for organic farming.

Namyangju Organic Farming Theme Park, which includes the Namyagju Organic Museum, is the only professional organic farming theme park around the world. The museum's opening coincided with Namyangju hosting the 17th IFOAM[9] Organic World Congress in 2011, and it is the world's first museum dedicated to the history and development of organic agriculture.

Organic Ssamchae[10] and strawberries are representative local specialties of Namyangju. In particular, an experience study program has been provided, allowing people to experience making organic strawberry jam and strawberry enzyme using organic strawberries. Similarly, organic lotus roots are one of the representative specialties of Namyangju. The lotus root, as a hypogeal stem, is prolific and has abundant proteins, vitamins, minerals, and other nutrition facts helpful for our health. In 2009 Lotus Village, which is a lotus theme village, opened. It represents an important tourist attraction, especially in the summer when lotuses are in full bloom. In addition, with the adaption of the eco-friendly programs, Lotus Village is considered as a meaningful eco-friendly ecological experience area in the metropolitan area (www.cittaslow.kr/).

The second initiative in the city consists of reducing transport–based pollution by promoting the use of alternative transportation such as bicycles. Thanks to a recovery plan of the old abandoned railway line, the Namyangju Bicycle Road has been developed. This project was undertaken as part of the policy "Making Urban Environment Better" by the Namyangju city government. The policy, promoted by Department of Roads, consists of checking leisure facilities – bicycle paths, walks and small parks – around roads (www .nyj.go.kr/english/index.jsp). The Namyangju Bicycle Road is part of a larger national "Four Rivers Cross-country Bicycle Roads Project." The roads are are bike trails constructed near the four major rivers of South Korea: Han River, Nakdong River, Geum River and Yeongsan River (Green Tourism Center, 2012). The Han River Bicycle Road is a 136 Km road reusing the former central railway and the 27 Km Namyangju Bicycle Road is part of it. The Han River Bicycle Road was opened in 2011 and in year after about 3,000 visitors used it on weekdays and 5,000 people during weekends (Korea JoongAng Daily, 2012). These bicycle roads have become more important than ordinary highways and constitute an alternative transportation mechanism that reduces automobile traffic jams, particularly during the holidays.

The third initiative refers to tourist attractions. In terms of tourism, the city of Namyangju features several attractions, both in the urban and suburban area, including the Silhak[11] Museum (Realist School of Confucianism), the Organic Farming Theme Park, the Lotus Village and Namyangju Studio Complex. The Silhak Museum is located in Dasan[12] historical site in Namyangju. Silhak Museum provides a variety of exhibitions and activities as well as educational and cultural programs, including Silhak Concert for Children, Silhak Travel and Silhak Camp. In addition to the Organic Museum, Organic Farming Theme Park also includes Ecological Pond, Theme Playground, Community Square, Green Rest Area, Farmer's

Market, Round-Glassed House and Experience Zone, where organic farming techniques are taught and experienced in a small area in the back of the park. Namyangju Studio Complex is the largest film production plant in Asia, covering an area of over 1,300,000 square meters. It contains outdoor filming sets, an indoor studio, and even a movie theater. Visitors can discover more about the conception of films, its evolution, and its future in the Film Culture Center while exploring the different ways films are put together in the Film Experience Center. A Prop and Costume Room displays actual props and costumes from films.

Although the eco-friendly methods promoted by the slow movement can be easily implemented in small towns and in a specific and reduced way, the coordination of ecological actions needs a wider territorial scale in order to reduce of the ecological footprint.[13] The experience of the city of Namyangju goes towards this direction. Namyangju is witnessing an environmentally friendly action on urban scale involving the biological aspect of production, marketing and consumption capacity, and also showing how larger urban environments can start productive networks dedicated to organic farming and produce green mobility paths.

Barcelona: many slow cities into a smart city

Slow cities are often environmentally friendly cities that tend to resemble the smart model. Currently, the issues of slow cities concern technological efficiency to enhance the quality of the urban environment, while smart cities focus on slowness as a parameter of eco-sustainability and urban livability. In these types of city, slowness means to safeguard resources through their wise use with the support of intelligent technologies, as well as the need to organize urban life in more qualitative ways. The most innovative technological dimensions are intertwined with eco-compatible development aspects, where the criteria of economic efficiency and socio-environmental equity become guiding principles for a comfortable, safe and intelligent city (Catalano & Tocci, 2012).

This is the case of the city of Barcelona with the project Many Slow Cities into a Smart City, created within the Master of Landscape Architecture at the Institute for Advanced Architecture of Catalonia (IAAC). The purpose of this plan is to transfer the slow philosophy to a metropolitan city like the Catalan capital (Institute for Advanced Architecture of Catalonia [IAAC], 2012). The project is based on the idea that it is possible to conceive of a smart city as a set of many slow cities (cf. Figure 8.2) in a multi-scale approach that breaks down the city, from the metropolitan scale to a smaller one made of districts and municipalities. It began as a holistic approach to the city reconsidered in several layers: from the environment to infrastructures, from water cycle to energy and mobility. Basically, the idea is based on the "decomposition" of the city in several slow areas where different identities are not just connected, but become "glocal". In this perspective the purpose of the city is not to centralize different peripheral cells in a single model, but to respect and enhance differences among all these areas, connecting them in a social and digital meaning.

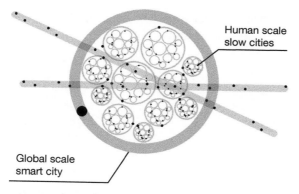

Figure 8.2 From the metropolitan level to the micro level. (From Guallart [2014]. *Barcelona 5.0, production, talent & networks, regenerating the cities of the future.* Retrieved from http://cba.mit.edu/events/11.08.FAB7/Tomas.pdf, p. 19).

The vision of Barcelona is meant as "the city of people," improving citizens' welfare and quality of life and the economic progress, where technology is an enabler for: a more efficient and sustainable urban mobility; environmental sustainability; integration and social cohesion; universal access to culture, education and health care. With regard to specific projects, some of the main ones focus on the creation of new sustainable urban infrastructures. Two examples are the Energetic Self-sufficiency Plan (self-sufficient blocks, smart grid, district heating and cooling) and Energetic Efficiency in Buildings Plan (building protocol, smart metering, corporate buildings). These projects aim at creating energy self-sufficient blocks, in order to improve practices related to consumption and production of energy. They are based on the incorporation of solar roofs, mixed uses, collective district heating, water recycling, and the use of electric vehicles, in order fit the maximum energy demand with local production (cf. Figure 8.3).[14]

Barcelona abounds in green areas and has approximately 18 m²/inhabitant of green surface. Others projects conducted by the city of Barcelona aim to protect and extend this. Indeed, they include the construction of urban gardens with growing plants and vegetables along streets and several management and rationalization systems of water resources, including water harvesting systems for irrigation. These include Smart Water (watering telecontrol, smart sewage system, phreatic water management, fountain telecontrol), which is based on the installation of a centralized remote management system to control automated irrigation infrastructure in order to monitor the duration and frequency of irrigation in each area, according to the needs.[15]

Through initiating several projects, Barcelona has been investing in the construction of a smart city with a high urban quality, and now the city is orienting its development strategy in order to guarantee quality of life for

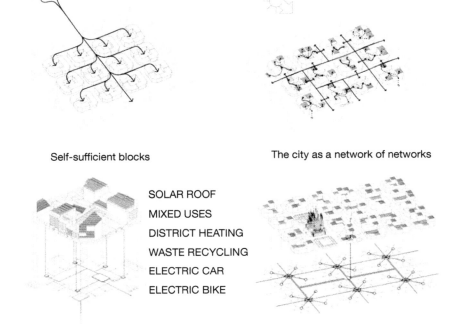

Figure 8.3 From centralized to distributed energy production. (From Guallart [2013]. *The self-sufficient city. FORUM CAT 21 SCOT.* Retrieved from http:// forum.scot.cat/downloads2/vicente_guallart.pdf, p. 8).

its citizens, social and urban improvement and added value in its neighborhoods, fostering all its urban potential towards sustainable development and green economy. As chief architect of the city of Barcelona, Vicente Guallart claims:

> This is what's happening in Barcelona, but – with the arrival of new technologies, ideas of sustainability – it has to change. And that's the idea, an idea of mixing many slow cities inside a smart city. Neighbourhoods should be the place where people live, with a high quality of life. (Szymczyk, 2014, p. 4)

From this point of view, Barcelona aims to become a city of productive neighborhoods, eco-efficient, energetically self-sufficient, inside a high-speed interconnected metropolitan area; i.e. "many slow cities inside the same smart city" where nature holds a prominent role for the balance of the city.

Conclusion

Based on the criteria used to define slow and smart cities, this work highlights several significant issues that can be considered as additional components in the vast and complex framework of urban sustainability. An increasing number of cities, large and small, are undertaking initiatives that are knowingly or unknowingly based on the philosophy of slow cities – such as the experiences of Namyangju and Barcelona demonstrate. According to Lindner (2013, p. 15):

> [G]iven the environmental excesses and precarious human and economic conditions now facing cities worldwide, sustainability is rightly a core concern within smart city design. (…) slowness – as concept, value, practice, and experience – needs to be incorporated more explicitly into future thinking about cities, including smart cities and their technologically-driven efforts to promote sustainability.

The chapter shows that slow and smart are mutually compatible and in fact, share many components and conceptions. Hence, being slow does not hinder from being efficient; if being slow greatly emphasizes the qualitative contents of urban living, being smart enhances the means to reach higher quality standards. Moreover, "what specifically characterizes Cittaslow movement is the willingness to apply the philosophy of slowness on the whole urban organism" (Rur, 2012, p. 28). The ambition of the network is to "contaminate" small towns and "districts of metropolitan cities through the quality of life, the world of relationships and sustainable socio-economic management practices" (Ibid., 31). Both the urban gardening experience (the village of lotuses and the organic farming theme park) of Namyangju, and the eco-friendly strategies adopted in Barcelona, fully comply with this perspective. Therefore, the concept of slow city can be associated, transferred and applied also to larger sized cities (Knox, 2005; Mayer & Knox, 2006). Finally, the innovative aspects implied by intelligent technologies – aimed at improving the quality of the environment and of the urban fabric, the sustainable mobility, and in general the quality of the urban life – represent a feature that deserves greater attention in the analysis of common elements between smart and slow urban models. According to Lindner (2013, p. 14) "as smart technologies and engineering have helped to make cities move and function faster and faster, they can also be used strategically and selectively to decelerate cities."

Notes

1 There is no common definition of a medium-sized city. The meaning of "medium-sized" depends on the scale one looks at. What appears medium-sized at the European scale may be considered large at the national scale or small on the global scale (Giffinger, Kramar, & Haindl, 2008). On a European scale, medium-sized cities are cities often also understood as "second cities": cities which are mainly not recognized very well on a European scale but often of crucial importance on a

national and regional scale. For example, on a European scale, medium-sized cities are cities with a population between 100,000 and 500,000 inhabitants (Centre of Regional Science, 2007).

2 For a thorough examination of social capital, consult Bourdieu (1980), Coleman (1988).

3 The research has been carried out on a sample of 70 cities with a population between 100,000 and 500,000 for the development of a new ranking tool of medium-sized cities (Centre of Regional Science, 2007).

4 Data updated March 2015. The list of member cities of Cittaslow is available on the web at www.cittaslow.org. The criteria to log in the network are selective and due to the continuous updating, some centers may be missing from the network. Policies are subject to periodical changes in order to update the benchmarks.

5 "Increased interest in the sustainability of tourism development initiatives has triggered expanding concerns about the capability of both tourism destinations and protected areas to accommodate recreational use" (McCool & Lime, 2001, p. 372).

6 For a thorough examination of environmental, territorial, social sustainability consult Magnaghi (2000).

7 According to Wirth (1938, p. 1),

[F]or sociological purposes a city is a relatively large, dense, and permanent settlement of heterogeneous individuals. Large numbers account for individual variability, (…) the segmentation of human relations which are largely anonymous, superficial, and transitory (…). Density involves diversification and specialization (…), distant social relations, glaring contrasts, a complex pattern of segregation (…). Heterogeneity tends to break down rigid social structures and to produce increased mobility, instability, and insecurity (…). The pecuniary nexus tends to displace personal relations, and institutions tend to cater to mass rather than to individual requirements. The individual thus becomes effective only as he acts through organized groups.

For a thorough examination of cities as social phenomena, consult also Amendola, 1997; Castells, 1989; Martinotti, 1993; Sassen, 1991.

8 These include technologies for energy saving in buildings and public systems, for public energy production from renewable sources: technologies for the eco-mobility and for the removal of architectural barriers (escalators, moving walkway), use of ICTs in the development of interactive services for citizens and tourists, and fiber-optics and wireless (cf. Table 8.2).

9 The International Federation of Organic Agriculture Movements (IFOAM) is an organization that aims to promote the practice of organic farming, the preservation of agricultural ecosystems and the production of healthy nutrition. IFOAM, founded in France in 1972, now unites more than 750 member organizations from 116 countries.

10 *Ssamchae* are vegetables, such as lettuce, green perilla, cabbage, pumpkin leaves, wild greens, medicinal herbs, used as *Ssam*, i.e. a Korean traditional food with rice wrapped in leaves.

11 *Silhak* was a Korean Confucian social reform movement in late Joseon Dynasty. *Sil* means "actual" or "practical" and *hak* means "studies" or "learning" (http://encyclopedia.thefreedictionary.com/) [Accessed 26 February 2015].

12 *Jeong Yak-yong*, often simply known as *Dasan* was one of the greatest thinkers of the later Joseon period. His philosophical position is often identified with the Silhak school (Ibid.).

13 The concept of ecological footprint refers to the amount of water, air, soil that we need to produce, consume and reabsorb the set of products originated by human activities.

14 www.slideshare.net/MicrosoftSuomi/city-next-smartbarcelona-28102013
[Accessed 18 February 2015].
15 Ibid.

References

Amendola, G. (1997). *La città post-moderna*. Roma-Bari: Laterza.
Amendola, G. (2007). I nuovi spazi pubblici tra agorà e mercato. *Sociologia urbana e rurale, 82,* 13–24.
Amin, A., & Thrift, N. (2002). *Cities: Reimagining the urban*. Oxford: Polity Press.
Augé, M. (1992). *Non-Lieux. Introduction à une anthropologie de la surmodernité.* Paris: Éditions du Seuil.
Berthon, B., & Guittat, P. (2011). Ascesa della città intelligente. *Outlook, 2,* 1–11.
Batty, M., Axhausen, K. W., Giannotti, F., Pozdnoukhov, A., Bazzani, A., Wachowicz, M., ... Portugali, Y. (2012). Smart cities of the future. *European Physical Journal. Special Topics, 214,* 481–518.
Bourdieu, P. (1980). Le capital social. Notes provisoire. *Actes de la recherche en sciences sociales, 31,* 2–3.
Castells, M. (1989). *The informational city*. Oxford: Oxford University Press.
Catalano, G., & Tocci, G. (2012). Le Comunità Urbane Ecocompatibili. Città lente e intelligenti. In V. Calzati & P. De Salvo (Eds.), *Le strategie per una valorizzazione sostenibile del territorio. Il valore della lentezza, della qualità e dell'identità per il turismo del futuro* (pp. 45–60). Milan: FrancoAngeli.
Caragliu, A., Del Bo, C., & Nijkamp, P. (2011). Smart cities in Europe. *Journal of Urban Technology, 18*(2), 65–82.
Centre of Regional Science. (2007). *Smart cities – ranking of European medium-sized cities*. Retrieved from www.smart-cities.eu/download/smart_cities_final_report.pdf
Cittalia. (2012). *Smart cities nel Mondo*. Reggio Emilia: Fondazione Anci Ricerche.
Cittaslow International Charter. (2014). Retrieved from www.cittaslow.org/download/DocumentiUfficiali/Charter_2014.pdf
Coleman, J. (1988). Social capital in the creation of human capital. *The American Journal of Sociology, 94,* 95–120.
Eurocities. (2007). *Knowledge society*. Retrieved from www.eurocities.org/main.php
Giddens, A. (1985). *A contemporary critique of historical materialism. The nation state and violence* (Vol. 2). Cambridge: Polity Press.
Giffinger, R., Kramar, H., & Haindl, G. (2008). The role of rankings in growing city competition. *Proceedings of the 11th European Urban Research Association (EURA) Conference,* 1–12. Retrieved from www.smart-cities.eu/download/city_ranking_final.pdf
Green Tourism Center. (2012). *Riverside bike trails in Korea*. Seoul: Korea Tourism Organization.
Grzelak-Kostulska, E., Holowiecka, B., & Kwiatkowski, G. (2011). Cittaslow International Network: An example of a globalization idea? In *The scale of globalization. Think globally, act locally, change individually in the 21st century*. Ostrava: University of Ostrava.
Guallart, V. (2013). *The self-sufficient city. FORUM CAT 21 SCOT*. Retrieved from http://forum.scot.cat/downloads2/vicente_guallart.pdf
Guallart, V. (2014). *Barcelona 5.0, production, talent & networks, regenerating the cities of the future*. Retrieved from http://cba.mit.edu/events/11.08.FAB7/Tomas.pdf
Haughton, G., & Hunter, C. (2004). *Sustainable cities*. London: Routledge.
Hollands, R. G. (2008). Will the real smart city please stand up? Creative, progressive or just entrepreneurial. *City, 12*(3), 303–320.

IAAC (Institute for Advanced Architecture of Catalonia). (2012). *Many slow cities into a smart city*. Retrieved from www.iaacblog.com

James, P. (2015). *Urban sustainability in theory and practice: Circles of sustainability*. London: Routledge.

Knox, P. L. (2005). Creating ordinary places: Slow cities in a fast world. *Journal of Urban Design, 10*(1), 1–11.

Komninos, N. (2011). Intelligent cities: Variable geometries of spatial intelligence. *Intelligent Buildings International, 3*(3), 172–188.

Korea JoongAng Daily. (2012). *Four rivers bicycle roads project*. Retrieved from http://koreajoongangdaily.joins.com/

Le Galès, P. (2002). *European cities. Social conflicts and governance*. Oxford: Oxford University Press.

Lindner, C. (2013). Smart cities and slowness. *Urban Pamphleteer, 1*, 14–16.

Magnaghi, A. (2000). *Il progetto locale*. Turin: Bollati Boringhieri.

Martinotti, G. (1993). *Metropoli. La nuova morfologia sociale delle città*. Bologna: il Mulino.

Mayer, H., & Knox, P. L. (2006). Slow cities: Sustainable places in a fast world. *Journal of Urban Affairs, 28*(4), 321–334.

Mayer, H., & Knox, P. L. (2010). Small town sustainability: Prospects in the second modernity. *European Planning Studies, 18*(10), 1545–1565.

McCool, S. F., & Lime, D. W. (2001). Tourism carrying capacity: Tempting fantasy or useful reality? *Journal of Sustainable Tourism, 9*(5), 372–388.

Miele, M. (2008). Cittáslow: Producing slowness against the fast life. *Space and Polity, 12*(1), 135–156.

Nam, T., & Pardo, T. A. (2011). Conceptualizing smart city with dimensions of technology, people, and institutions. *Proceedings of the 12th Annual International Digital Government Research Conference*, 282–291.

O'Reilly, A. M. (1986). Tourism carrying capacity: Concept and issues. *Tourism Management, 7*(4), 254–258.

Osti, G. (2010). *Sociologia del territorio*. Bologna: il Mulino.

Pink, S. (2008). Sense and sustainability: The case of the slow city movement. *Local Environment, 13*(2), 95–106.

Polese, M., & Stren, R. (2000). *The social sustainability of cities: Diversity and the management of change*. Toronto: University of Toronto Press.

Ritzer, G. (1997). *Il mondo alla McDonald's*. Bologna: il Mulino.

Rur. (2012). *Cittàslow: Dall'Italia al mondo*. Milan: FrancoAngeli.

Sassen, S. (1991). *The global city: New York, London, Tokyo*. Princeton: Princeton University Press.

Szymczyk, E. (2014). Interview with Vicente Guallart, chief architect of Barcelona. *ArchDaily*. Retrieved from www.archdaily.com/?p=471732

Thimothy, D. J., & Boyd, S. W. (2003). *Heritage e Turismo*. Milan: Hoepli.

United Nations. (2010). *State of the world's cities 2010/2011. Cities for all: Bridging the urban divide*. New York, NY: UN-HABITAT.

Van Der Meer, A., & Van Winden, W. (2003). E-governance in cities: A comparison of urban information and communication technology policies. *Regional Studies, 37*(4), 407–419.

Véron, J. (2008). *L'urbanizzazione del mondo*. Bologna: il Mulino.

Wirth, L. (1938). Urbanism as a way of life. *American Journal of Sociology, 44*(1), 1–24.

9 Between slow tourists and operators

Expectations and implications of a strategic cross-border proposal

Moreno Zago

Introduction

The decline of mass tourism has introduced the figure of the post-tourist, one who is no longer identified in a collective dimension, but seems to seek confirmation of existence and identity through diversity of the holiday experience. Leed (1992) showed that the tourist journey induces socialization, as well as being a means of transforming social identities. Today politicians and tourism operators talk about responsible tourism, which requires adherence to a logic of sustainability where territory is a common cultural heritage. Slow tourism supports an alternative holiday based on these criteria, shifting the attention from each specific landmark and symbolic places (the beach, the main cultural resource, the old town, etc.) to the many paths and routes that cross the territory.

This chapter analyzes the results achieved by the European cross-border cooperation project Slowtourism: Implementation and Valorization of Slow Itineraries between Italy and Slovenia. The project, which was implemented between 2007 and 2013, sought to increase cross-border cooperation through coordination and promotion of tourism offerings in the region with a specific focus on the niche market of slow tourism. Notably, through interviews with the operators who have joined the network Slowtourism and slow tourists, the chapter highlights the system of expectations that both have had towards the project, services and territorial development. Furthermore, attention is given to the links with other cross-border projects that enhance typically slow activities (cycling, walking, food and wine, fishing, etc.), highlighting the spatial planning of the Upper Adriatic in supporting a tourism industry based on sustainability, authenticity, uniqueness and environmental protection, keys for long-term economic development.

The Upper Adriatic in policies of cross-border cooperation

The present study focuses on the Upper Adriatic cross-border area between Slovenia and the Italian Friuli Venetia Giulia Autonomous Region. Border conditions gave a kind of imprinting to these areas, of cultural complexity and cohabitation of different ethnic groups (Italian, German and Slovene speaking) that have always inhabited the area. This complexity played itself out violently through nationalist conflict during the first half of the twentieth century. However, this area has also been able to handle the border specificity directing relations to local hinterlands at Italian-German and Slavic-Hungarian prevalence or towards the Mediterranean and the imperial lands (Valussi, 2000).

Within the European Territorial Cooperation (ETC), this has been one of several areas to benefit in 2007–13 from the opportunity to participate in many European funding programs: Central Europe, South Eastern Europe, Mediterranean, Alpine Space, Interreg IVC, Urbact II, Espon. With a total budget of over €2 billion, these programs promote competitiveness, growth and integration through the creation of transnational partnerships and joint actions (De Felice, Fioretti, & Lanzilli, 2009; Nadalutti, 2015).

Historically the European Economic Community and subsequently the European Union (EU) have promoted policies aimed at reducing disparities among different regions and member states. Especially since the 1990s, considerable attention was paid to border areas where 38 percent of the European population lives. The promotion of cross-border cooperation (CBC), which arose with the recognition of the border served as a limit or obstacle to the development of an area as well as to a single European Market and political unit, has become the instrument for the reconstruction of administrative and economic fractures. The capacity attributed to CBC to recenter an area is greater where there is a balance between activities carried out in the economic and cultural spheres and between indirect and direct relations by which such activities are enacted (Del Bianco, 2010).

Implemented by the European Regional Development Fund and national funds, ETC has several objectives, including (a) help to transform regions located on either side of internal or external EU borders into strong economic and social poles (i.e., Cross-border cooperation), (b) promote cooperation among European regions, including those surrounding sea basins (e.g., Baltic Sea Region, North Sea, Mediterranean and Atlantic Area) or mountain ranges (e.g., Alpine Space), and (c) provide a framework for local and regional actors from across Europe to promote the exchange of experiences and the identification of good practices (i.e., Interregional cooperation). Financial resources allocated to the ETC have been about €8 billion – 2.5 percent of the resources allocated to cohesion policy (approximately €350 billion) – of which 74 percent to 6,000 cross-border cooperation projects focused on 60 EU border areas (European Commission, n.d.).

Notably, great attention was paid to the tourism sector in view of the fact that it is the third most valuable economic activity in Europe in terms of turnover and number of employees. In addition, it was viewed as the productive sector that could most effectively develop a cross-border area (see the Madrid Declaration of 15 April 2010 signed by the ministers of tourism of the member states). The programs mentioned above significantly targeted the growth of sustainable tourism, improving the quality of products offered and promoting new brand of international appeal.

Features, actors and projects of tourism cooperation

The Operational Programme of the Cross-Border Cooperation Italy-Slovenia 2007–2013, "Strengthening the attractiveness and competitiveness of the programme-area" received final approval by the European Commission on 20 April 2010, with a public funding of about €137 million in tourism. It favored specific niche segments as alternatives to mass tourism. The program aimed at promoting the production and marketing of local products, agriculture and fishing, the development of agritourism and the promotion of resources and tourist destinations in compliance with sustainability principles and focused on specific segments, such as cultural, environmental, river, spa and wellness, active, enogastronomic and accessible tourism (VV.AA, 2010).

The cross-border area includes the provinces of Ravenna, Ferrara, Rovigo, Padua, Venice, Treviso, Pordenone, Udine, Gorizia and Trieste in the Northeast of Italy and the statistical regions of Gorenjska, Goriška, Obalno-Kraška, Osrednjeslovenska and Notranjsko-Kraška in Western Slovenia. With a population of about 6 million inhabitants in an area of 31 thousand km^2, the area draws about 40 million tourists per year, often of a seasonal nature. Overall, the cross-border area, which can count on a strategic positioning on key transport routes between East-West and North-South European corridors, includes a wide variety of landscapes - coasts, plains, alpine reliefs – including the Adriatic Sea, which is an important factor for commercial activities and a driving force for the tourist. The area has significant naturalistic landscape attractions; a rich biodiversity; important endemic species; many parks (the Po Delta, Triglav); seaside resorts with a good state of coastal waters in terms of bathing (Adriatic Riviera, Jesolo, Lignano Sabbiadoro, Grado) and skiing (Tarvisio, Sella Neva, Kranjska Gora, etc.); numerous shopping centers and historic towns, castles (Miramare, Duino, Udine, Gorizia, Bled) and archaeological sites (Aquileia); religious sites (Castelmonte, Monte Lussari, etc.); and natural (Po Delta, Dolomites, Škocjan Caves) and cultural (Ravenna, Ferrara, Venice and its lagoon, some Palladian villas, Aquileia, Cividale del Friuli, the Botanical Garden of Padua) sites recognized by UNESCO, accompanied by various expressions of the local handicraft (majolica of Faenza, Murano glass), the maritime, wine (Collio, Vipava, Prosecco) and gastronomic culture (Gasparini & Zago, 2011).

Given these characteristics, cross-border cooperation has been oriented to strengthen and promote sustainable tourism as a distinctive brand identity of the program area. With a public contribution of about €26 million, projects in tourism sector were substantial and varied. Among them, some aimed at achieving several objectives related to the reorganization of transport accessibility of the whole cross-border area (Adria A, Tip): constructing cross-border cycling circuit to promote integration between the cities and rural areas and reduce the volume of traffic (Bimobis, CroCTaL, Idago, Interbike); decreasing the negative impact of intensive agriculture on the environment and improving the quality and recognition of indigenous products and crafts (Agrotur, Lanatura, Pesca,

Solum, Ue-Li-Je II Trecorala with attention to marine biodiversity), in order to stimulate the development of rural tourism (Enjoy Tour, Rural); improving economic competitiveness in tourism and cultural cooperation through the promotion of thematic routes (Heritaste) or the development of an integrated market of agricultural products (OGV); developing new ideas to improve the supply of tourist attractions and offerings, increase the flow of information, and improve access to the best technologies and improve collaboration (Motor, T-Lab); and enhancing and promoting itineraries featuring natural elements of value such as the salt pans (Saltworks) or the water by developing forms of slow tourism, paying particular attention to the concepts of sustainability, responsibility and eco-compatibility (Slowtourism) (see Table 9.1).

Thanks to the information found on the website of the CBC program (http://www.ita-slo.eu) and provided by the Joint Technical Secretariat, it is possible to reconstruct the significant transfrontier network of actors created by the implementation of these projects. The graph in the Figure 9.1 draws the

Table 9.1 Italy–Slovenia 2007–13 cross-border funded projects in tourism

Acronym	Title	Partner n.		Budget €
		Ita	Slo	
Adria A	Accessibility and Development for the Re-launch of the Inner Adriatic Area	18	11	2.838.872
Agrotur	Kras Agrotourism	3	3	1.022.915
Bimobis	Bike Mobility Between Italy and Slovenia	6	8	1.468.947
CroCTaL	Cross-border Cycling Tracks and Landscape	6	8	1.286.268
Enjoy Tour	Bon Appetit on the Cross-border Routes of Flavors	6	5	391.374
Heritaste	The Routes of Knowledge and Tastes	6	4	1.152.610
Idago	Improving Accessibility and the Attractiveness of the Cross-border Mountain Area	1	3	1.159.762
Interbike	Cross-border Intermodal bike Network	12	11	3.027.535
Lanatura	Tradition and Innovations in the Use of Animal Materials	6	6	386.961
Motor	Mobile Tourist Incubator	5	4	1.156.618
OGV	Gorizia's Vegetable Garden	6	6	487.561

Acronym	Title	Partner n.		Budget €
		Ita	*Slo*	
Pesca	Food Educational Project to a Healthy Eating	6	6	903.028
Rural	Cross-border Development of Rural Tourism and Joint Promotion of Local Products	2	1	446.750
Saltworks	Eco-touristic Valorization of the Salt-pans Between Italy and Slovenia	3	2	1.084.070
Slowtourism	Valorization and Promotion of Slow Tourism Itineraries Between Italy and Slovenia	16	14	3.590.571
Solum	Joint Itinerary Through Traditional Taste	4	4	1.103.901
Tip	Transborder Integrated Platform	5	5	1.150.865
T-Lab	Laboratory of Touristic Opportunities in Cross-border Regions of Slovenia and Italy	4	3	1.104.332
Trecorala	Rocky Outcrops and Coralligenous Formations in the Northern Adriatic: Enhancement and Sustainable Management in the Gulf of Trieste	8	3	1.430.000
Ue Li Je II	Olive Oil: A Symbol of Quality in the Cross-border Area	4	9	870.591
	Total	*127*	*116*	*26.063.531*

Source: VV.AA. (2010). Programma per la cooperazione transfrontaliera Italia-Slovenia 2007–2013. *Programma Operativo.* Retrieved from http://www.ita-slo.eu/progetti/progetti_2007_2013.

network based on the regional location of the beneficiaries. The values along the lines represent the number of partners involved in cross-border projects, while those inside the circles the number of partners involved on the basis of their national belonging. The greatest number of cross-border collaborations is between the organizations of Friuli Venetia Giulia and Goriška (n. 137) and between the latter and Veneto (n. 59). Furthermore, the region Friuli Venetia Giulia has 79 collaborations inside its territory while 61 are inside the Goriška region. The graph shows a greater participation among Italian operators rather than among Slovenian operators. The graph in Figure 9.2, however, reconstructs the network on the basis of the main types of beneficiaries: local

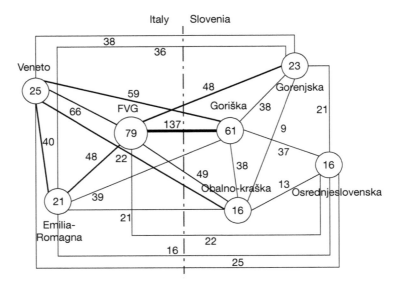

Figure 9.1 The cross-border cooperation network: list of beneficiaries by region.

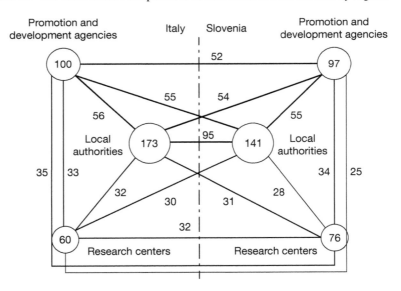

Figure 9.2 The cross-border cooperation network: list of beneficiaries by organization.

government (municipality, province, region), promotion and regional development agencies, research institutes and universities. In this case, cross-border cooperation takes place primarily among the authorities (numbering 95 partners), although the Italian partnership network seems to be stronger than that of Slovenia (n. 173 vs. n. 141 partners).

The *Slowtourism* project

In May 2010, the EU funded *Slowtourism*, a strategic project of cross-border cooperation for the enhancement and promotion of slow tourist itineraries between Italy and Slovenia. The project, led by the Local Development Agency of Emilia-Romagna Delta 2000, led to the participation of 30 institutional partners including regions, provinces, municipalities, development and promotion agencies, natural parks, and universities. Taking into consideration the fact that the area is characterized by a significant natural, historical and cultural heritage and by a wide range of tourism products and services, the aim of the project was to produce a strategy for cross-border slow tourism through the implementation of joint products of "slow" activities such as cycling, fishing, bird-watching and water-related tourism products, thus defining the Upper Adriatic as an area for slow tourists.

The traditional mass tourists have increasingly since the 1980s been replaced by post-modern tourists who, through their leisure and vacation, search for experience, diversity, and confirmation of their own identity. The growth of alternative forms of tourism confirms the importance of the dimension of consciousness, as *knowledge* of self and others - the locals who host, places, cultures, and so on – and as *awareness* of the impact that the presence has on the environment (Lavarini, 2008; Nocifora, de Salvo, & Calzati, 2011). Although taking on many labels, these new forms of responsible, ethical and sustainable tourist combine recreation and learning (edutainment), recognize the central importance of the host communities, pay attention to the environment, hold respect for different cultures, and support local development. The relevance of these types of tourism is confirmed by some data. At European level, the answer "Nature (landscapes, mountains, etc.)" was for Europeans the second most popular reason for going on holiday in 2014 (31 percent), following the answer "Sun/beach" (48 percent) and preceding the answer "Culture" (religious, gastronomy, arts, etc.: 27 percent) (European Commission, 2015, pp. 6–7).

A more specific survey implemented by the project on a sample of 800 tourists of the Italian-Slovenian border area underlined the appreciation of the following activities: doing outdoor activities and contemplating landscapes (61 percent, response category *very much appreciated*); visiting castles, churches, historic buildings or ruins (48 percent); visiting nature reserves and visitor centers in the parks (44 percent); walking, hiking and trekking (42 percent); tasting local products in agritourism or winery (40 percent). These are all activities that well embody aspects of slow tourism (Zago, 2012, p. 162). Applying factor analysis on a list of 20 items reveals five latent dimensions that reproduce 57 percent of total variance of the original variables.

1 *Practicing sport activities* (24.1 percent): the stay, either short or long, is seen as a chance to free one's energies and to find one's psycho-physical equilibrium through sport practice.
2 *Diving into the local* (11.3 percent): the tourist is seduced by typical rhythms and values of local life, tempted by local products

and attending courses on local culture, such as on wine and food, environment, history, etc.

3 *Living in nature* (8.3 percent): using one's own feet only, the tourist observes wild plants and animals within natural or protected environments, such as nature reserves, visitor centers, etc.

4 *Looking at the past* (6.4 percent): for the tourist, means to visit the vernacular heritage, which includes churches, castles, ruins, architectonic styles but also the reproduction of the past in historical, ethnographical, archaeological, etc. museums.

5 *Getting possession of time again* (5.7 percent): the tourist is seduced by those rhythms that are imposed in a place where there are no fast practices or means. They stay in accommodation facilities that are different from hotels, such as agritourism facilities, mountain huts, campsites, etc. and time is driven by the speed of his or her pace or, at most, by the speed of their push on a pedal (ibid., pp. 163–166).

A follow-up quantitative-qualitative survey carried out in 2013 on a sample of 245 tourists visiting the border area has evaluated these five dimensions and put in evidence the meaning of slow living and travel. On a Likert scale, the top response was "Living in nature." Some 69 percent of respondents answered that this category was *very important* on the item. Next was "Getting possession of time again" (63.3 percent), followed by "Diving into the local" (60.8), "Looking at the past" (50.4) and "Practicing sport activities" (11.4). When asked what slow tourism means to them, among notable responses were as follows:

- "to know the country, the city, the mountain in all their entirety; to live the vacation as a local citizen, not as a tourist, watching and visiting only the important things for locals" (Female, 18–35 years old);
- "to leave the motor vehicles to pay special attention to the most relaxing vehicles (such as the legs!) that allow you to enjoy with your eyes and your heart what you have around, experiencing the time without timetables or conditions of too many movements" (Female, 36–50 y.o.);
- "to give the right time to see and learn about the place you visit; less things to visit but deeper and it is better to visit with someone of the place able to capture different aspects of the local life" (Male, 18–35 y.o.);
- "to choose and prepare a travel itinerary, looking for little or strange things or that nobody cares, at your own pace" (Female, 51–65 y.o.);
- "to be able to organize the contents of the trip according your own needs" (Male, 18–35 y.o.);
- "to get in touch with local flavors, attending local wine and food tastings itineraries and the production of natural products" (Female, 36–50 y.o.); and
- "to travel in an environmentally friendly manner, thoughtful and appropriate with a strong respect of the territory and taking home feelings and values perhaps a little lost" (Male, 51–65 y.o.).

On the basis of these results, the study considered that the classification of an experience (supply and demand) of slow tourism must simultaneously satisfy the following six dimensions (ibid., pp. 167–169):

1　*Social Exchange*: This dimension is the sphere of relationships among individuals (with different opinions, beliefs, knowledge, cultures) and the capability of the supply system to create fruitful opportunities of more genuine exchange among them. Even if tourism has become the leading economic sector in the world, we still have the problem of cultural dialogue between the culture of those who leave and those who welcome. Travel could be the opportunity to understand ourselves through the eyes of others and this is the best way to deal with otherness (Lucchesi, 1995). Considering that 80 percent of international travel concerns residents of only twenty richest countries, practicing slow tourism also means to be able to build a society of different people based on equality. The relationships under consideration are in particular those between guests and the local people and among the guests themselves.

2　*Authenticity*: The concept of authenticity is eclectic and changes over time. Today, travelers and tourists are brought together by hunger for uncontaminated places and cultures. According to recent studies (Sedmak & Mihalic, 2008), authenticity has proved to be an important factor of choice, a factor that will tend to be regarded as increasingly important in the future. If the traveler and the tourist share the same desire, what changes is the way they interpret and enter into relationship with the different situations and environments. Those who practice slow tourism wish to be in a unique place, where they seek out peculiarities that characterize exclusively the chosen destination and the people who live there. Authenticity is the capability to create and offer a non-artificial experience strongly connected with local culture and traditions, and non-standardized products and services.

3　*Sustainability*: According to the Brundtland World Commission on Environment and Development (1988), development is sustainable if it meets the present needs without compromising those of future generations: "A development capable of future" (Ronchi, 2000).

　　Sustainable tourism development meets the needs of present tourists and host regions while protecting and enhancing opportunity for the future. Sustainable tourism operates in harmony with the local environment, community and cultures, so that these become the permanent beneficiaries and not victims of tourism development (UNWTO, 1996).

　　Slow tourism shares this concern with the impact of tourism on the local environment. It claims the need for a sustainable approach in the long term that is economically viable, and ethically and socially fair toward local people.

4　*Time*: Modern society is characterized by an accentuated acceleration of the present and the loss of the future: we make fewer plans, we have less hope, and relationships are less stable. The reflection arising from the literature is that in the society of acceleration it is more gratifying to orientate to the present rather than the future (Crespi, 2005). Thus, time here deals with the capacity of taking (the organization) and giving (to the guest) the right time to understand and act properly. Slow tourism seeks to dedicate time to analyze, understand, and plan quality improvements (for the customers and the employees), following a strategic orientation with an explicit medium-long-term planning, timely opening of the services, and offering the guest a comfortable experience.

5 *Length*: Related to the point in the previous paragraph, Bauman (2009) argues we live in a society that has lost a sense of time and that has emptied the criteria by which it is possible to distinguish the enduring from the ephemeral, the essential from the superfluous. The real waste of time is deceived by speed, even on vacation. Often the journey is seen as an obligation. Get the plane, take just two photos and then move on to the next exhibit, ultimately coming home to show them to friends. Slow travel teaches, instead, to enjoy the luxury of "wasting" time, to understand, to enter into the travel, not to do it: an experience that involves all the senses. Thus, the supply of services and products of slow tourism with non-frenetic rhythms, enable the guest to engage in a more complete experience that allows them to gradually assimilate and build relationships with local people. Slow means to reduce quantity and focus on quality of experiences.

6 *Emotion*: Slow tourism must rise, first of all, from the desire to get involved. The journey is not just the final destination, but it is the valuing of many experiences and sensations. The contemporary tourist is a multisensory tourist (Costa, 2005) looking for playful, liminal, experiential component and of sense gratification. As described by Bruno (2006), places become generators of moods, feelings, and emotions: emotional geography. Thus, place holds the capability to generate memorable moments and emotions, giving to the tourist a true involving and gratifying experience. By acknowledging and acting upon this, service providers may facilitate tourists' desired emotions.

In this sense, slow tourism is an approach to the use of tourism products that stimulate interactions with the host community (contamination), enhance the specificity of places (authenticity), minimize the impact on the environment (sustainability), require a planning aimed at improving the quality (time), prefer not frenetic rhythms (length), involve in a multisensory experience (emotion) (Castle model).

Classifying activities as "slow" requires all six criteria. The presence of one or more is not enough. Instead all must be present, although this can be done with different degrees of intensity. Without meeting all these criteria, one is probably in the presence of other types of tourism, already widely recognized and codified by institutions, traders, travelers, media and general public (see Figure 9.3).

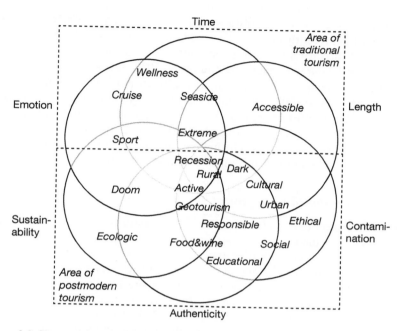

Figure 9.3 Slow tourism dimensions and types of traditional and post-modern tourism.

Project outcomes

With a budget of approximately €4 million, the *Slowtourism* project put together 23 pilot projects between 2010 and 2013 in the fields of cycling, river tourism, bird-watching and environmental tourism, and sport tourism and identified 32 separate itineraries. More than 600 stakeholders and tourist operators attended 24 organized workshops for the dissemination of the guidelines. The project also organized two educational tours for travel agencies and disseminated and promoted the project and slow routes through slow moments/events. In addition, it carried out 30 meetings of training activities for tour operators (over 1,000 participants) and four meetings for school managers (about 60 participants), aimed at spreading the concepts of slow tourism at professional and education level. For schools, the project produced two manuals for elementary school pupils and for middle and high school students.

The *Slowtourism* project has also participated in several international travel and tourism fairs in China, Japan and Italy, where it utilized brochures, apps and multivisual materials in order to promote the project and the larger philosophy. In Beijing, at the COTTM (China Outbound Travel and Tourism Market) fair held in 2012, considered as a leading outbound tourism fair in China, the Slow Tourism project received first prize in the category "Product innovation" of the CTW Chinese Tourists Welcoming Award as a recognition for successful collaboration between the two countries and for the interest for the Asian market. This recognition took place in a particularly important venue, as China recently became the world's top tourism sending country and the World Tourism Organization estimates the total number of outbound tourists from China will reach 100 million by 2020 (Delta 2000, 2014).

In the end, the project created a new slow tourism network in order to not just publicize slow travel in the region but also to guarantee quality and consistency of the services offered, to allow accessing the regional and national funds for quality projects, and to guarantee the continuation of the project activities by private operators. The network has been joined by 133 operators (hotels, bed-and-breakfasts, restaurants, tour guides, etc.).

Assessing the *Slowtourism* project

As the EU project closed at the end of 2015, questions were submitted to the operators who joined the *Slowtourism* network. The goal was to understand how enhancing the cross-border area according to the feelings, the interests and the specificities of the activities and territories and to gather all opinions and ideas about further encouraging cooperation and partnerships. In all, 75 interviews have been completed: 36 operators in services (guided tours, learning activities, boat and bike rental, etc.), 22 in accommodation and food services, 13 in accommodation services only and four in food services.

For the most part, operators agree that there is not enough coordination at cross-border level, which is ironic, given that cross-border cooperation was *the* primary motivation behind the project. Interviewees responded that operators would be instantly recognizable if they could present themselves under the same umbrella, with a single slow brand. They would be recognizable to the tourists looking for a slow holiday, those who take their first steps in this kind of experience and those who intend to mix the traditional holiday with naturalistic, cultural, sport activities, enogastronomic aspects. In fact, the cross-border area allows them to diversify offerings because it contains the characteristics of a singular natural environment, the variety of food and wine that combines the flavors of the sea and the mountain with the Austro-Hungarian, Istro-Venetian and Slavic traditions, elements of the long and troubled borderland history, crossroads of people and cultures. Operators also require a promotional network that publicizes the various initiatives highlighting the relevance for the tourist to find in each structure a specific space devoted to information and distribution of materials on initiatives that can be taken by the tourist independently or with the help of specialized guides.

On the other hand, many operators report having developed synergies with other institutions in the area not only linked to tourism, but also to parks, marine reserve, botanical gardens, natural history museums, and so on. Many initiatives have found fertile ground and initial cooperation has continued. For others cooperation between operators is not always successful. Coordination and management of activities proves to be difficult in both promotional and organizational terms. It may be that this kind of experience requires some time to show concrete results. Finally, most attraction operators require the intervention of travel agencies that deal with incoming tourists, and many contend the agents present the area insufficiently given the nature of the project. Many incoming agencies often do not have anything structured to offer to the tourist who is looking for things to do, see and experience from a slow perspective.

Operators insist on using different tools to promote the area and especially to facilitate structured tour packages utilizing the language of slow. They have also pushed public institutions responsible for promoting tourism to erect billboards even outside the program area – at railway stations, airports, national and international fairs – dedicated to tourism. They consider of primary importance the creation of a website that can act as a clearinghouse for slow tourism attractions in the area. Some operators also insist on promotion through the media: press, press conferences, promotional videos to be run on local television networks and on Internet sites in other regions. A small group of operators talk about Consumer-to-Consumer (C2C) e-commerce promotional tools that, they argue, are the best way to meet the needs of tourist today – well-informed, innovative, faithless and impatient - by the interaction through online auctions. In general the operators know the potential of the Internet, but lack the skills and training to handle this form of promotion with certainty and autonomy. For this reason, operators feel a need for entrusted promotion management with competent people who can support the launch of this innovative new experience offered by the *Slowtourism* project.

As a result of the *Slowtourism* cross-border initiative and the subsequent transformation of the marketing strategy of Friuli Venetia Giulia 2014–18 from "live" to "slow" (Four Tourism, 2014), operators now aim to a formalize the network, registering a *Slowtourism* trademark in order to distinguish specific slow tourism offerings and identify the participants who joined the *Slowtourism* program. Further, operators have worked to create structured tour packages to be included in the cross-border tourist offers using the regional and national Tourism Agency's web portal as a promotional channel, very attentive to the slow proposals and convinced to focus on this kind of tourism.

At present, it is not possible to quantify results of the initiative in terms of slow tourists to the area. In part this is due to classificatory challenges. The spatial proximity makes the area attractive for tourists who, for different reasons, spend a few days and come from nearby places: Croatia, Austria, Germany and which seem to reveal more interest in local events and naturalistic activities. Tourists from Poland, Hungary and Czech Republic have long been a presence in the area and now they seem involved in the slow tourism; many Russian vacationers, staying in seaside destinations, like to move within a day's time to visit a historic center, a castle, a cave, a winery or to walk along nature trails. The activities related to the slow tourism – that work on elements of authenticity, original experiences, emotion – can contribute to a real increase in the perceived value of a vacation in the area.

The *Slowtourism* project tried to analyze results by three types of tourists who border on slow tourism:

1 Slow tourism as the main reason for their visit: this segment is made of people who visit the destination in order to do activities which are naturally slow (trekking, cycling, nature tourism, river tourism, outdoors sports, etc.) as the main reason of their stay (11 percent of current flows).
2 Slow activities in traditional tourism products: this segment is made of those who, even though they do not state a slow motivation as the main reason for their travel, still engage in activities related to slow tourism (17 percent).
3 Slow trekkers who live in the nearby areas: they are people who live in the area and in the nearby areas, inclined to do activities close to the slow tourism (7.5 percent of the resident population for the in or up to 1-hour travel range and of 3.7 percent for the between 1- and 2-hour travel range).

The analysis highlighted that the slow tourism product can move almost 3.7 million people each year in the project area (Dall'Aglio & Zago, 2011, pp. 55–57).

Conclusion

In the future, if the Upper Adriatic area wants to capitalize on slow tourism, there are some strategies that should be supported or implemented at the level of central and peripheral administrations. Slow tourism cannot be separated from well-informed local organizations and operators and a shared social responsibility in a territory which is an *affair of all* (Citterio & Lenzi, 2007). The uniqueness of a place depends on "the innovative strategies implemented simultaneously by residents, local and external operators and consumers developed on the basis of an efficient and open system (not exclusive) of information and communication among different types of subjects" (Savelli, 2003, p. 145).

The following guidelines highlight the issues needed to be addressed in the process of the creating offerings, managing them in an effective and cohesive manner, and promoting them systematically:

1 *Territory and environment*: support the recovery and the conservation of the natural and cultural heritage, especially of the rural areas in order to avoid their deterioration, compromise the offer of slow products and the economic development on local population's behalf; support the use of transport alternative to automobiles, stimulating the use of public transportation, in order to reduce environmental and crowding impacts on the area.
2 *Economy and society*: develop the local competences and skills in order to fight against the creative and intellectual impoverishment of the area, which ultimately leads to depopulation; support the local entrepreneurship in non-tourist fields in order to strengthen the identity of places in terms of traditions, skills, lifestyles.

3 *Accessibility*: use the central position of the cross-border area in Europe and the several road and infrastructural connections in order to increase the number of tourists in emerging countries; supplement the local road network in order to develop short-break tourism and the connections between coasts or mountains and hinterland; support the transformation of information centers into service centers in order to offer tourist the opportunity to stop and prolong his stay; support the image of slow tourism product on the web, outside, in order to communicate with potential tourists, and inside, to exchange information between operators.

4 *Institutional support and image*: support the creation of uniform quality standards for services, infrastructure and resources in order to meet the increasing demand for quality; support the creation of network models between operators, through a centered coordination that performs planning activities, in order to diversify and personalize the offer; support and spread the image of slow tourism product in a coordinated and unitary way, though highlighting the specificities of each area; support and spread the image of an area rich in cultural and natural heritage and where to live unforgettable moments outdoors or practicing sports to intercept the increasing demand for sport, walking, cycling and wine and food; explore marketing plans in order to support traditional tourist fields (development of slow tourism product) in order to fight against the competition of emerging destinations, of new and far attractions but easily reachable; support and spread slow tourism principles through an effective information circulation system in order to develop a common view of operators and local people; support the specialist training of the people in charge in the tourist field in order to offer a service from a slow perspective.

5 *Tourist fruition*: utilize the attractions of sea, mountains and cities in order to develop an additional occasion to visit the area from a slow perspective; develop common strategies aimed at the extension of tourist offerings and at the de-seasonalization of tourist flows; spread slow tourism principles between operators and population in order to improve the welcoming skills (opening times flexibility, willingness to talk with the client, etc.); support the uniqueness of the slow tourism product in order to avoid the fragmentation of supplies at a promotional level; support local wine and food offerings and protect food farming productions in order to safeguard culinary traditions and to intercept the increasing demand from gastronauts.

References

Bauman, Z. (2009). *Vite di corsa. Come salvarsi dalla tirannia dell'effimero*. Bologna: il Mulino.

Bruno, G. (2006). *Atlante delle Emozioni. In Viaggio tra arte, architettura e cinema*. Milan: Bruno Mondadori.

Citterio, A., & Lenzi, I. (2007). Il territorio 'affare di tutti.' Esperimenti di responsabilità sociale condivisa. *Equilibri. Rivista per lo sviluppo sostenibile, 2*, 261–270.

144   *Moreno Zago*

Costa, N. (2005). *I Professionisti dello Sviluppo Locale*. Milan: Hoepli.
Crespi, F. (Ed.). (2005). *Tempo vola. L'Esperienza del Tempo nella Società Contemporanea*. Bologna: il Mulino.
Dall'Aglio, S., & Zago, M. (Eds.). (2011). *Guidelines for the slow tourism*. Retrieved from www.slow-tourism.net
De Felice, F., Fioretti, C., & Lanzilli, P. (Eds.). (2009). *I fondi strutturali 2007–2013. Il nuovo ciclo di programmazione dell'unione Europea*. Rome: Carocci.
Del Bianco, D. (2010). Prospettive euroregionali per il futuro della governance dei territori transfrontalieri. *Studi di Sociologia, 47*, 445–470.
Delta 2000. (2014). The slowtourism project. Short description and results. *Newsletter*, p. 12. Retrieved from www.slow-tourism.net
European Commission. (2015). Preferences of Europeans towards tourism. *Flash Eurobarometer*, p. 414. Retrieved from http://ec.europa.eu/public_opinion/flash/
European Commission. (n.d.). *Regional policy*. Retrieved from http://ec.europa.eu/regional_policy
Four Tourism. (2014). *Piano del Turismo della regione autonoma friuli venezia giulia per il periodo 2014–2018*. Retrieved from www.regione.fvg.it
Gasparini, A., & Zago, M. (Eds.). (2011). Relazioni transfrontaliere e turismo. Sinergie e strategie di cooperazione e sviluppo turistico nell'Alto Adriatico, Gorizia in *IUIES Journal*. Quadrimestrale di Studi Internationali, 1–2.
Lavarini, R. (Ed.). (2008). *Viaggiar lento. Andare adagio alla scoperta di luoghi e persone*. Milan: Hoepli.
Leed, E. J. (1992). *La mente del viaggiatore. Dall'Odissea al turismo globale*. Bologna: il Mulino.
Lucchesi, F. (Ed.). (1995). *L'esperienza del viaggiare. Geografi e viaggiatori del 19° e 20° secolo*. Torino: Giappichelli.
Nadalutti, E. (2015). *The effects of Europeanization on the integration process in the Upper Adriatic region*. Dordrecht: Springer.
Nocifora, E., de Salvo, P., & Calzati, V. (Eds.). (2011). *Territori lenti e turismo di qualità. Prospettive innovative per lo sviluppo di un turismo sostenibile*. Milan: FrancoAngeli.
Ronchi, E. (2000). *Uno sviluppo capace di futuro. Le nuove politiche ambientali*. Bologna: il Mulino.
Savelli, A. (2003). Mutamenti di significato dei luoghi e degli sguardi turistici. In R. Bonadei & U. Volli (Eds.), *Lo sguardo del turista e il racconto dei luoghi*. Milan: FrancoAngeli.
Sedmak, G., & Mihalic, T. (2008). Authenticity in mature seaside resorts. *Annals of Tourism Research, 4*, 1007–1031.
UNWTO. (1996). *Guide for local authorities on developing sustainable tourism*. Madrid: World Tourism Organization.
Valussi, G. (2000). *Il confine nordorientale d'Italia*. Gorizia: Isig.
VV.AA. (2010). Programma per la cooperazione transfrontaliera Italia-Slovenia 2007–2013. *Programma Operativo*. Retrieved from www.ita-slo.eu
Zago, M. (2012). Definire e operativizzare lo slow tourism: Il Modello Castle. In V. Calzati & P. De Salvo (Eds.), *Le Strategie per una Valorizzazione Sostenibile del Territorio*. Milan: FrancoAngeli.

10 Cittàslow

The Emilia-Romagna case

Gabriele Manella

Introduction

This aim of this chapter is to focus on the Emilia-Romagna towns that are certified Cittàslow members, in order to show the importance of tourism in their choice of joining as well as the eventual impact on this sector after they joined. There are many reasons why localities may choose to join Cittàslow. This research, undertaken in the Emilia-Romagna region of Italy, shows that a primary motivation is that of promoting tourism as an economic development strategy. This Italian region has a strong local production and tourism system, both of which are rooted in a social fabric characterized by cooperation and solidarity networks. These elements have probably provided a strong base for the success of Cittàslow in this region, but it is interesting to see if tourism has been important in this choice and if this membership affected the hospitality policies of the certified cities.

In the first part of the chapter I examine some recent trends of global tourism and their possible effects on local development; I stress that quality of urban life and the promotion of local heritage are important factors for implementing local tourist policies. This is particularly true for the so-called minor territories as well as the Cittàslow certified cities. The second part focuses on the general development of Cittàslow in Italy and a preliminary investigation of the certified towns in Emilia-Romagna; I consider their territorial distribution, the reasons for joining Cittàslow, and the measures they implemented in order to meet the hospitality requirements. The third part examines the case of Santarcangelo di Romagna, in order to highlight the effects of Cittàslow membership on local tourism.

New tourism strategies: the slow dimension in "minor territories"

One of the effects of globalization on tourism is that new destinations are emerging, many of which were totally unknown before (Michaud, 1996, pp. 467–468). Sometimes, their model is very similar to the most well-known destinations; in such cases, their tourism consist in offering the same product at a lower price. Sometimes, however, these newer destinations try to offer an alternative through their own heritage and the unique features of their region. Slow tourism can probably be included in the latter trend; it represents a new opportunity for many areas as well as a new way to enjoy holidays instead of following the so-called 4S model (Sun, Sea, Sand, Sex) of mass tourism.

Calzati (2011) points out that although there are no dominant models in the academic literature on slow tourism, there are three frequent theoretical approaches: "sustainability/new types of tourism/slow tourism," "slowness/experience/transport" and "slow tourism/slow food/Cittàslow." The first approach stresses the rise of new forms of tourism inspired by environmental concerns and the search for sustainability. This approach pays attention to the dramatic impact of tourist activity as well as the importance of respecting the territory and the society we visit. Slow tourism is part of this broader turn toward sustainable tourism (Edgell, 2006; Weaver, 2006). The second approach focuses on slowness as a new kind of experience (Honoré, 2005; also see the slightly different conceptions noted by McGrath and Sharpley in this collection). Travel, according to this view, becomes important as the rest of the holiday. In this sense, engaging in slow tourism is looking for viable transport options to enjoy the places you cross instead of something to do as quickly as possible. The third approach places slow tourism along with the Slow Food and Cittàslow movements along with many other slow alternatives to aspects of modern life. Slow Food is a frame to consider a new way of life and a new territorial strategy; at the same time, this approach stresses the link between Slow Food and Cittàslow as a spin-off for urban government. In this chapter I will rely mainly on the third approach, concentrating on the reference to Slow Food and territories on the one hand but also seeking to put the phenomenon of slow tourism into the context of the recent changes in the tourist sector.

Modern tourism emerged with industrialization and, for 200 years, it has followed a dominant logic based on the clear division between work time and leisure time corresponding to a distinct specialization and spatial distinction of tourist and entertainment areas. The industrial economy was concentrated in industries, downtowns, factories, stations, and harbors; tourism was concentrated in archaeological ruins, monuments, historic buildings, natural and coastal areas. In other words, the areas outside industrial economy frequently became tourist spaces (Savelli, 2008). Over the past several decades, a dramatic change has occurred: the clear distinction between tourist areas and productive areas is gradually fading. At the same time, as we said before, many new destinations emerge every year on the global market. Capturing tourists becomes more and more difficult and there is a strong need for territorial marketing using strategies of communication and information. As a result, many well-established traditional tourist areas are suffering a crisis while new areas with potential tourist resources emerge; tourism is more and more an "experiment" instead of being a "show," because people are increasingly searching for the authentic instead of the sensational (Benini, 2008). Homogenization and standardization were two core elements for mass tourism; now, differentiation seems to be the dominant model. As a result the global tourism market has become highly segmented demographically, spatially and by activity. In turn, tourist destinations are now required to promote originality and authenticity; the quality of local products and the strengthening of local identity are two key factors in this sense (Battaglini, 2012).

While challenging, this change in tourism markets also provides new opportunities for the so-called minor territories (*territori minori*). These territories are located at the edge of sizeable urban and tourist areas; they see themselves as promising for new local development because differences are valued, networks are strong and best practices are easy to disseminate; all these elements contribute to the removal or mitigation of several constraints that previously made these places hostile to innovation (Calzati, 2012).

Tourism and "minor territories": the Cittàslow association

Cittàslow was born in 1999 through an initiative of the mayor of the town of Greve in Chianti (Tuscany). Nearby towns of Orvieto, Bra, and Positano immediately joined. Since 2008, this association became international through the approval of a new statute in Orvieto. By the end of 2014 this Association included 189 certified cities from 29 countries. Not surprisingly, Italy leads the way with most certified cities at 74 (25 in the North, 34 in the Center and 15 in the South). Tuscany is the region with most members (14), followed by Emilia-Romagna (13), Umbria (11) and Campania (8). The Cittàslow network is also strong in Poland (18 cities), Germany (12 cities), and South Korea (11 cities). The total breakdown is summarized in Table 10.1.

Table 10.1 Cittàslow certified cities by country (December 2014)

Country	Cittàslow certified cities
Italy	74
Poland	18
Germany	12
South Korea	11
France	8
Turkey	7
Holland	7
Belgium	6
Portugal	6

(*Continued*)

Table 10.1 Cittàslow certified cities by country (December 2014) (*Continued*)

Country	Cittàslow certified cities
Spain	6
Great Britain	5
Australia	3
Austria	3
Norway	3
USA	3
Canada	2
China	2
Denmark	2
Cyprus	1
Finland	1
Ireland	1
Iceland	1
Japan	1
New Zealand	1
Sweden	1
Switzerland	1
South Africa	1
Taiwan	1
Hungary	1
Total	189

Source: Author elaboration on Cittàslow International data.

It is also interesting to note that, although the maximum population allowed for joining Cittàslow is 50,000 residents, the average of these cities is much lower (Table 10.2). This is especially true in Italy: Cittàslow towns average about 11,300 residents versus 16,400 in the other countries (Roma, 2012, p. 63). At the same time, the Italian-certified cities show a lower growth rate of population (6.6 percent versus 22.9 percent), a relatively higher percentage

Table 10.2 Demographic data on Italian Cittàslow certified cities

Demographic data	Cittàslow Italy	Cittàslow rest of the world	Cittàslow total
Average number of residents	11.302	16.369	13.711
Variation % population over the last 10 years	+6.6	+22.9	+12.2
% over 65 people	23.0	20.1	21.6
% under 14 people	12.9	17.2	14.9
% migrant people	7.8	5.9	7.0

Source: Elaborated from Roma, 2012.

of residents over age 65 and a relatively lower percentage of residents aged under 14. Italian Cittàslow members have also a slightly higher percentage of foreigners as residents than slow cities elsewhere.

We can best understand Cittàslow as a specific practice within a more general trend: the rise of slow territories and their connection with local and tourism development. Calzati (2011, p. 60) defines "slow territories" as those characterized by low population density, a strong agricultural tradition, a relatively unknown but attractive historical and artistic heritage, accommodation facilities which are well integrated with local landscape (bed-and-breakfast, holiday homes) and many cultural activities for the enhancement of local identity and traditions. These territories are very common in Italy, and they provide a good setting for the flourishing of "slow products" as a niche area in the overall tourism market.

Cittàslow is one of the many associations and networks that strongly support this new "way of life" in experiencing holidays. Slow Tourism (website) is another example. The association was founded in 2007 and headquarter is in Acqualagna (Umbria). Slow Tourism aims at promoting travel itineraries able to enhance stronger relations between tourists and places they visit. Most of the proposed routes include lesser-known destinations, with the aim of discovering or rediscovering their natural and cultural attractions. Slow Tourism is not only interested in enhancing territorial resources; the encounter between residents and travellers is another important aspect of its philosophy, together with the idea of respect for natural and cultural diversity. Another best practice I would like to mention is the transnational network SlowTourism.net: this consortium is the most important example in Italy as regards transnational cooperation focused on slow tourism. Originally funded in large part with and EU development and cross-border cooperation grant, today it constitutes a public-private partnership that includes 125 tour operators from Slovenia and Northeastern Italy (Zago, 2011). Both Slow Tourism and SlowTourism.net are examples of supplier-based networks that attempt to coordinate and draw would-be slow tourists into new regions.

The most significant step for Cittàslow, however, is in relation to Carlo Petrini and Slow Food. This movement originated in 1986 and was formalized in Paris (1989) through the signature of an Official Manifesto by delegates from 20 countries. Today, Slow Food involves more than 40,000 people in Italy and more than 60,000 in the rest of the world; its members belong to 130 countries, with about 1500 local offices all over the world and hundreds of events organized each year. Within the larger slow movement Slow Food is by far the most institutionalized segment. Slow Food is not a tourist movement; nevertheless, there is a clear link between tourism and the aims of this association. If we look at some excerpts from the Manifesto, we can see that Slow Food helps the younger generation to establish a proper relation with food, promote a tourism respectful of the environment, and promote initiatives of solidarity (De Salvo, 2011, p. 49). In these aims, we can find many elements that can contribute to the development of slow tourism: the focus on sustainability, the promotion of local heritage, the stress on host-guest solidarity and the social and ethical implications of our everyday behavior.

Slow Food has also promoted and supported the creation of Cittàslow as an urban spin-off. This association aims at pursuing actions for environmental and social sustainability. The Cittàslow project proposes a different concept of living, producing and consuming; it is an alternative model, more inclusive and less corporate (Mayer & Knox, 2006). Slowness becomes a credible metaphor for rejecting the dominant logic of speed, an antidote to the fast imperatives of global capitalism (Honoré, 2005; Humphrey, 2010).

Cittàslow strategy considers "slowness" as attention to urban quality of life, as well as the effort to preserve some elements of local traditions. It becomes the base of territorial planning, a metaphor of development against the fast imperatives of global capitalism (Honoré, 2005; Humphrey, 2010). Economic growth, environmental protection and social equity are all taken in high regard in the agenda of certified cities (Mayer & Knox, 2006). Cittàslow is a combination of local and global. On one side, several international issues are part of its mission, like environmental crisis or the negative impacts of globalization; on the other side, the implementation of strategies is local and there is not just an emphasis on slow spaces and slow living, but also local economic development (Pink, 2008, p. 97).

Cittàslow is based on three main principles (Roma, 2012, pp. 32–33): first is the size of member cities. There is a maximum of 50,000 inhabitants in order to apply for membership.[1] At the same time, the certified cities cannot be capitals of regions or provinces. Both these elements clearly stress the "minor nature" of the territories that are part of Cittàslow, as well as the intention of favoring the development of small cities. Areas with a population of over 50,000 inhabitants, however, can be eligible to become Cittàslow supporters.

Second is promoting local traditions and identity: both are important in Cittàslow philosophy and potentially strategic in the ever more globalized world. The third principle is the encouragement of hospitality. Cittàslow-certified cities must promote the encounter of local community with visitors, removing obstacles that affect access to physical and cultural resources; there is also the requirement to promote a model that avoids any practice associated with standardized mass tourism and instead encourage a slow, deliberate enjoyment of the physical territory and community.

Cittàslow has become institutionalized over the years, with headquarters in Orvieto and a formal process for joining the network. In order to achieve Cittàslow certification, applicant cities must meet at least 50 percent of all the specific association requirements. These requirements cover specific benchmarks within six areas: environmental policy, infrastructural policy, technology and design for urban quality, promotion of local production, support for Slow Food activities, hospitality and commitment. Meeting these requirements implies a process where not only the administrators but also the entire local community participate (Heitmann, Robinson, & Povey, 2011).

Cittàslow-certified cities must meet at least one parameter in each area. The evaluation process is different whether cities are in a state where a Cittàslow network is already present or not. There are several common steps, however. Applicant cities must submit a request with their history, the reason of submission, a list of the accomplished requirements, and a plan to meet the not accomplished ones. After the submission, the Cittàslow coordinating committee (*Comitato di Coordinamento*) manages the whole process, in collaboration with Slow Food and a local delegate. As a next step, a national or international staff delegation visits the applicant city to further check their accomplishment (evaluators give a rating from 1 to 3 to every requirement). The international coordinating committee has also the task to review the final report of applicants. Every five years there is a check to see if certified cities are still meeting the requirements (further checks can be done without notice, however).

These requirements affect tourism in various ways. First, certification requirements themselves reveal consistency with several principles of sustainable tourism (Heitmann et al., 2011). The World Tourism Organization in 1988 considers sustainable tourism those activities implemented with no time limits, without affecting the natural, social and cultural environment and without affecting the rise of other social and economic activities. In other words, the base of sustainable tourism is the respect of local territory and community; both of them are clearly part of Cittàslow requirements. In the Charter of Cittàslow, the desire to make these cities visitor friendly is also evident (Nilsson, Svärd, Widarsson, & Wirell, 2010, p. 4). Tourism is one of the sector characteristics of this new form of city government involving both citizens and guests (De Salvo, 2011). In addition, a slow city can also develop a reputation as a tourist destination specifically because of its relation with Slow Food (Dietz, 2006. See also Corvo and Matacena, this volume).

Cittàslow and tourism in Emilia-Romagna: general trends

Over the last several decades, the economic development literature has paid increasing attention to intangible and relational factors: trust, sense of belonging, creativity and local identity become essential elements for local development (Boschma, 2005; Calzati, 2012; Granovetter, 1985; Trigilia, 1999; Tura & Harmaakorpi, 2005). In many Italian regions, these factors have contributed to the growth of industrial clusters in which tacit knowledge is a competitive resource, encouraging the circulation of information and entrepreneurial trust relationships (Becattini, 2000). Emilia-Romagna is one of the most striking examples of this phenomenon: numerous small enterprises, often artisan, are located side by side with a high number of medium-sized enterprises, in many cases leaders in niche markets, and with about 300 large-sized companies with over 250 employees. Together they constitute a productive system in which the larger companies can rely on a network of subcontractors and dedicated services which, in turn, provide an enrichment of know-how and innovation (Regione Emilia-Romagna, 2013, pp. 32–33).

Emilia-Romagna is located between northern and central Italy; with almost 22,500 sq/kms and 4.45 million inhabitants, it ranks sixth out of 20 Italian regions with on regards to size and population. With a very strong industrial, agricultural and commercial system, Emilia-Romagna is one of the richest regions of the country and, until a few years ago, some provinces within the region had full employment. With respect to tourism, the eastern part of the region has traditionally been the most important one, with a prominent presence of mass coastal tourism on the Adriatic Sea (Rimini, Cervia, Cesenatico, and Riccione are the most famous sites). After the opening of the first bathhouse in Rimini (1843), mass characteristics emerged in the early twentieth century and strengthened during the "Glorious Thirty" (1950s–1970s), a boom time in Italy's economy as well as within the mass coastal tourism market. The sea is not the only attraction, however; there are several cities known for art and culture (Ravenna and Ferrara, but also Bologna, Parma and Modena), spa destinations (Salsomaggiore, Castrocaro, Riolo) and some winter destinations on the Apennines. These alternatives have contributed to diversify the tourist supply of Emilia-Romagna, and mitigate the decrease of tourist flows in more recent years.

Such a decrease has taken place, however. The region is suffering competition from cheaper locations throughout the world. The globalization of mass coastal tourism has affected Emilia-Romagna in two different ways. First is growing competition with places that are able to offer a similar product at a lower price. This threatens the traditional tourist model of the region. Second, however, is the growing segmentation and specialization of tourism markets and products mentioned above, which provide and opportunity to launch new proposals through the recovery of local heritage and identity. Both these factors are something that "others cannot copy," a possible way through which developing innovative tourist products. They could be a resource for well-established tourist destinations as well as the ones that are still not part of this market. Even in a prominent tourist region like Emilia-Romagna, the locations excluded from the tourist market were considerable until a few years ago: many areas of the hinterland of Ferrara, for example, but also many Romagna villages and even some coastal towns (Fiorucci, 2004, p. 187). In the new global context, these places can find the opportunity for development; the globalized mass tourism model passed them by but they are now taking advantage of new developing forms of tourism such as slow tourism. Such places, indeed, may provide something that is difficult to find in well-established areas already too crowded for allowing for authentic relationships.

These trends contribute towards providing a suitable context for understanding the growth of Cittàslow in Emilia-Romagna. As regards this region, one of the peculiarities is the signature of a Regional Protocol of Agreement in 2011. This document was the result of a shared need: all the Cittàslow-certified cities encouraged an integrated and more effective strategy of local development. Three key elements of this document are local identity, defense of natural and social environment, sustainability, civic sense, and the attention to good living. This document also includes a number of issues that members intend to pursue together. Some of them affect tourism, and they must be accomplished within three years:

- organize at least two events per year related to the promotion of local production, preferably in collaboration with Slow Food;
- lay out a common plan of paths and a map connecting all the Cittàslow members in Emilia-Romagna and their trails (hiking, biking, horse riding);
- identify tourist and recreation trails for slow motorcycling;
- create a tourist guide unique to Emilia-Romagna Cittàslow cities.

These issues are a first indicator of the cohesion among the Cittàslow towns in this region, as well as a demonstration of the intention to share tourism development strategies. To further investigate these points, however, local governments of these towns have been contacted regarding their relationship with the Cittàslow Association and the measures they have implemented.[2]

While Table 10.3 presents a general profile of the certified Cittàslow cities in Emilia-Romagna, which indicates a wide variability of surface, population and density with no particular territorial concentrations, Table 10.4 particularly focuses on the reasons behind the decisions of the various local administrations to join Cittàslow.

Regarding the year of membership, we can see that the first certified cities are located in the western provinces of the region: Parma (Zibello and Pellegrino Parmense) and Reggio Emilia (Castelnovo ne' Monti). The first

Table 10.3 Cittàslow members in Emilia-Romagna

Province	City	Residents at 01/01/2014	Surface in sq kms	Density people/sq kms
Bologna	Castel San Pietro Terme	20,634	148,42	139.97
Forlì-Cesena	Galeata	2,527	63,13	40.11
Forlì-Cesena	Santa Sofia	4,198	148,87	28.26
Parma	Borgo Val di Taro	7,218	151,49	47.18
Parma	Fontanellato	7,038	53,98	133.58
Parma	Pellegrino Parmense	1,081	82,08	13.38
Parma	Zibello	1,820	23,62	81
Ravenna	Brisighella	7,688	194,33	39.61
Reggio Emilia	Castelnovo ne' Monti	10,496	96,68	111.51
Reggio Emilia	Novellara	13,541	58,11	240.6
Reggio Emilia	Scandiano	25,071	50,05	507.71
Rimini	Santarcangelo di Romagna	21,101	45,01	473.76

Source: Author elaboration on Istat data.

Table 10.4 Reported motivations to join Cittàslow in Emilia-Romagna towns

Town	Year of membership	Motivations
Borgo Val di Taro	2004	-Starting a local, regional and national collaboration with similar cities. -Implementing policies to promote our territory through the brand Cittàslow, which identifies many features of our community.
Brisighella	2005	-To pursue a slow philosophy.
Castel San Pietro Terme	2005	-Establishing good practices about sustainability, governance and the defense of local typical products. -Establishing networks as soon as possible.
Castelnovo ne' Monti	2001	-Joining practices and guiding principles of Cittàslow. -Enhancing the Parmigiano-Reggiano district. -Protecting our landscape.

Town	Year of membership	Motivations
Fontanellato	2006	-Being in touch with other towns that promote similar policies. -Identifying good practices. -Enhancing and improving our political and administrative action.
Galeata	2007	-Enhancing our historical/archaeological/artistic heritage. -Promoting our Slow Food districts. -Strong confidence in renewable energy. -Promoting healthy lifestyles that are compatible with our territory.
Novellara	2010	-Collaborating and exchanging proposals and projects about environment, culture and tourism.
Pellegrino Parmense	2001	-Maintaining and developing the local characteristics and our social fabric. -Promoting the quality of hospitality and safeguarding our environment. -Encouraging the use of food produced with eco-friendly techniques. -Preserving local productions that are rooted in our culture and traditions and contributing to our territorial identity.
Santa Sofia	2004	-Enhancing our environmental and natural heritage. -Promoting our Slow Food districts. -Promoting healthier lifestyles compatible with our territory.
Santarcangelo di Romagna	2010	-Joining the basic principles of Cittàslow. -Sharing the reference values of Cittàslow policies. -Increasing our vocation for hospitality and prestige, with positive effects on local tourism.
Scandiano	2007	-Promoting our typical products.
Zibello	2000	-Promoting our prominent food product, the *culatello*.

Source: *Author's elaboration.*

members from the eastern part joined a few years later (Castel San Pietro, Santa Sofia, Brisighella and Galeata). The general impression, however, is that Cittàslow membership is scattered throughout the region. At the same time, this movement seems strong but steady. As we can see from the table, Santarcangelo di Romagna was the last certified town in 2010. Almost five years with no new members suggest that there has not been any "cascade effect" in joining.

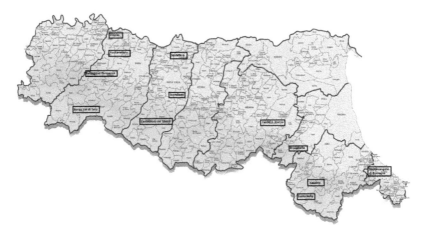

Figure 10.1 Map of Cittàslow certified cities in Emilia-Romagna.

With respect to motivations for joining Cittàslow, many of them reflect an awareness of the need to rethink local development. Such rethinking includes an enhancement and promotion of local features, the attention to good living, and the skill of proposing innovative measures to reach these goals. As we have seen, all these elements are part of Cittàslow and Slow Food, and they are probably a good motivation to join.

Another commonly reported reason for joining Cittàslow is the networking opportunity. New local development takes place not only through independent innovative measures, but also through sharing of knowledge and best practices with the other towns engaged in this project. Cittàslow is a very important movement as it represents growing, learning and reinforcing reciprocally. Looking at the regional Protocol of Agreement I mentioned before, we can clearly see that intention; exchanging practices about promotion of typical products, defense of environment or tourism policies for example. Other motivations include strategies of economic development, namely the opportunity of using Cittàslow as a sort of "slow brand" in order to boost the local economy. This aspect emerges clearly in towns with a strong wine and food heritage and also reflects the standing of the Slow Food organization. In other words, there exists a complementarity between Cittàslow and Slow Food here. For example, the local government of Zibello sees Cittàslow as a promoting agent of their local *culatello* sausage, while Castelnuovo ne' Monti aims at promoting their particular brand of Parmigiano-Reggiano cheese. Other motivations concern the desire for the tourist promotion of environmental and cultural heritage, specifically in the towns of Novellara and Santarcangelo di Romagna.

It is interesting to note that almost all these towns base their economy on typical products and the artistic and environmental heritage. Industry is not important for them (with the partial exceptions of Novellara, Castel San Pietro, and Santarcangelo). This trend reinforces the impression that certified cities are not trying to "use" Cittàslow to reorient their economy, but to stress further some typical aspects of their local production system. In other words, within the economic development side of the motivation for Cittàslow status, the marketing aspect is what stands out.

Table 10.5 indicates the measures implemented by Cittàslow towns in Emilia-Romagna. The structure of the survey schedule took into account both the six major categories and the 50 subcategories of the requirements of the Charter of the Cittàslow Association; for reasons of synthesis, however, I have reported only the six major categories in the table.

Table 10.5 Cittàslow requirements met in the towns of Emilia-Romagna

Areas	CSP	N	SDR	B	SS	G	CNM	Z	F	S	PP	BVT
Environmental policies (11 requirements in the Cittàslow statute)	7	11	11	8	10	7	9	9	6	9	9	7
Infrastructure policies (13 requirements)	8	11	10	7	7	6	8	9	11	12	8	9
Technology and facilities for urban quality (9 requirements)	5	9	7	4	4	4	6	7	4	6	6	3
Safeguarding autochthonous production (9 requirements)	9	7	7	9	4	3	7	8	7	7	4	8
Hospitality (5 requirements)	5	3	4	4	5	5	4	5	5	3	3	2
Awareness (3 requirements)	1	1	1	2	3	3	3	3	3	1	3	2
Total (50 requirements)	35	42	40	34	33	28	37	40	36	38	33	31

Source: Author's elaboration (CSP: Castel San Pietro; N: Novellara; SDR: Santarcangelo di Romagna; B: Brisighella; SS: Santa Sofia; G: Galeata; CNM: Castelnovo ne' Monti; Z: Zibello; F: Fontanellato; S: Scandiano; PP: Pellegrino Parmense; BVT: Borgo Val di Taro).

A first important observation is that all of these towns have accomplished most of the Cittàslow requirements (even if certified cities have to meet at least 50 percent of total requirements and in addition at least one in each area). We can also see, however, a variation in the accomplishment of these requirements: Zibello, Novellara and Santarcangelo have already fulfilled 80 percent or more, while Santa Sofia, Pellegrino Parmense, Borgo Val di Taro and Galeata have fulfilled 60 percent of or less. As we can see, finding a general trend to explain the variation is very difficult: the most virtuous cities are different in size, geographical location and sectors of excellence, as well as the less virtuous ones.

Table 10.6 illustrates the five requirements related to hospitality, the first two of which are obligatory for becoming certified Cittàslow cities:

Table 10.6 Cittàslow in Emilia-Romagna: hospitality requirements

Hospitality	CSP	N	SDR	B	SS	G	CNM	Z	F	S	PP	BVT
1. Training courses for tourist information and quality of hospitality	Yes	Yes	Yes	Yes	Yes	Yes	Yes	Yes	Yes	Yes	Yes	Yes
2. International signs for tourist in the city centers with guided itineraries	Yes	Yes	Yes	No	Yes	Yes	No	Yes	Yes	Yes	No	No
3. Reception policies to facilitate the approach of visitors to the city	Yes	Yes	Yes	Yes	Yes	Yes	Yes	Yes	Yes	Yes	Yes	Yes
4. "Slow" itineraries	Yes	No	No	Yes	Yes	Yes	Yes	Yes	Yes	Yes	No	No
5. Campaigns for transparency of prices for tourism operators and storekeepers	Yes	No	Yes	Yes	Yes	Yes	Yes	Yes	Yes	Yes	Yes	No
Total	5	3	4	4	5	5	4	5	5	3	3	2

Source: Author's elaboration.

1 Training courses for public and private operators and entrepreneurs as regards tourist information and quality of hospitality.
2 International signs for tourists in the historical city centers with guided itineraries.
3 Reception policies and plans to facilitate the approach of visitors to the city and their access to information and services (parking, extension of opening hours of public offices, etc.), with particular regard to events.
4 "Slow" itineraries of the city (available through brochures, websites, etc.).
5 Awareness campaigns for operators in tourism and storekeepers regarding transparency of prices and their public exhibition outside the premises.

Five towns have fulfilled all the hospitality requirements: Castel San Pietro Terme, Santa Sofia, Galeata, Zibello and Fontanellato. On the other hand, only one town has accomplished the two mandatory requirements and nothing more (Borgo Val di Taro). In more detail, the first and second requirements are obligatory for participating in the Association and all the Cittàslow towns have necessarily accomplished them. However, all these towns also have reception plans and policies (third requirement). As regards the fourth and fifth requirements, eight out of twelve towns have planned a system of international signs for the city centers, eight of them have slow itineraries for their territory and ten of them have implemented awareness campaigns for tourism operators and storekeepers. This accomplishment possibly reflects that many of these towns are particularly interested in the benefits that Cittàslow can have specific to tourism. It seems that rather than simply meeting the minimum requirements the towns are going much further here. The logical conclusion is that the hospitality category is seen as a mean toward economic development.

At this point we must ask whether being part of Cittàslow really helps the development of local tourism. In other words, if tourism grows, is this due to inclusion of the Cittàslow network? Santarcangelo, one of the Cittàslow towns, is a very interesting case with respect to this question.

Tourism in Cittàslow cities: the Santarcangelo case

Santarcangelo is located in the hinterland of the eastern coast of Emilia-Romagna, to the north of Valmarecchia. This town is about 20 kilometers from Rimini, the most important city in the region (and probably in the country) for mass coastal tourism. With a population of about 21,000 residents, Santarcangelo is the second most populated Cittàslow town in Emilia-Romagna. Population has slowly but steadily increased since 1951 (around 1500–2000 residents every 10 years). Such growth is primarily connected to the commercial and industrial expansion during this period. As we will see, however, tourism development also played a role.

Since medieval times, the base of local economy was agricultural and particularly reliant on the production of wine, which was the main trade in local markets and seasonal fairs. Historically, other important contributors to the local economy were small workshops that deal in hemp, ceramics and bricks, as well as silkworm breeding. In the second half of the twentieth century, Santarcangelo also saw a steady expansion in industrial development with the appearance of many small and medium enterprises, which, together with the existing family-run craft ones, contributed to the growth of the city and its population. Investments in tourism have been more recent, but they began before the town joined Cittàslow in 2010. The first significant public and private tourist initiatives were undertaken in the 1970s and increased in the 1990s. We can probably consider these initiatives a consequence of the trends already mentioned about minor territories and new spaces for global tourism. In particular, the recent changes in mass coastal tourism in Rimini has affected many inland areas, including Santarcangelo. After having been a mass seaside tourism destination for almost a century, new products began to emerge in Rimini hinterland. This was an important opportunity for sites like Santarcangelo, a town with a well-preserved heritage.

For example, Santarcangelo preserves its own old fairs of San Martino and San Michele. The latter has also been recently promoted for Cittàslow Sunday (on September 29), a day in which every town of the international Association organizes some events. As regards cultural events, the most important one is probably the international festival of street theatre (*Festival Internazionale del Teatro di Piazza*) which has been celebrated every July in the squares and streets of Santarcangelo center since 1971. Other attractions preserve and promote local heritage: the ethnographic museum, which was opened in 1981 (*Museo Etnografico degli Usi e Costumi della Gente di Romagna*), and the museum of history, which was opened in 2005 (*Museo Storico-Archeologico*). Another tourist resource is the museum dedicated to buttons (*Museo del Bottone*); it was opened in 2008 and it is unique in Italy.

In the area of accommodation in Santarcangelo, the twenty bed and breakfasts, most of which are very small, with 2 to 5 beds on average, and only two relatively larger, with 6 and 11 rooms, and the five small hotels are consistent with the typical accommodation capacity of "minor territories." However, there is no direct relationship between this element and using Cittàslow to promote slow tourism; most of these facilities opened before Santarcangelo joined Cittàslow, and most of the owners do not know anything about the town's membership in Cittàslow.

From our direct observations in the city center, we were able to perceive this tie with the past and a certain "slow attitude": we noted a very well-preserved artistic heritage, as well as a considerable presence of about 120 commercial activities, most of which are typical restaurants and retailers of local products.[3] We often saw groups of old men playing cards outside their homes and shops closing at lunchtime, all of which demonstrate a relaxed attitude to living with no stress and in direct contrast to "shopping mall logic," with its 24hr opening, which is more and more frequent everywhere. Local government has also reinforced this attitude by pedestrianizing the whole city center and introducing other traffic limitations in 2013. The qualities of this town, moreover, had already been documented in a study carried out a few years ago (Mussoni, 2008). Many of the 108 people interviewed in that study[4] stressed the quiet life of Santarcangelo, considered a place of "virtues of the small": a small town with little traffic, almost no crime and hardly any stress. The interviewed particularly appreciated its historical and cultural heritage: the number of attractions and the peculiarity of some of them, with particular reference to the tufa caves. They also mentioned the strategic location of Santarcangelo, which is very close to Rimini and the Adriatic Sea. It is the ideal destination for a 1-day visit before going back to the coast.

In many respects, therefore, Santarcangelo is the typical slow city and orientations of local government definitely confirm this. An employee of the local tourist office mentioned the decision made 25 years ago to avoid the construction of a shopping mall and to promote instead the development of a "natural mall" composed of the many small shops of the city center. It was a clear choice to preserve the historical, cultural and production heritage of Santarcangelo. Such choice was very different from what was occurring in many other areas of Emilia-Romagna and Italy. The same employee stressed the influence of local intellectuals. The local poet Tonino Guerra, together with other intellectuals and artists, advised against building, in the early 1960s, a sanatorium that the administration was going to approve, because it would have meant the demolition of several small traditional houses. They also suggested closing to traffic the streets of the center and planting a cherry tree and erecting a fountain in Piazza Ganganelli, which was being used as a parking lot. Both tree and fountain are still there. A further accepted proposal was the displacement of the benches in Piazza Scarpellini in order to promote the admiration of landscape. These examples give an idea of how the special atmosphere in this town is the result both of decisions taken in the past and the continuation of these aims in present policy at avoiding the homogenization processes so evident in nearby Rimini.

Given all these factors, the request of the town for admission to Cittàslow is not surprising. The same local tourist office employee reminds us that he was the first to contact the Association in 2009. The decision to join, as evidenced by the municipal act of 2009, was almost unanimous (20 votes for and one vote against); the only concerns that emerged concerned the eventual costs connected to Cittàslow membership or its actual benefits. Santarcangelo fulfilled the requirements of the Association and was granted the "sign of the snail" on November 6, 2010.

How important is tourism for Santarcangelo? How important is Cittàslow membership? Local government officials pointed out that their territory was already a tourist destination that could be enhanced by new ideas and attractions connected to Cittàslow membership. In 2010, when Santarcangelo officially entered the Cittàslow network, the then mayor's comment was enthusiastic:

> We are truly honoured that Santarcangelo has become a member of Cittàslow since it is an acknowledgment of our concern for good life, respect for the environment, wine and food tradition, food production using natural techniques and the attention to visitors of our town.

Despite everything that has been mentioned up until now, about tourism and Cittàslow seems to be extremely positive, some perplexing factors do emerge and results have been mixed. With the broader financial and economic crisis in recent years, attracting tourists is difficult everywhere. Tourism to Santarcangelo grew very quickly shortly after the turn of the century, with overnight stays in the town increasing from about 19,000 annually to almost 42,000 from 2000 to 2004 (Istat data). Since then there has been a slow but steady decline of tourists over the past years; there were just 27,000 overnight stays in 2012, even with a slight increase of arrivals from the year before. In addition, the average stay per visitor has decreased: from 3.9 days in 2004 to 2.1 in 2012. The impression from this data, therefore, is that Santarcangelo remains a one-day tourist destination "in the shadow" of Rimini and the Adriatic coast. As long as this remains the case, the economic benefits from tourism will remain limited.

A further critical issue emerges regarding the awareness of the Cittàslow brand among tourist operators and tourists. As we have seen, the local government strongly supported joining Cittàslow, but none of the bed and breakfast websites in the town refers to it. Our interviews have confirmed that the Association is not so well known. Only two of the six accommodation proprietors, two of the four restaurant owners and four of the six shopkeepers we contacted knew that Santarcangelo was member of Cittàslow. The most striking result, however, emerged in the interviews held with tourists; we contacted 11 tourist groups with a total of 31 people, and only one of them knew about Cittàslow membership. If joining Cittàslow is so important for promoting a town or region, it seems odd that residents and businesses have been left out of the loop!

Conclusion

This study focuses on two tendencies that, in recent decades, have contributed towards the establishment of both slow tourism and the Cittàslow movement. The first concerns the changing attitudes to the relationship between growth and well-being, a cultural and political trend that facilitates local development initiatives in highlighting the particular identity of a territory, its genius loci and its history. The second has to do with global tourism trends which open new opportunities for "minor territories" able to exploit network skills and information strategies. Some local governments have therefore invested on slowness as a factor of tourist competitiveness, as an asset rather than a hindrance. Cittàslow, born in the wake of the Slow Food movement, is one form of this investment and proposes an innovative model of "slow" and sustainable urban governance.

On the base of these considerations, this study presents the case of the certified cities of Cittàslow in Emilia Romagna, a region already characterized by a strong model of local development and a sound tourist tradition. These cities have joined the movement for several reasons. A common attraction to Cittàslow as a brand that can aid in promoting tourism takes first place. Concerning the actions taken by the local governments, they have all proved coherent in their aims to meet almost all the requirements necessary to join the Association, especially in the field of hospitality. This suggests tourism is a primary motivator for joining. Nevertheless, the case of Santarcangelo di Romagna shows that the membership to Cittàslow is not necessarily an add-on or the initiating push for tourism development. We have seen that this town has all the credentials to be part of the Association: an important and well-preserved heritage, many cultural attractions and strong support from the local government in applying for membership. Tourist promotion is also the most important reason for joining Cittàslow. However, examining recent data on tourist movements, the results have been modest and even ambivalent. Moreover, as revealed by our interviews, awareness of being part of Cittàslow is at best partial in the tourism market: neither operators nor tourists realize that they embrace the Cittàslow brand.

Perhaps it is premature to make definitive judgments here; membership of Santarcangelo to Cittàslow is relatively recent and coincided with a larger economic crisis in the country and region. As a result tourism more generally has suffered. Slowness remains a possible development strategy for many cities, and this is particularly true for "minor territories" such as the one where Santarcangelo is located. Nevertheless, there would seem to be considerable gaps between institutional efforts as regards Cittàslow and the awareness of local operators and citizens. Perhaps a stronger collaboration between public and private actors is necessary to fill this gap.

Notes

1 Also see www.Cittàslow.org.uk/supporters/. There are also Italian associations open to larger cities, however. The most important one is ANCI (association of Italian municipalities), with more than 7300 members throughout the country.
2 I carried out this part of my study in collaboration with Viviana Calzati and Paola de Salvo (University of Perugia). We took our contacts with local administrators from October 2013 to February 2014. We contacted 13 towns but one of them, Bazzano, had temporarily suspended the membership as they are merging with other municipalities in a larger union, Valsamoggia. All Cittàslow towns accepted to participate our preliminary survey and sent us back the survey form. In a few cases, a further contact was necessary because some items were missing.

164   *Gabriele Manella*

3 I would like to thank Marco Filanti, M.A. student in Sociology at the University of Bologna, for his help in the field observations (from June to September 2014, 30 observations for a total of 45 hours) and the 28 interviews.
4 The research sample was stratified in 9 groups, with 12 people interviewed for each group (hotel owners, barmen, restaurant owners, shopkeepers, members of associations, citizens, local politicians, excursionists and tourists).

References

Battaglini, E. (2012). Senso, legami, valori dello sviluppo territoriale sostenibile: Una sfida teorica e metodologica. *Economia e società regionale, 114*(3), FrancoAngeli, Milan, 122–131.
Becattini, G. (2000). *Dal distretto industriale allo sviluppo locale.* Turin: Bollati Boringhieri.
Benini, E. (2008). Superare l'evidenza, rompere l'omologazione dello sguardo. In A. Savelli (Eds.), *Spazio turistico e società globale* (pp. 24–32), Milan: FrancoAngeli.
Boschma, R. A. (2005). Proximity and innovation: A critical assessment. *Regional Studies, 39*(1), 61–74.
Calzati, V. (2011). Territori lenti: Nuove traiettorie di sviluppo locale. In E. Nocifora, P. de Salvo, & V. Calzati (Eds.) (2011), *Territori lenti e turismo di qualità. Prospettive innovative per lo sviluppo di un turismo sostenibile* (pp. 62–72). Milan: FrancoAngeli.
Calzati, V. (2012). Il ruolo dell'identità, del capitale sociale e delle certificazioni territoriali nello sviluppo locale dei territori minori: Il caso di Pitigliano nella Regione Toscana. *PASOS. Revista de Turismo y Patrimonio Cultural, 10*(3), 265–279.
De Salvo, P. (2011). Cittàslow: un modello alternativo di sviluppo urbano lento e sostenibile. In E. Nocifora, P. de Salvo, V. Calzati (Eds.), *Territori lenti e turismo di qualità. Prospettive innovative per lo sviluppo di un turismo sostenibile* (pp. 47–58). Milan: FrancoAngeli.
Dietz, A. (2006). *Cittàslow: Das gute Leben. Kulturelles Erbe, Nachhaltigkeit und Lebensqualitatin Kleinstadten.* Magisterarbeit: Universität Tubingen.
Edgell, D. L. (2006). *Managing sustainable tourism: A new legacy for the future.* New York, NY: Haworth Hospitality Press.
Fiorucci, O. N. (2004). Sistemi di offerta e reti distributive. In A. Savelli (Eds.), *Città, turismo e comunicazione globale* (pp. 181–188). Milan: FrancoAngeli.
Granovetter, M. (1985). Economic action and social structure: The problem of embeddedness. *American Journal of Sociology, 91*(3), 481–510.
Heitmann, S., Robinson, P., & Povey, G. (2011). Slow food, slow cities and slow tourism. In P. Robinson, S. Heitmann, & P. Dieke (Eds.), *Research themes for tourism* (pp. 114–127). London: MPG Books Group.
Honoré, C. (2005). *In praise of slow: How a worldwide movement is challenging the cult of speed.* London: Orion.
Humphrey, K. (2010). *Excess: Anti-consumerism in the West.* Cambridge: Polity Press.
Mayer, H., & Knox, P. L. (2006). Slow cities: sustainable places in a fast world. *Journal of Urban Affairs, 28*(4), 321–334.
Michaud, J. L. (1996). Village globale et identités culturelles. In Aiest (ed.), *Globalisation et tourism* (pp. 467–478), St. Gall: Aiest.
Mussoni, A. (2008). Cosa vuol dire turismo a Santarcangelo di Romagna. I risultati di una ricerca sul campo. *I quaderni di Tutto Santarcangelo, 5*, 5–21.
Nilsson, J. H., Svärd, A. C., Widarsson, Å., & Wirell, T. (2010). Cittàslow' ecogastronomic heritage as a tool for destination development. *Current Issues in Tourism, 14*(4), 373–386.
Pink S. (2008). Sensing Cittaslow: Slow living and the constitution of sensory city. *The Senses & Society, 2*(1), 59–77.

Regione Emilia-Romagna. (2013). *Il quadro di contesto della regione Emilia-Romagna. Parte 1: I macrotrend su dinamiche demografiche, economiche e produttive in Emilia-Romagna.* Bologna: Bologna, Regione Emilia-Romagna.

Roma, G. (Ed). (2012). *Cittàslow dall'Italia al mondo: La rete internazionale delle città del buon vivere.* Milan: FrancoAngeli.

Savelli, A. (2008). Alla ricerca di nuovi spazi per il turismo. In A. Savelli, (Ed.), *Spazio turistico e società globale* (pp. 11–32). Milan: FrancoAngeli,.

Trigilia, C. (1999). Capitale sociale e sviluppo locale. *Stato e Mercato, 57*, 419–440.

Tura, T., & Harmaakorpi, V. (2005). Social capital in building regional innovative capability. *Regional Studies, 39*, 1111–1125.

Weaver, D. B. (2006). *Sustainable tourism: Theory and practice.* Amsterdam-Oxford: Elsevier Butterworth Heineman.

Zago, M., (Ed.). (2011). *Le linee guida per lo slow tourism. Rapporto di ricerca del progetto di cooperazione transfrontaliera Italia-Slovenia Slow Tourism, 2017–2013.* Retrieved from www.slow-tourism.net.

Part III

Comparative perspectives

11 Successful integration of slow and sustainable tourism

A case study of food tourism in the alpine region of Algovia, Germany

Katia Laura Sidali and María de Obeso

Introduction

Tourism is an important economic sector that has a complex relationship with the environment, society and culture. Many studies have investigated the relationship between sustainability – divided into the economic, environmental and sociocultural pillars – and tourism. Although challenging (Cooper, 2012a; UNEP, 2014), the recent trend within the tourism industry has been the rise of new, particularly sustainable forms, such as the development of the slow tourism approach (Matos, 2004). This can be considered a reaction to the broader Western way of life, and it takes the form of tourism that operates at a more leisurely pace, respecting nature and human beings. Starting from a brief description of this approach in tourism, we will present a specific case based on food tourism in Germany. Specifically, it deals with Algovian Emmentaler tourism and is based on data derived from 12 in-depth interviews with different participants (producers, policy-makers, etc.) from the Algovian Alps. Results provide evidence on how food tourism can be considered a best practice within slow and sustainable tourism. The remainder of the paper is structured as follows. We first discuss the three pillars of sustainability in tourism. Following that, we offer a brief description of slow and food tourism and we present the results of the qualitative case study on Algovian Emmentaler. Finally, we draw some conclusions.

Sustainability dimensions

Tourism is recognized to be one of the fastest growing economic sectors according to the United Nations World Tourism Organization (UNWTO, 2014). International tourist arrivals grew in 2013 to 1.087 billion, and are projected to grow in 2030 to 1.8 billion. Furthermore, tourism represents 9 percent of the world's GDP, is responsible for 1 of every 11 jobs in the world and represents 6 percent of the world's exports (UNWTO, 2013). However, tourism is also recognized to cause environmental harm (Cooper 2012a; Scarlett 2005; Sinclair & Stabler, 1997; UNEP, 2014) and to have mixed social and cultural consequences in the host communities (Cooper, 2012b). As a result, tourism and sustainable development still appear to be a contradiction in terms.

Over the years the sustainable development term has spread in legislation and research articles, but it has not yet been consensually defined. The term "sustainable development" was popularized after the report "Our Common Future of the World Commission on Environment and Development" (WCED, also known as the Brundtland Report) in 1987. That report argued that sustainable development would be achieved by ensuring that humanity "meets the needs of the present without compromising the ability of future generations to meet their own needs" (WCED, 1987). Clearly, this definition is general. For that reason, given the complex relationships between economic development, environmental quality and society, around 57 definitions have been published (Rogers, Jalal Kazi, & Boyd John, 2006). Lastly, different theories (Munasinghe, 2009; Senge, 2008; Weber & Savitz, 2006) on how a business can achieve sustainable development have emerged.

The implementation of the term "tourism" in combination with "sustainable development" has followed a different path. First, there is no mention of tourism in the two most influential publications in the development of the term "sustainable development" (Rachel Carson's *Silent Spring* of 2002 [1962] and Club of Rome Report Limits to Growth of 1972). Similarly, the 1980 World Conservation Strategy publication by the International Union for Conservation of Nature and Natural Resources (IUCN) mentions a one-way relationship between wildlife and tourism, remarking that tourism needs wildlife, but neglects the impacts of tourism on wildlife. In addition, *Our Common Future* also indicates a one-way relationship between tourism and wildlife, implying that tourism is a beneficial activity that brings earnings of foreign exchange to national parks and that governments need to do "more promotion of wildlife-based tourism" (WCED, 1987). Nevertheless, the concerns about the relationship between tourism and environment quality rose in the 1990s.

The potential for tourism to contribute towards the achievement of sustainable development and its principles has been gaining momentum since the 1990s, but not yet succeeded. On the one hand, international organizations such as the Commission on Sustainable Development (CSD) recognize the importance of potential for tourism to eradicate poverty, which is principle five in the Rio Declaration on Environment and Development (www.un.org/documents/ga/conf151/aconf15126-1annex1.htm). In addition, the World Travel & Tourism Council, the World Tourism Organization and the Earth Council joined to create the Agenda 21 for the Travel & Tourism Industry: Towards Environmentally Sustainable Development in 1996. Furthermore, alternative tourism niche areas have emerged; examples include ecotourism, pro-poor tourism and Slow Tourism. Nevertheless, international organizations (UNEP, 2011; UNWTO, 2000) suggest that there is still a misconception that only ecotourism can be considered sustainable tourism, when in fact all forms of tourism should move towards becoming more sustainable by focusing on the three pillars of sustainability: economic, environmental and sociocultural.

Economic, environmental and sociocultural benefits

Tourism brings a variety of benefits to each of the pillars of sustainability. Considering that tourism is an economic sector, the benefits to the economic pillar of sustainability are easy to identify. Examples of the main benefits are inflow of foreign currency, job generation, infrastructure development and income generation (Cooper, 2012c; Scarlett, 2005; Sinclair & Stabler, 1997; UNWTO, 2013). In addition, tourism is recognized to have the potential to alleviate poverty (Cooper, 2012a; UNEP, 2011; UNCSD, 2011a), which is a principle of sustainable development. Additionally, tourism is recognized as a fundamental sector to make a transition towards a green economy (UNCSD, 2011b; UNCTAD, 2011; UN Division for Sustainable Development, 2012; UNEP, 2011). Therefore, tourism is recognized to create positive benefits.

Contrary to the benefits to the economic pillar, however, tourism benefits to the sociocultural and environmental pillars are more difficult to find. On the one hand, the benefits to the social pillar are directly related to improving the economic component of the community, which might contribute incrementally to the quality of life of the locals. Similarly, tourism has social benefits related to helping to maintain cultural traditions, such as traditional food, festivities, language and practices. Furthermore, some scholars have argued that tourism promotes peace by generating tolerance and understanding of cultural differences between the host community and tourists (Cooper, 2012b). On the other hand, the benefits to the environmental pillar are related to supporting the conservation of natural and heritage areas (Cooper, 2012a; IUCN, 1980; WCED, 1987). In addition, it encourages the preservation of traditional know-hows that are more environmentally friendly. However, the alleged social and environmental contributions are more controversial and uncertain, and considering that the world has limited resources, tourism's benefits to one pillar may lead to a trade-off of another pillar.

Slow and food tourism as a means towards environmental and sociocultural sustainability

In the pursuit to identify forms of tourism that are particularly environment-and-society friendly, two main phenomena have drawn attention within the tourism literature in the past years: slow tourism and food tourism. The former is an underlying principle that includes many forms of tourism to which we postulate that food tourism belongs. Slow tourism has received increasing appreciation because poverty is increasing in Western countries, thereby generating social cost such as a decrease in quality of life and emotional well-being (García Martin, 2014; Spinney & Millward, 2010). As a result, the slow tourism phenomenon has arisen as a reaction to the Western way of life. Basically, the slowness component can affect the distribution channel (such as slow travel tour operators instead of conventional ones), the product (a rural destination instead of city-sightseeing), the service (transport organized by a combination of walking and bicycle tours instead of car), the price (volunteering as a part of the holiday payment) or a combination of these.

On the other hand, food tourism is often referred to as "the development and promotion of prepared food/drink as an attraction for visitors" (Wolf, 2006, p. ix). When set in the frame of slow tourism, the food component is related with products that are often neglected by the ordinary tourist (who belongs generally to individuals that suffer from a lack of free time), such as regional specialties, ingredients derived from rare cattle or plant species, and other types of "slow foods" which are particularly appreciated and searched by slow tourists. In the remainder of this article we will propose food tourism in the alpine mountains as a possible best-practice that synthetizes both slow and sustainable tourism traits.

Case study: PDO Algovian Emmentaler

This study explores whether food tourism could benefit from principles of slow and sustainable tourism. To this end, the focus is the Algovian Emmentaler cheese from the Algovian region. The name "Algovia" does not technically indicate any geographical or political region. It is rather a label that demarcates an administrative alpine region in the Southern part of Germany that is mostly located in the Bavaria state, and, to a smaller extent, in the state of Baden-Wurttemberg.

According to Gschwender (2011), the success of the milk economy and of the tourism sector in Algovia dates back to the second half of the nineteenth century. In the case of the former, immigrants who came in the region began producing cheeses by using the traditional methods of their countries of origin: so, the Swiss cheese-maker Johann Althaus introduced the Algovian cheese by using the Emmentaler method of production, whereas Dutch immigrants started the production of the soft cheeses which are nowadays known as Limburger and Romadur (ibid.). Tourism developed in the region during the 1880s when the railways coverage reached the Algovian territory. In this early stage the main trigger for the tourism growth was alpinism since alpine associations supported the construction of the first tourism infrastructure (Gschwender, 2011, p. 3).

Nowadays, both the dairy and the tourist economies work in synergy to position the region as a hallmark of food tourism. This successful combination is probably due to the special role that local food plays in the territorial identity of Bavaria as well as of Baden-Wurttemberg. In fact, historically both states put lots of effort into supporting their culinary heritage (May, unpublished). Especially the Bavarian state has strongly invested in labeling its regional specialties and supporting its local agriculture (ibid). One of its recent initiatives is named Weltgenusserbe (World Culinary Heritage of Bavaria) and consists of a database for Bavarian specialties and the advertising campaign "World Culinary Heritage of Bavaria" (cf. www.weltgenusserbe.de/) (May, 2013). Furthermore, both Bavaria and Baden-Wurttemberg lead in their number of registered food products in the German ranking of EU-products protected by geographical indications (ibid.), namely Protected Denomination of Origin (PDO) and Protected Geographical Indication (PGI).[1] As May (unpublished) points out, of the altogether 90 products with geographical indications (PDO or PGI), Baden-Wurttemberg holds 18 whilst Bavaria has 30. In the case of the Algovian Emmentaler cheese the PDO label dates back to 1997. It helps small-sized dairies to signal their unique selling proposition consisting in the artisanal method of production (raw milk, prohibition of using silage for feeding cows, etc.) and in this way to differentiate from the large-sized dairies. Nowadays, only the dairies that are settled in the Algovian region and have certified the traditional production method are allowed to name this cheese Allgäuer Emmentaler (Algovian Emmentaler) and to use the PDO label.

Many tourist initiatives have been launched by policy-makers of both Bavaria and Baden-Wurttemberg around local food and specifically around the Allgovian Emmentaler cheese. Among these the Algovian cheese-cup (Allgäuer Käse-Cup) is perhaps the most emblematic. It holds more than 25 cheese operations, which present around 40 different variants of Allgäuer Emmentaler cheese. According to the co-founder of the event and member of the Bavarian Office for Agricultural and Forestry settled in Kempten, the initiative was sponsored by the European Union's program LEADER and it has increased popularity throughout the years. In 2011, for instance, it attracted more than 60,000 visitors in the 3 days of the competition.[2]

Methodology

In order to conduct the study we adopted a qualitative approach based upon open-ended interviews (Mason, 2002). These were conducted by one of the authors together with an anthropologist of the University of Tuebingen as part of a 3-year interdisciplinary project on Cultural Property of the University of Goettingen (http://cultural-property.uni-goettingen.de). The questionnaire consisted of three main sections, namely, "initiation and application processes, the establishment of geographical indications, the interrelations between the geographical indications and tourism as well as structures of government and policy-making" (May, unpublished). The overall goal of the interviews was to analyze how the meta-cultural practices of different actors concur to set up the culinary heritage of a territory characterized by agricultural and food products protected by Denomination of Origin. All the interviews were transcribed in the German language. In total, 12 participants linked to the Algovian cheese with different roles were interviewed. Specifically, seven cheese-makers, two representatives of the consortium of Algovian cheese (one for the Baden-Wurttemberg state and one for the German state of Bavaria), one representative of the Office for Agricultural and Forestry and two Slow Food members who worked on a voluntary basis in Slow Food Convivia were interviewed in Germany between March and October, 2012.

Results

In the following, the results of the data collected through interviews are presented and then systematically sorted according to the three pillars of sustainability: economic, environmental and sociocultural.

Economic sustainability

As already mentioned, Algovian Emmentaler is protected by PDO from the EU. The decision to apply for this European certification scheme was made during the 1990s to protect it from the increasing success of the industrial Emmentaler, which consisted mainly of pasteurized milk (Jeanneaux, Meyer, & Barjolle, 2011). In fact, as described in the Case Study section above, the Algovian Emmentaler cheese is based on a traditional method of production that embraces, among other things, the use of raw milk from cows that have a diet based on grass and hay. As a consequence, the production of Algovian Emmentaler is more expensive, due to the extra costs implicit in the artisanal method of production. The PDO certification scheme helped Algovian Emmentaler producers to set a premium price and, in this way, to keep on producing it. Nowadays, the actual production is organized as it follows: the small dairies sell to local customers and rural tourists while the big-sized dairies devote their production to specialized wholesalers. Therefore, the horizontal competition is rather weak (Jeanneaux et al., 2011).

On this line, the vice-director of the consortium of Algovian Emmentaler Baden-Württemberg declared:

> Here in Baden-Wurttemberg we have the highest merging rate behind us, I forecast it remains stable for the next 10, 20 years. In between, all dairies are so specialized; they have their market segment, (…) their own product niche [so that] they can, if quality does not change, keep staying on the market for a long time. This also in the case of competition against even bigger operations from the Northern of Germany or from abroad.

On the other hand, due to the increasing global market importance of such European schemes as PDO in the food sector, in recent years leading international manufacturers, such as the biggest French dairy Lactalis, Emmi plc or the Swiss sausage company Bell plc, have been trying to build up a portfolio of attractive protected foods through the involvement of food specialists (Bramley & Kirsten, 2007). This trend did not spare the Algovian region. One of the biggest regional dairy, Allgäuland, was bought by the milk manufacture ARLA from Denmark. Although many interviewees, who were producers, considered this dynamic a matter of concern, most dairies-operators did not seem concerned by this situation since, according to the interviewees, "big enterprises cannot fulfil consumers' desires for niche products." Furthermore, big enterprises must also respect the code of practice of the protected product, which in most cases represents a disincentive for them.

Environmental sustainability

The protection of a food product by means of a PDO such as the Algovian Emmentaler is possible only when the production is so deeply rooted in the region that the quality or characteristics of the product are essentially or exclusively due to its particular geographical environment (Reg. 510/2006). In addition, the uniqueness of the products depends not only on the geographical origin – for example, the climate or the soil composition – but also on the human factors, such as the know-how of producers that has passed from one generation to another along time. This combination of geographical and human factors is generally called "terroir." In the interviews, when asked about the relationship between the region, its people and the product, it emerged that it was clear that producers are well aware of the cheese tradition deeply rooted in the region:

> Interviewer: "What do you think: are the associations of people living in this region more likely linked to the Algovian region or to the Algovian Emmentaler?" Participant: "First of all, individuals associate the name "Algovia" with the landscape. Only afterwards they associate it with the Algovian Emmentaler (...); also the regional milk sector contributes to the creation of the landscape's image (...). Personally, I associate the Algovian Emmentaler with the region (...) This is also a piece of my mother country."

Most participants agreed that the PDO scheme has a direct, positive impact on the environment. In fact, in the code of specification of this cheese specialty the use of silage is strictly forbidden. As a consequence, cows graze most part of the year and this process, in turn, help to maintain the biodiversity of regional ecosystem. Most respondents agree that the landscape remaining unspoiled give an aesthetic that attracts rural tourists.

Sociocultural sustainability

As mentioned above, the linkage between the environment and the Algovian Emmentaler is broadly recognized as very closed. When asked whether human factors contribute to forging a sense of uniqueness around this cheese specialty, most interviewees agreed and justified it with the particular character of Algovian people, who are described as "rude but genuine." The representative of the Bavarian association of Algovian Emmentaler synthetized it with a slogan: "If it is not blustered, it is enough praise" (from the German: *Nicht geschimpft ist genug gelobt*, translation of one of the authors). Apparently, tourists recognize such characteristics and, when they visit the Algovian region, they appreciate this sense of harmony among the food product, the landscape and the people.

> Yes, here we have a piece of cultural landscape, something like a pristine landscape. The individuals, who live here and make their existence of this environment – that is, who live from agriculture – formed this landscape. [there is still] the same harmony with nature, environment and people [who] live here happily as it was 100 years ago even if today's agriculture is mechanized. That's why tourists are coming here to relax.

Surely, the tourism sector is well aware of the attractiveness of the linkage between Algovians, their landscape and the Algovian Emmentaler cheese. An example of this is the rising number of food and cheese festivals that take place almost monthly from springtime to autumn in most Algovian cities and even in small villages of the Algovian region. One of the most relevant is the Algovian cheese-cup, organized since 2010 in Algovia, to which around 200 consumers yearly enroll to taste around 40 cheese types. When asked whether this commodification of the Algovian culture could be seen as a menace to the place's identity, the majority of interviewees disagreed. To this respect, one of the two Slow Food members synthetized this concept in a rather picturesque manner:

INTERVIEWER: "Might tourism have a negative influence on the perceived tradition of a place among locals?"
RESPONDENT: "Only because a couple of fat tourists stroll across, this does not change tradition."

On the other hand, many respondents do perceive a steady increase of such events in comparison to the past 10 or even 20 years, what is commonly attributed to the tourist offices of the region.

Integrating sustainability pillars with slow tourism

According to Matos (2004), slow tourism consists of two main characteristics: the deceleration of time and the attachment to a place, which is to be experienced with all human senses. The need to decelerate is a consequence of the fast pace of modern life, which is increasingly perceived as a menace to human well-being. According to several authors, this tendency is related to an increasing dissatisfaction toward current capitalism (Cederholm & Hultman, 2010; Sidali, Kastenholz, & Bianchi, 2015), which pushes tourists to pursue an "interlude of quiet serenity to recollect energies and genuinely enjoy the holiday" (Matos, 2004).

In the interviews, this tendency on the supply side was also detected. For instance, one producer of Algovian Emmentaler cheese introduced himself as a man who is "not made for the big industry." Another declared that many retired people choose this tourism destination to pass the last part of their life. Also when describing Algovian cheese, the interviewees made many references to time. For example, during guided tours in Algovian dairies, cheese-makers continuously reinforce people's awareness of the laborious steps followed in the production of the Algovian Emmentaler cheese, highlighting the amount of time that is necessary to create a good cheese, what, in turn, is manifested in the higher premium price.

On the other side, the transmission of a sense of place and its perception with all human senses is offered to tourists in many different ways. An increasing number of people (especially in the Bavarian Algovia) who used to wear typical regional costumes (Tracht) in the past, have started wearing them again. This phenomenon is gathering momentum not only during the increasing number of food festivals but also in day-to-day life. Many of our interviewees welcomed the authors in their typical "Tracht"; others declared to use it on a broad range of occasions. Also, the mentioned guided tours are an occasion to allow tourists to experience the whole "world around cheese," viewing and smelling the product in its different phases of production and, above all, tasting it at the end of the visit.

All in all, it seems that the combination of sustainability and slow tourism in the case of Algovian Emmentaler provokes in tourists an emotional attachment to the place that results in frantic purchasing behavior that contributes to ensure the existence of small-sized dairies. This was confirmed by a very well-known producer of Algovian Emmentaler:

Definitely tourists buy irrational quantities of cheese, when they come here, what I mean is that they buy [in such] bulks, that they will never ever eat. It is a very strange phenomenon, and this happens above all when it is written "sold directly from the dairy," absolutely irrational.

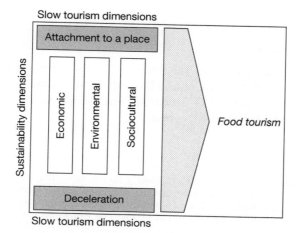

Figure 11.1 Food tourism as the integration of sustainability and slow tourism.

Discussion and conclusions

This paper presents a review on the sustainability issue of tourism. As an economic sector, food tourism in the Algovian mountains brings benefits to the three pillars of sustainability. However, it may also cause negative effects. For example, if the number of food festivals keep increasing, this will lead to congestion of mountain streets, as well as irritate locals' sensitivity. The permeating habit to wear regional costumes could be read as locals' defensive reaction to reaffirm their identity towards an increasing number of tourists coming from outside the Algovian region. All in all, the interviews with different participants involved directly or indirectly in the marketing of Algovian Emmentaler show that the tensions caused by tourism in the small Algovian region are not very high. On the contrary, the incoming trend of tourists from outside the region has been very beneficial in social-economic terms for the small-sized dairies. Furthermore, in our case study we have identified two slow tourism dimensions, namely attachment to the place and deceleration of time, confirming the results of Matos (2004).

Both dimensions are part of the tourism experience in Algovia. For instance, in the case of Algovian Emmentaler cheese, producers present themselves as laborious artisans and offer a detailed explanation of each step of the cheese production, trying to transmit the essence of their work by using techniques of sensory marketing. The case study showed that the combination of both sustainability and slow tourism characteristics can be very beneficial for food tourism operators. In a period characterized by globalization of agrarian market, these characteristics have the potential to contribute to the economic sustainability of artisan dairies, as well as to be a fundamental sector in the transition to a green economy. In conclusion, if successfully implemented, the combination of sustainability and slow tourism characteristics may concretely contribute to balance the interests of the different actors involved in food tourism.

Acknowledgments

The first author acknowledges the financial support from the DFG for the project "The Constitution of Cultural Property: Actors, Discourses, Contexts, Rules" Interdisciplinary DFG Research Unit 772 (http://cultural-property. uni-goettingen.de) for part of this research.

Notes

1   Geographical indications (GIs) are quality labels, since they signal a close link between geographically and traditionally identified origin (*terroir*) and specific product characteristics (quality, production method, reputation, product particularities etc.) of food or agricultural products. The European Union has two main qualified distinctive labels to protect traditional food: Protected Denomination of Origin (PDO) and Protected Geographical Indications (PGI). The main difference

between them relies on the geographical link of the product with the territory of origin: whilst in the case of PDO the entire value-added chain is situated in the region, for a PGI protection only one of the production steps must take place in the region. The European Union has created the DOOR database which is a platform displaying all products registered as PDO or PGI within the EU or awaiting possible registration (http://ec.europa.eu/agriculture/quality/door/list.html).

2   Interview at the Office for Agricultural and Forestry, Kempten, May 9, 2012.

References

Bramley, C., & Kirsten, J. F. (2007). *Exploring the Economic Rationale for Protecting Geographical Indicators in Agriculture*. Retrieved from http://purl.umn.edu/10128

Carson, R. (2002 [1962]). *Silent spring*. Boston, MA: Houghton Mifflin Harcourt.

Cederholm, E. A., & Hultman, J. (2010). The value of intimacy – negotiating commercial relationships in lifestyle entrepreneurship. *Scandinavian Journal of Hospitality and Tourism, 10*(1), 1–17.

Club Of Rome. (1972). *The Limits to Growth: A Report for the Club of Rome's Project on the Predicament of Mankind*. Retrieved from www.clubofrome.org/

Cooper, C. (2012a). The environmental consequences of tourism. In *Essentials of tourism* (chap. 4, pp. 74–94). London: Pearson.

Cooper, C. (2012b). The social and cultural consequences of tourism. In *Essentials of tourism* (chap. 5, pp. 97–117). London: Pearson.

Cooper, C. (2012c). The economic consequences of tourism. In *Essentials of Tourism* (chap. 3, pp. 55–73). London: Pearson.

García Martín, J. A. (2014). *Behaviour and market segmentation. Three contributions from a multidisciplinary perspective*. PhD thesis, University of Castilla-La Mancha.

Gschwender, L. (2011). *Synergien im Lebensmittel und Tourismusmarketing am Beispiel Allgäuer Bergkäse*. Bachelor, Hochschulschriftenserver HAW University of Hamburg.

IUCN. (1980). *World Conservation Strategy, Living Resources Conservation for Sustainable Development. IUCN-UNEP-WWF*. Retrieved from http://cisdl.org/natural-resources/public/docs/wcs.pdf

Jeanneaux, P., Meyer, D., & Barjolle, D. (2011). *Gouvernance des filières fromagères sous AOP et origine des prix de lait: un cadre d'analyse*, 5 Journée de recherches en sciences sociales – AgroSup Dijon, Dec. 2011, pp. 1–19.

Mason, J. (2002). *Qualitative researching*. London: Sage.

Matos, R. (2004). Can slow tourism bring new life to alpine regions. In K. Weiermair & C. Mathies (Eds.), *The tourism and leisure industry* (pp. 93–103). New York, NY: Haworth Press.

May, S. (2013). Cheese, commons, and commerce. On the politics and practices of branding regional food. *Ethnologia Europaea, 43*(2), 62–77.

May, S. (unpublished). Shaping borders in culinary landscapes: European politics and everyday practices in geographical indications (in review).

Munasinghe, M. (2009). *Sustainable development in practice, sustainomics methodology and applications*. London: Cambridge University Press.

Rogers, P. P., Jalal Kazi, F., & Boyd John, A. (2006). *An introduction to sustainable development*. London: Earthscan.

Scarlett, C. (2005). *The global tourism system: Governance, development and lessons from South Africa*. London: Ashgate.

Senge, P. M. (2008). *The necessary revolution: How individuals and organizations are working together to create a sustainable world*. New York, NY: Doubleday.

Sidali, K. L., Kastenholz, E., & Bianchi, R. (2015). Food tourism, niche markets and products in rural tourism: Combining the intimacy model and the experience economy as a rural development strategy. *Journal of Sustainable Tourism, Special Issue: Rural Tourism: New Concepts, New Research, New Practice*, *23*(8–9), 1179–1197.

Sinclair, M. T., & Stabler M. (1997). *The economics of tourism*. London and New York: Routledge.

Spinney, J., & Millward, H. (2010). Time and money: A new look at poverty and the barriers to physical activity in Canada. *Social Indicators Research*, *99*, 341–356. doi:10.1007/s11205-010-9585-8

UN Division For Sustainable Development. (2012). *A guidebook to the Green Economy*. Retrieved from http://sustainabledevelopment.un.org/content/documents/GE%20 Guidebook.pdf

UNCSD. (2011a). *Rio+20 issues briefs finance for the transition to a green economy in the context of sustainable development and poverty eradication*. Retrieved from http://sustainabledevelopment.un.org/sdissuesbriefs.html

UNCSD. (2011b). *Rio+20 issues briefs trade and green economy*. Retrieved from http://sustainabledevelopment.un.org/sdissuesbriefs.html

UNCTAD. (2011). The green economy: Trade and sustainable development implications. Retrieved from http://unctad.org/en/docs/ditcted2011d5_en.pdf

UNEP. (2011). Towards a green economy: Pathways to sustainable development and poverty eradication. Retrieved from www.unep.org/greeneconomy/Portals/88/documents/ger/ger_final_dec_2011/Green%20EconomyReport_Final_Dec2011.pdf

UNEP. (2014). *Environmental impacts of tourism – Global level*. Retrieved from www.unep.org/resourceefficiency/Business/SectoralActivities/Tourism/FactsandFiguresaboutTourism/ImpactsofTourism/EnvironmentalImpacts/tabid/78775/Default.aspx

UNWTO. (2000). *Sustainable development of tourism: a compilation of good practices*. Madrid, Spain.

UNWTO. (2013). *Tourism highlights*. Retrieved from http://dtxtq4w60xqpw.cloudfront.net/sites/all/files/pdf/unwto_highlights13_en_hr.pdf

UNWTO (2014). *Why tourism?* Retrieved from http://www2.unwto.org/content/why-tourism.

WCED. (1987). *Report of the world commission on environment and development: Our common future*. UN documents. Retrieved from http://conspect.nl/pdf/Our_Common_Future-Brundtland_Report_1987.pdf

Weber, K., & Savitz, A. W. (2006). *The triple bottom line: How today's best-run companies are achieving economic, social, and environmental success – and how you can too*. San Francisco, CA: Jossey-Bass.

Wolf, E. (2006). *Culinary tourism: The hidden treat*. Iowa: Kendall/Hunt Publishing Company.

12 The experiential value of slow tourism
A Spanish perspective

*José Manuel Hernández-Mogollón, Elide
Di-Clemente, Ana María Campón-Cerro and
José Antonio Folgado-Fernández*

New trends in tourism: slowness, sustainability, experientiality

Today the slow philosophy is receiving increasing attention from an academic and entrepreneurial perspective. It promises the opportunity to experience quality and return to natural rhythms. In the tourism context, the assumption of a slower pace is defining a new trend expressing a broader sociocultural phenomenon, the slow movement. It favors a change both in daily life and in leisure/holiday time in order to achieve healthier lives and environments. Slow travel and tourism has been mainly defined by the experiential value of travel and the environmental consciousness of tourists who avoid fast means of transport such as aircrafts and cars, motivated by a personal environmental concern (Dickinson & Lumsdon, 2010; Fullagar, Markwell, & Wilson, 2012; Lumsdon & McGrath, 2011).

These dual aspects provide slow tourists with a more satisfactory and enjoyable trip and with a sense of personal fulfillment and well-being (Gardner, 2009). Rediscovering slowness and natural rhythms while on holiday gives travellers the chance to enjoy time, to appreciate the authentic sense of touring, to talk to local people and to experience local lifestyle. In this context, slow mobility is both a "green choice" and a way to enjoy the travel itself as part of the experience (Dickinson, Lumsdon, & Robbins, 2011). Slow tourism proposes a new alternative tourism system, one that focuses on qualitative more than the quantitative aspects of travel. Far beyond the temporal value of time, slow tourism interprets slowness as a rich and suggestive concept which encapsulates the idea of quality, social and environmental responsibility, permeability to other cultures, uniqueness of experiences and self-expression of tourists and guests (Dickinson & Lumsdon, 2010). Therefore, slow tourism amounts to an alternative style of traveling that combines the pleasant experiential component of holidays with responsible and ethical behaviors (Moore, 2013).

This chapter critically analyses slow tourism, focusing on its experiential component. At the same time, the importance of giving slow tourism more attention leads to the need of assessing some important questions: Is there a consistent correspondence between theory and practice? Is practice suggesting a new evolving conceptualization of slow tourism? Do slow-tourism-labeled experiences really encapsulate the value of slowness? How is slow tourism being offered on a practical level? The geographical area chosen for the analysis is Spain for two major reasons: First, according to Euromonitor International (2007, as cited by Dickinson, Lumsdon, & Robbins, 2010, p. 482) "slow travel will be a key growth area in the European Market." Although slow tourism is hardly confined to Europe, the continent appears to constitute the leading edge of the activity. Second, we turn to Spain. Spain is one of the top tourism destinations in Europe and the world. According to the World Tourism Organization (WTO, 2014), in 2013 Spain ranked third after France and the United States, drawing more than 60 million international visitors. Therefore, due to its position in the international tourism ranking, Spain will likely respond to new trends such as slow tourism, putting forward attractive offerings and proposals along these lines.

Although slow tourism is growing both as a phenomenon and subject for academic inquiry, on a practical level it is being interpreted in many different ways and its fundamental precepts sometimes misunderstood by practitioners and tourism operators. Slowness is not easily reconciled with existing tourism services and offerings, so the feasibility of slow tourism is difficult to achieve. Specifically, while the experiential value of travel and tourism can be more or less easily proposed in practice, environmental consciousness and slow mobility are the hardest components of slow tourism to achieve.

Environmental consciousness is a fundamental pillar in the conceptualization of slow tourism (Lumsdon & McGrath, 2011). Slow mobility gives the tourism industry the chance to reduce its huge impact on climate change, for example, through the generation of a lower carbon footprint, and, at the same time, maintains the enjoyable aspects of the tourism and travel experience (Dickinson & Lumsdon, 2010; Dickinson et al., 2010). However, slow tourism represents a major constraint for slow tourists in that it reduces the territorial range of destinations to be visited and activities to be done during a holiday period (Dickinson et al., 2010). This is a "price" that even the most convinced slow tourists are in many cases not willing to pay (Dickinson et al., 2010). Therefore, tourists welcome the sustainable and responsible component of slow tourism as long as it does not represent what is perceived to be excessive impediment to travel (Dickinson et al., 2011). However, it is worth noting that having the chance of assuming environmentally responsible behaviors while on holiday, even if not in the pure form of slow mobility, contributes to providing ethically gratifying experiences and higher satisfaction among modern tourists (Lumsdon & McGrath, 2011). Slow tourism is in this sense closer to other forms of alternative tourism, such as ecotourism, responsible tourism or ethical tourism.

On the other hand, the experiential value of the slow trip is what makes slow tourism an attractive proposal for many modern tourists, as it evokes the chance to create memorable experiences, through a deeper and more involving contact with places and people (Kim, 2010; Lumsdon & McGrath, 2011;

Moore, 2013). Experiential aspects of tourism consumption are so relevant because they create some link between the leisure time and the tourist's quality of life, well-being, happiness and life satisfaction (Bimonte & Faralla, 2012, 2013; Dolnicar, Lazarevski, & Yanamandram, 2013). Slow travel promises the opportunity for greater engagement through slower pace, deeper knowing of place and more significant people-to-people connections. Definitions of slow travel describe it as an enjoyable activity, in part through pace alone, but also through the environmental practice that contributes to "saving the planet." In contrast, fast tourism does not possess these features. Therefore, this environmentally friendly type of tourism can enhance the well-being of travelers (Moore, 2013).

In this way slow tourism represents a new style for travel and holidays that enhances tourists' quality of life, while providing life-changing experiences, and can be therefore conceptualized within the recently growing theoretical stream of tourism and quality of life (Bimonte & Faralla, 2012, 2013; Uysal, Perdue, & Sirgy, 2012; Sirgy, Kruger, Lee, & Yu, 2011). In this context, a remarkable number of studies regarding the contribution of tourism to the quality of life of travelers and local community have appeared. Moreover, issues – such as the effectiveness of tourism in supporting quality of life as related to poverty reduction, the revitalization and preservation of cultural and natural heritage and sustainability – have emerged as topics for an interesting research agenda (Uysal et al., 2012). The studies about tourism experience recognize the pivotal role that meaningful holiday experiences have on life satisfaction and on personal and social growth (McCabe & Stokoe, 2010). At the same time, the sustainability of slow tourism appears to suffer important impediments to being fully achieved on a practical level due to (i) the lack of disposition of the majority of tourists to avoid long-haul flights and car driving; and (ii) the lack of tourism infrastructure, services and institutionalized arrangements in line with slow tourism philosophy (Dickinson et al., 2010).

Based on the preceding discussion, the linkages that relate the research on happiness and quality of life and the experiential content of slow tourism, together with the impediments to the practical fulfillment of its environmental precepts, suggest the need to reconceptualize slow tourism, providing new theoretical sources to the topic. The remainder of the chapter is structured into five sections. After this introduction, the second section focuses on the experiential value of slow tourism/travel and its benefits on tourists' quality of life and happiness. The third and fourth sections are dedicated to the Spanish case, which will be approached from both a scientific and practical perspective. Finally, the last section will present the major conclusions of the study.

Tourism experiences and happiness: time and rhythm

Nowadays the tourism and travel industry is expected to provide much more than rest, relaxation and a superficial knowledge of places and cultures. Holidays have been charged with the more ambitious purpose of being

184 Hernández-Mogollón et al.

meaningful, life-changing experiences (Björk & Kauppinen-Räisänen, 2014; Crouch & Ritchie, 2005; Manthiou, Lee, Tang, & Chiang, 2012; Oh, Fiore, & Jeoung, 2007). In this way, the time spent and the activities undertaken while on holiday are increasingly conceived of as constituting functional elements to achieve and enhance personal well-being and quality of life for both hosts and guests (Uysal et al., 2012). Tourism has started to be considered as a means to achieving happiness and for improving the quality of social relationships, life, personal esteem, and cultural background, rather than simply providing a break from everyday stresses. In this context, the traditional approach to travel experiences through mass tourism is unavoidably insufficient to fulfill the new expectations of tourism activities and to ensure the overall satisfaction of tourists.

While traditional tourism focuses on functional and quantitative aspects of the travel experience, recent trends in tourism stress the actual interest about the qualitative, emotional and moral content of holidays. In this context, Moore (2013) asserts that new forms of tourism have appeared, such as sustainable tourism, responsible tourism, ecotourism and ethical tourism, types of tourism in which tourists have to get involved. Values, beliefs, ethical and moral convictions together with feelings, emotions and moods started to be conceived of as important components of the tourism experience, capable of turning a holiday into a transformative and enriching experience which leads to happiness and an increasing sense of well-being.

Several researchers have addressed the relationship between the tourist experiences and the perception of increasing personal happiness. Bimonte and Faralla (2012, 2013) demonstrate that tourists who practice activities which respect the environment and local communities and register higher level of happiness than highly consumptive tourists. Their results show that tourism has a beneficial effect to well-being in general, but that certain specific activities (appreciative) are more beneficial to local communities, places, environment and visitors themselves than others (consumptive activities). Along the same lines, Letho, Choi, Lin, and MacDermid (2009) found that family travels exert a strong influence on personal well-being as this kind of activity facilitates communication between family members and enhances their cohesion. Neal, Sirgy, and Uysal (1999) measured the effects of tourism on travelers' quality of life, and confirm the positive relationship that exists between a satisfactory travel/tourism experience and satisfaction with life in general. Gilbert and Abdullah (2004), show how leisure travel contributes to the personal life satisfaction of travelers. Similarly, the results of Sirgy et al. (2011) demonstrate that satisfaction with the travel experience may impact not only on satisfaction with the leisure domain of life, but on satisfaction with life in general. More importantly, these authors suggest that tourists who perceive an increase in personal well-being are more likely to assume positive future behaviors such as repeating the experience and recommending it to friends and relatives, which have important managerial implications for tourism enterprises and operators. These studies are just a representative sample of an increasingly important line of research that sheds light on a new interpretation of the holiday and travels as constructive and life-changing experiences.

It is important to point out that not all kinds of travel activities positively impact the affective and subjective sphere of life and well-being (Bimonte & Faralla, 2013). The emotional aspect of travel requires special "ingredients" to be provided on both the supply and demand side. Traditional tourism services and offerings are likely to match the functional requirements of a trip or travel but they are not able to satisfy the actual expectations of the modern tourist, who is increasingly interested in unique, impressive and memorable experiences that enrich not just the journey itself, but also the personality, education and self-esteem of travelers (Chen & Chen, 2010; Kao, Huang, & Wu, 2008). In this context, the affective reactions of tourists to a specific destination or activity become pivotal elements for the modern tourism industry. They satisfy travelers' psychological needs and influence their future purchases and behavior (Lam & So, 2013; Sirgy et al., 2011). Arousal, involvement, attachment, and other emotions trigger the experiential and memorable value of the travel experience, which in turn affect leisure satisfaction (Chen, Li, & Chen, 2013), life satisfaction (Neal et al., 1999), and loyal behaviors (Kao et al., 2008; Lee & Shen, 2013; Manthiou et al., 2012).

Little attention has been assigned to the role of time and rhythms as determining the role holiday factor into increasing happiness and quality of life. The lack of consideration of the time variable is surprising, considering that all the crucial elements necessary to achieve the affective and emotional dimension of the trip are not likely to be experienced in a hurried and superficial context. Gilbert and Abdullah (2004, p. 103) point out that "holidays represent a period when people can have the time of their life." Slowness and the adoption of a slow pace on holidays are propitious elements for stronger emotions and meaningful experiences. One exception is Neal, Sirgy, and Uysal (2004, 2007), who have recently introduced the "length of stay" variable in their predictive model on travel experience and overall life satisfaction. They assume that the "length of stay" is a moderating variable between travel experience and life satisfaction. This is the first attempt to introduce "time" as a determinant variable for leisure and life satisfaction. Results by these authors show that people who stay longer at a destination have higher chances to engage with places, local communities and services and, therefore, to achieve more satisfactory experiences (Neal et al., 1999, 2004, 2007). This new consideration of time is in line with slow tourism and travel assumptions, as standardized touristic packages cannot provide tourists with valuable experiences. Thus, the time and rhythms tourists decide to adopt during holidays are crucial to maximizing the positive impact that tourist experience can have on personal happiness and quality of life.

Dickinson et al. (2010, 2011) state that slowing down on holiday and adopting a new pace encourage people to have deeper contact with places, cultures and local communities. This, they argue, provides benefits for hosts, guests and the environment. For tourists themselves, this new focus on pace provide emotional and memorable experiences, which are arguably those having a stronger impact on quality of life and happiness. Therefore, the search for happiness and an increased quality of life through holiday experiences need to be considered fundamental elements of slow tourism, which is probably more incisive in its conceptual definition and practical expressions than in its environmental assumptions. The latter are relevant and consistent on a theoretical level, but they are weak in practice. This raises the question of reconceptualizing slow tourism. With slowness as a determinant element in achieving increased happiness and quality of life through tourism (Neal et al., 2007), these aspects have to be introduced explicitly in both the *conceptualization* and *practice* of slow tourism. This rethinking places a less prominent role on the environmental component, which, nonetheless, has to be figured in as a functional element in order to achieve the experiential value of slow tourism, in turn, itself a determinant for increased happiness and well-being. Figure 12.1 explains the conceptualization proposed.

Much of the early focus on slow tourism has generally supported the concept with strong environmental arguments, defending slowness as a valuable opportunity to reduce tourism's high pollution and carbon footprint. Instead, the tourist industry has mainly focused on the experiential and regenerative power of the slow tourism experience. However, it is possible to identify a continuum of slow travellers that goes from the "hard slow traveler," who has strong environmental motivations, to the "soft slow traveler," who also cares about the environment but is more motivated by experiential goals

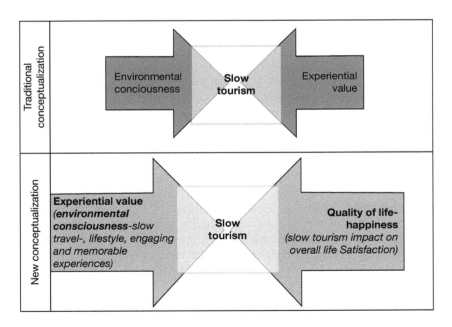

Figure 12.1 Reconceptualizing slow tourism.
Source: Authors.

(Dickinson et al., 2011). In the next section we demonstrate how slow tourism and travel has been interpreted by one of the major international tourism destinations, Spain, assessing both the scientific and practical perspective. We believe that results arising from the Spanish context provide an initial confirmation of the new conceptual framework proposed for slow tourism.

Slow tourism: the Spanish perspective

According to the WTO (2014), in 2013, Spain was the third largest tourism destination, after France and the United States and followed by China and Italy. Based on the Hotel Occupancy Survey carried out by the National Institute of Statistics of Spain in 2013, Spain received 83,820,919 tourists. Some 50.8 percent of them were Spaniards, and the remainder were foreigners. Spain's major outbound markets in the same year were the United Kingdom (19.6 percent), Germany (17.1 percent), France (11.0 percent), followed, at a distant fourth and fifth, by Italy (5.3 percent) and the United States (4.7 percent). Concerning its contribution to the Spanish GDP, tourism represents one of the main industries, contributing about 11 percent of the national economy in recent years, according to the Tourism Satellite Account of Spain.

For several decades, Spain has focused its attention on sun and beach tourism, centered on a strong standardization of this product in response to a generalized tourist profile. Spain has become a primary beach destination for northern Europe during this time. This traditional model has not been adequately adapted to meet new tourism demands. However, other types of tourism have been recognized as excellent ways to balance the potential of inland tourism versus coastal tourism. Hence, cultural, urban, natural or rural tourism have experienced greater development in more recent years (General Secretariat of Tourism, 2007). According to the major current tourism planning policy document, Spanish Tourism Plan Horizon 2020, the emphasis is "to develop successfully a new tourism positioning – the 'experiential Spain' – based on high quality tourism products made available to customers based on the identity and singularity of destinations" (General Secretariat of Tourism, 2007, p. 42). Considering the important role that the tourism industry has in the Spanish economy, it is particularly interesting to investigate slow tourism/ travel and its place within this vibrant tourism market. Specifically, it is useful to ask whether conceptual contributions on slow tourism are giving birth to innovative touristic proposals which, in line with the slow tourism principles, will lead to higher levels of sustainability, attractiveness of destinations, satisfaction and guests' and hosts' well-being.

First, we will focus on the Spanish literature about slow tourism, devoting special attention to scientific publications. This section will include those contributions edited by Spanish journals or, alternatively, written by Spanish authors or authors belonging to Spanish institutions. Secondly, a webpage analysis of content will be conducted in order to check the importance slow tourism acquired in practice and which kind of proposals are being marketed at the present time.

Slow tourism in the Spanish academic literature

Although the main contributions to slow tourism have originated in Italy (Calzati & De Salvo, 2012), the United Kingdom (Dickinson & Lumsdon, 2010) and Australia (Fullagar et al., 2012), there is increasing interest in the subject in Spain. Table 12.1 below provides a short list of literature pertaining to slow tourism developed by Spanish authors, in some cases in collaboration with Italian researchers. Although the slow philosophy dates back to the 1980s (Slow Food originated in 1986), specific literature on slow tourism/travel is quite recent. The majority of publications can be found within the last five years. The Spanish literature follows this trend. The first Spanish publication specifically focused on slow tourism is by De Luis Blanco (2011) who analyzed slow tourism in the Spanish cities that are part of the Cittáslow Network. Results showed that Spanish Cittáslow centers do not yet provide a slow-oriented touristic system, mainly due to their recent membership of the Cittáslow network.

In general, the Spanish academic approach to slow tourism is in line with international conceptualizations of slow tourism, even if each author or work emphasizes one particular aspect over others. De Salvo et al. (2013) focus on the slow tourist's profile and his/her permeable attitude versus the "impermeable" attitude of the non-slow tourist. Hernández-Mogollón et al. (2012b, c) and Di-Clemente et al. (2012) empirically tested the perception of slowness and responsible behaviors of tourists visiting Spanish rural areas that can potentially be considered "slow tourism destinations" due to their characteristics. Their results show that tourists do consider that relaxed rhythms of rural lifestyles, together with quality of natural heritage, are main motivators for visiting certain destinations. Spanish destination infrastructure is not ready to satisfy the slow tourism requirements, as those that Dickinson et al. (2010) point out as essential and identify as potential barriers to the development of slow tourism. The tourism infrastructure needs to take into account the type of activity, equipment carried, time frame, tour group characteristics and tour operator options, among others. Similarly, tourists who do appreciate slower rhythms on holiday often behave inconsistently with slow tourism and travel assumptions (for example, they often stay few hours at a destination, use car for daily trips, etc.).

Spanish literature proposes a conceptual framework for slow tourism that, apart from sustainability and experience, explicitly includes quality and degrowth as main characteristics of slowness in tourism (Di-Clemente et al., 2012; Hernández-Mogollón et al., 2012c). This puts Spanish contributions in line with Italian (Calzati & De Salvo, 2012), English (Dickinson & Lumsdon, 2010; Dickinson et al., 2010, 2011; Lumsdon & McGrath, 2011) and French (Babou & Callot, 2009) contributions to the topic. In summary, Spanish literature, rather than providing an innovative perspective on slow tourism, proposes a general conceptual arrangement of the issue and opens up critical discourses around the need of measuring slowness and testing its practical feasibility (Hernández-Mogollón et al., 2012c).

Table 12.1 Spanish literature on slow tourism

Authors	Title	Year	Journal/editorial
Di-Clemente, Hernández-Mogollón, De Salvo, & Campón-Cerro	Slow tourism: an alternative model for local and tourist development. In J. Mondéjar-Jiménez, G. Ferrari, M.D.V. Segarra-Oña and A. Peiró-Signes (Eds.), *Sustainable Tourism: A Collection of Tools and Best Practices.*	2014	Chartridge Books Oxford
De Salvo, Hernández-Mogollón, & Di-Clemente	"Repellent" tourists vs. "Slow" tourists	2013	European Journal of Tourism, Hospitality and Recreation
Hernández-Mogollón, De-Salvo, & Di-Clemente	Verso il turismo slow: il caso della Sierra de Gata, Spagna[1]	2012c	Sinergie Rivista di studi e Ricerche
Hernández-Mogollón, Campón-Cerro, Folgado-Fernández, & Di-Clemente	Turismo rural: concepto, evolución y nuevas tendencias. In J. Ortega, E. Pérez and P. Milanés (Eds.), Estudios de Investigación sobre turismo y medioambiente.	2012a	Editorial Académica Española
Hernández-Mogollón, De-Salvo, & Di-Clemente	Una aproximación al concepto de slow tourism: el caso del territorio del Valle del Jerte	2012b	Turismo & Desenvolvimento
Di-Clemente, De-Salvo, & Hernández-Mogollón	Slow Tourism o Turismo de la Lentitud: Un nuevo enfoque al desarrollo de territorios lentos	2011	Encontros Científicos – Tourism & Management Studies
Di-Clemente, Hernández-Mogollón, Folgado-Fernández, & Campón-Cerro	La Experiencia de la lentitud: Un estudio comparativo entre el viajero slow y el turista rural de Extremadura	2012	Proceedings of the AECIT conference: Creación y desarrollo de productos turísticos: innovación y enfoque experiencial
De Luis Blanco	Una aproximación al turismo slow. El turismo slow en las Cittáslow de España	2011	Investigaciones Turísticas

Source: authors.

Apart from academic studies, the specialized tourism press in Spain has recognized the interest of slow tourism. The Spanish online professional tourism journal *Hosteltur* has published articles on slow tourism and travel focusing on the practical efforts made by the Spanish government and private operators to achieve more sustainable touristic practices related with the slow travel philosophy (Hosteltur, 2009, 2010, 2014). Finally, it is worth noting that in 2014 slow tourism was the main topic of the V International Congress of Rural Tourism of Navarra. In this context, slow tourism has been proposed as a new marketing and promotional means for ecotourism and rural tourism, stressing the importance of living and traveling in a more relaxed style for the benefit of local people, the environment, and the quality of the tourism experience (www.congresoturismorural.es on line 26/09/2014).

Slow tourism/travel offerings in Spain

Slow tourism, as an alternative way of conceiving the tourist experience, promises to enhance not only the quality of traveling but also, and more importantly, the quality of life of both tourists and local communities. The results from Andereck and Nyaupane's (2010) study reveal that residents perceive tourism as exerting a positive influence on their quality of life. This effect is related to the availability of recreational amenities, positive impacts on the economy, the preservation of natural and cultural heritage and greater community pride and wellbeing. On a practical level, at times slow tourism has been used to brand offerings and proposals that do not share any similarity with the slow tourism precepts, except for the "slow" label. Within the Spanish context, it is possible to identify some initiatives that are in line with slow tourism. Some of them make an explicit reference to the value of slowness, while others embrace the slow philosophy with no specific hint at slow tourism. In this section we will not provide an inventory of slow tourism proposals in Spain, as this is not the aim of this work. We prefer to show the most representative initiatives that advance the slow philosophy in the Spanish tourism industry and analyze how close they are to the theoretical traditional or new interpretations of slow tourism. We differentiate between public and private initiatives.

Public initiatives undertaken by Spanish government or regional institutions

Recently, the Spanish government made several efforts to improve the sustainability and the experiential value of tourism practices. Both aspects are distinctive for slow tourism development. First of all, it is noteworthy that Spain boosts a large range and variety of routes and itineraries (8,700 Km.) that are suitable for exploring places by trekking, cycling, horse-riding, etc., and, in general, through non-motorized paths. Among the most famous are The Natural Paths and The Green Ways, the cattle routes, and the pilgrims' route to Santiago de Compostela (www.magrama.gob.es online el 26/09/2014). All of these together comprise a non-motorized itineraries network which is spread out over the national territory and that represents a valuable potential infrastructure to enhance slow traveling and to avoid high-polluting means of transport.

The *pilgrims' route to Santiago de Compostela* ("The Camino") is the most well-developed and frequently renewed itinerary, and it contains complementary services and infrastructure which make it possible for tourists to cover the entire itinerary with non-motorized transports means. As a slow travel route, this itinerary has a meaningful content which, in part, is routed in the religious, cultural and educative value of the pilgrimage practice (Fullagar et al., 2012) while also providing deep contact with a high-quality environment. Finally, the arduousness of the route itself creates the chance of experiencing a sense of fulfillment for the physical effort sustained and for the achievement of the "finish line."

Another slow example has to be seen in *Territors Serens*. It is an initiative developed by local administrations of a few villages in the interior of Barcelona, with the aim of giving an alternative response to the increasingly massive urbanization of the spaces surrounding the metropolis and preserving social, environmental and cultural qualities of the area. On the 28 March 2009 the representatives of a number of rural municipalities came together to sign a manifesto aiming at protecting the uniqueness of local villages and natural heritage. Territors Serens wishes to promote a specific lifestyle that is focused on changing patterns in relation to economy and work, life cycle and territory and environment. It is not a specifically touristic project, but it includes itineraries designed to allow tourists to get to know the area on foot and enjoy places, times and locality. It seeks to be a pleasant place to live and to travel to (http://territoriserens.suporttic.com online 26/09/14).

Within Spanish public initiatives about slow tourism we have to include *Menorca Slow*, a brand created by the local administration of the Spanish Island of Menorca to promote a different tourism experience. The webpage for tourism in Menorca included the "Slow" concept within the distinguishing characteristics of the island. At the beginning of 2014, a comprehensive catalogue of slow accommodation has been edited and presented at the most renewed Tourism International Fairs, such as the World Travel Market in London, where it has received a large acceptance by tour operators of foreign markets (Hosteltur, 2014).

Private initiatives

Private initiatives are characterized by efforts aimed at turning slow tourism into a marketable, concrete tourism reality. Spain boasts some valuable initiatives, while some others are not worth mentioning, as they just use the suggestive slogan of slow tourism without a corresponding slow content. Below, the most representative initiatives are presented in order to show the status of the development of slow tourism in Spain, which is still in its infancy when compared, for example, with Italy, the leader of the slow philosophy.

Les Martines Slow Tourism (www.lesmartines.es) is a private initiative in Vilafames (Valencia) that proposes different touristic services which encourage the slow approach of the stay (not of the travel). The experiences are focused on relaxing and enjoying the authentic atmosphere of their rural houses, as well as typical dishes and landscapes. Their main philosophy is to experiment with *serendipity* and to avoid strict and exhausting travel planning.

Con Calma Viajes and Slow Travelling are tour operators, established respectively in Madrid and Barcelona. Their aim is to respond to an increasing demand from travelers who desire to experience freedom, relaxation and escape stress on holidays. Both agents emphasize the importance of avoiding compressed itineraries and enjoying time and location, staying longer at the destination. Con Calma Viajes proposes alternative means of transport, such as trains, boats and camper vans. However, environmental concern about the reduction of greenhouse gasses emitted by traditional means of transport is not the main justification for these proposals, but rather the experience associated with the use of slower means of transport. Slow Travelling, on the other hand, is more focused on accommodation, providing a detailed catalogue of hotels and resorts favoring the slow experience. This tour operator promotes journeys all over the world and makes no reference to the ecological assumptions of slow travel. It promotes the importance of staying in the vicinity of the destination, but again it is considered to be a functional choice for enhancing the experiential value of the holiday and not the expression of an ecological concern. *Ambulare* (www.ambulare.es) and *Caminando Caminando* (www.caminandocaminando.com) are tour operators specializing in trekking experience in Spain and focusing on cultural, rural and gastronomic offerings. Ambulare specializes in small group trekking experiences at the Ribeira Sacra, in Galicia, a destination rich in culture, gastronomy, natural heritage and craftwork. Caminando Caminando is also established in Galicia and is keen on the Way of St. James (The Camino). It leads different tours, both trekking and cycling, and occasionally uses buses for larger itineraries. These highlight slow tourism, slow travel or slow food as the key elements of the organization's tourism offerings, and the descriptions related to these are permeated with the slow philosophy.

The aforementioned initiatives are just representative examples of how slow tourism is being interpreted and implemented by the Spanish private and public sector. The webpage analysis shows that many references to slow tourism can be found. They mainly promote calm, relaxation and quality rhythms that make the traveler envision an alternative holiday, with a deeper connection to the environment and natural resources, cultures and local communities. One of the most important results that emerged from the web analysis is that a strong trend to "sell" as slow tourism whatever is rural and includes any kind of contact with natural resources exists, which often involves just walking in the countryside or contemplating suggestive landscapes.

Those proposals that appear more consistent with what the academic literature has defined as slow tourism tend not to emphasize the ecological value of slow travelling and the importance of utilizing alternative transport to get to the destination and to move *in situ*. This is in line with results by Dickinson et al. (2011, p. 283) who, with reference to the pioneering Slow Travel Website (www.slowtrav.com) funded by Pauline Kenny in 2000, stated, "This advocated staying in one place to enjoy the local life but made no reference to the journey to the destination." Spanish slow tourism proposals are all based on the experiential importance of walking, cycling and horse riding as activities to be done *once at the destination*, and these aspects are mainly seen as experience enhancers, more than consciously green behaviors resulting from personal environmental concern. In summary, the Spanish web page analysis shows how web proposals celebrate the experiential value of the slow tourism experience, with slow travel and soft mobility being either completely omitted or considered to be a functional element within the richness of the whole slow tourism experience.

Conclusions

Slow tourism has been proposed as an alternative tourism system that can potentially address the two major problems that the tourism industry faces at the present time: the sustainability of tourism activities and the competitiveness of destinations and touristic products. In light of these, slow tourism presents an attractive option deserving more attention from both scholars and the tourism industry. Slow tourism has been conceptualized on the basis of two major pillars: the sustainable value of soft mobility and the experiential value of a relaxed and slow approach to travel and holiday time. On the other hand, there are some trends that suggest the need for slow tourism to be critically analyzed and ultimately reconceptualized:

1 The feasibility of pure soft mobility: many self-described slow tourists are not willing to completely avoid fast and polluting means of transport such as cars or planes. Related are distance concerns. How far, physically, can tourists travel before slow tourism becomes fast?
2 The practical interpretation of slow tourism on the ground appears to be mainly omitting the soft mobility assumptions of slow travel and instead exalting the experiential value of slowness.
3 New tourism trends aim to present holiday and travel as fulfilling and meaningful experiences which can positively impact on life satisfaction, happiness, self-esteem and quality of life (Dolnicar et al., 2013; Sirgy et al., 2011; Uysal et al., 2012). These goals need specific conditions to be achieved and slowness and relaxed rhythms appear to be suitable components for memorable and enriching tourism experiences (McCabe & Stokoe, 2010; Sirgy et al., 2011).

Based on these three observations, slow tourism can be reconceptualized introducing the concept of happiness and quality of life as main determinants of the slow tourism experience and rearranging the contribution of the environmental consciousness component as a functional element for the slow experience (see Figure 12.1).

The aim of this chapter has been to critically analyze the slow tourism concept and practice, paying special attention to the Spanish tourism industry. Spain, as a major international destination, should be leading the way in new trends in tourism, both from a conceptual and a practical perspective. Literature analysis showed that Spanish theory on slow tourism is in line with international conceptualization. Very few authors treat the topic and approach it in a basically descriptive way. From the practical perspective, webpage analysis showed that a large number of supposedly slow initiatives exist both in the public and the private sector, but in fact just a few of them succeed in bringing the real meaning of slow tourism to life. Apart from these, the initiatives of slow tourism are in an introductory stage in the Spanish market. Probably, in the coming years, more initiatives will appear, and time will tell if all of them will include a genuine philosophy of slow travel to satisfy the increasing demand for this approach. Moreover, a gap between the traditional conceptualization of slow tourism and the way Spanish institutions and operators translate it into concrete offerings persists. Slow tourism initiatives are primarily focused on the experiential value of the holiday. The ecological value of slow traveling and soft mobility is rarely fundamental to the slow tourism product.

In general terms, the slow components of travel have been partially interpreted and taken in by the tourism industry. Moreover, the academic literature has already questioned the feasibility of the ecological and sustainable principles asserted by slow travel (Dickinson et al., 2011). However, empirical research on this topic needs to be considered emergent and, currently, noteworthy contributions are being published that seek to conceptualize the viability of slow tourism (Di-Clemente et al., 2014). All this, together with the new touristic trends, points to interpreting the tourism experience as a path for happiness and increasing quality of life, suggesting the need to reconceptualize slow tourism and bring it in the direction of the experiential tourism and happiness/quality of life research field.

Note

1   This study has been carried out together with researchers pertaining to the Italian University of Perugia, with Spain (Sierra de Gata) the geographical context chosen for empirical works.

References

Andereck, K. L., & Nyaupane, G. P. (2010). Exploring the nature of tourism and quality of life perceptions among residents. *Journal of Travel Research*, *50*(3), 248–260.

Babou, I., & Callot, P. (2009). Slow tourism, slow (r)evolution? *Nouvelles Mobilités Touristiques, Cahier Espaces*, *100*(56), 48–54.

Bimonte, S., & Faralla, V. (2012). Tourist types and happiness a comparative study in Maremma, Italy. *Annals of Tourism Research, 39*(4), 1929–1950.

Bimonte, S., & Faralla, V. (2013). Happiness and outdoor vacations appreciative versus consumptive tourists. *Journal of Travel Research, 12,* 1–14.

Björk, P., & Kauppinen-Räisänen, H. (2014). Exploring the multi-dimensionality of travellers' culinary-gastronomic experiences. *Current Issues in Tourism, 19*(12). doi:10.1080/13683500.2013.868412

Calzati, V., & de Salvo, P. (coord.). (2012). *Le strategie per una valorizzazione sostenibile del territorio. Il valore della lentezza, della qualità e dell'identità per il turismo del futuro.* Milan: FrancoAngeli.

Chen, C.-F., & Chen, F.-S. (2010). Experience quality, perceived value, satisfaction and behavioral intentions for heritage tourists. *Tourism Management, 31,* 29–35.

Chen, Y.-C., Li, R.-H., & Chen, R.-H. (2013). Relationships among adolescents' leisure motivation, leisure involvement, and leisure satisfaction: A structural equation model. *Social Indicators Research, 110,* 1187–1199.

Crouch, G. I., & Ritchie, J. R. B. (2005). Application of the analytic hierarchy process to tourism choice and decision making: A review and illustration applied to destination competitiveness. *Tourism Analysis, 10*(1), 17–25.

De Luis Blanco, A. (2011). Una aproximación al turismo slow. El turismo slow en las Cittáslow de España. *Investigaciones Turísticas, 1,* 122–133.

De Salvo, P., Hernández-Mogollón, J. M., & Di-Clemente, E. (2013). "Repellent" tourists versus "Slow" tourists. *European Journal of Tourism, Hospitality and Recreation, 4*(2), 131–148.

Dickinson, J., & Lumsdon, L. M. (2010). *Slow travel and tourism.* London: Earthscan.

Dickinson, J., Lumsdon, L. M., & Robbins, D. (2010). Holiday travel discourses and climate change. *Journal of Transport Geography, 18*(3), 482–489.

Dickinson, J., Lumsdon, L. M., & Robbins, D. (2011). Slow travel: Issues for tourism and climate change. *Journal of Sustainable Tourism, 19*(3), 281–300.

Di-Clemente, E., De-Salvo, P., & Hernández-Mogollón, J. M. (2011). Slow tourism o turismo de la lentitud: Un nuevo enfoque al desarrollo de territorios lentos. *Book of Proceedings vol. I – International Conference on Tourism & Management Studies* (pp. 883–893). Algarve.

Di-Clemente, E., Hernández-Mogollón, J. M., De Salvo, P., & Campón-Cerro, A. M. (2014). Slow tourism: An alternative model for local and tourist development. In J. Mondéjar-Jiménez, G. Ferrari, M. D. V. Segarra-Oña, & A. Peiró-Signes (Eds.), *Sustainable tourism: A collection of tools and best practices* (pp. 23–36). Oxford: Chartridge Books Oxford.

Di-Clemente, E., Hernández-Mogollón, J. M., Folgado-Fernández, J. A., & Campón-Cerro A. M. (2012). La Experiencia de la lentitud: Un estudio comparativo entre el viajero slow y el turista rural de Extremadura. *Proceedings of the XVII AECIT Conference: Creación y Desarrollo de Productos Turísticos: Innovación y Enfoque Experiencial* (pp. 409–417). O Carballiño, Ourense, España.

Dolnicar, S., Lazarevski, K., & Yanamandram, V. (2013). Quality of life and tourism: A conceptual framework and novel segmentation base. *Journal of Business Research, 66,* 724–729.

Fullagar, S., Markwell, K., & Wilson, E. (2012). *Slow tourism. Experience and mobilities.* Bristol: Channel View Publications.

Gardner, N. (2009). A manifesto for slow travel. *Hidden Europe Magazine, 25,* 10–14.

General Secretariat of Tourism. (2007). *Spanish tourism plan horizon 2020.* Madrid: Ministry of Industry, Tourism and Commerce.

Gilbert, D., & Abdullah, J. (2004). Holidaytaking and the sense of Well-being. *Annals of Tourism Research, 31*(1), 103–121.

Hernández-Mogollón, J. M., Campón-Cerro, A. M., Folgado-Fernández, J. A., & Di-Clemente, E. (2012a). Turismo rural: Concepto, evolución y nuevas tendencias.

In J. Ortega, E. Pérez, & P. Milanés (Eds.), *Estudios de Investigación sobre turismo y medioambiente* (pp. 65–88). Saarbruken: Académica Española.

Hernández-Mogollón, J. M., De-Salvo, P., & Di-Clemente, E. (2012b). Una aproximación al concepto de Slow Tourism: El caso del territorio del Valle del Jerte. *Turismo & Desenvolvimento, 3*(17/18), 1681–1693.

Hernández-Mogollón, J. M., De-Salvo, P., & Di-Clemente, E. (2012c). Verso il turismo slow: Il caso della Sierra de Gata, Spagna. *Referred Electronic Proceeding Del Convegno CITTÁSLOW: Il Valore Della Lentezza per Il Turismo Del Futuro* (pp. 83–94). Sinergie.

Hosteltur. (2009). *España creará una marca turística para potenciar el 'slow travel.'* Retrieved from www.hosteltur.com

Hosteltur. (2010). *El slow travel avanza sin prisa pero sin pausa en Europa.* Retrieved from www.hosteltur.com

Hosteltur. (2014). *Menorca Slow, un nuevo producto turístico que inicia su promoción.* Retrieved from www.hosteltur.com

Kao, Y.-F., Huang, L.-S., & Wu, C.-H. (2008). Effects of theatrical elements on experiential quality and loyalty intentions for theme parks. *Asia Pacific Journal of Tourism Research, 13*(2), 163–164.

Kim, J.-H. (2010). Determining the factors affecting the memorable nature of travel experiences. *Journal of Travel & Tourism Marketing, 27*(8), 780–796.

Lam, D., & So, A. (2013). Do happy tourists spread more word-of-mouth? The mediating role of life satisfaction. *Annals of Tourism Research, 43*, 646–650.

Lee, H. T., & Shen, Y. L. (2013). The influence of leisure involvement and place attachment on destination loyalty: Evidence from recreationists walking their dogs in urban parks. *Journal of Environmental Psychology, 33*, 76–85.

Letho, X. Y., Choi, S., Lin, Y.-C., & MacDermid, S. M. (2009). Vacation and family functioning. *Annals of Tourism Research, 36*(3), 459–479.

Lumsdon, L. M., & McGrath, P. (2011). Developing a conceptual framework for slow travel: A grounded theory approach. *Journal of Sustainable Tourism, 19*(3), 265–279.

Manthiou, A., Lee, S., Tang, L., & Chiang, L. (2012). The experience economy approach to festival marketing: Vivid memory and attendee loyalty. *Journal of Services Marketing, 28*(1), 22–35.

McCabe, S., & Stokoe, E. (2010). Have you been away? Holiday talk in everyday interaction. *Annals of Tourism Research, 37*(4), 1117–1140.

Moore, K. (2013). On the periphery of pleasure: Hedonics, eudaimonics and slow travel. In S. Fullagar, K. Markwell, & E. Wilson (Eds.), *Slow tourism. Experiences and mobilities* (pp. 25–35). Bristol: Channel View Publications.

Neal, J. D., Sirgy, J., & Uysal, M. (2004). Measuring the effect of tourism services on travelers' quality of life: Further validation. *Social Indicators Research, 69*, 243–277.

Neal, J. D., Uysal, M., & Sirgy, J. (1999). The role of satisfaction with leisure travel/tourism services and experience in satisfaction with leisure life and overall life. *Journal of Business Research, 44*, 153–163.

Neal, J. D., Uysal, M., & Sirgy, J. (2007). The effect of tourism services on travelers' quality of life. *Journal of Travel Research, 46*, 154–163.

Oh, H., Fiore, A. M., & Jeoung, M. (2007). Measuring experience economy concepts. *Tourism Applications, 46*, 199–132.

Sirgy, M. J., Kruger, P. S., Lee, D. J., & Yu, G. B. (2011). How does a travel trip affect tourists' life satisfaction? *Journal of Travel Research, 50*(3), 261–275.

Uysal, M., Perdue, R., & Sirgy, J. (2012). *Handbook of tourism and quality-of-life research.* New York, NY: Springer.

UNWTO. (2014). *Tourism highlights* (2014th Ed.). Madrid: UNWTO United Nations World Tourism Organization.

13 Embedding slow tourism and the "Slow Phases" framework

The case of Cambridge, UK

Michael B. Duignan and Chris Wilbert

This chapter addresses current and future tourism opportunities and challenges for Cambridge (UK) and illustrates the potential role of "slow" tourism as an antidote to what the authors previously referred to as the "one-day tourist" problematic (see Wilbert & Duignan, 2015). It outlines how the historic and internationally famous city of Cambridge is considering a reworking of its perspective on tourism management and the development of its destination experience. This process is currently under way with the 2016 introduction of Cambridge's new regional Destination Management Organisation (DMO): "Visit Cambridge and Beyond" (VCB). Decisions that regional tourism policy makers take will partly determine how visitors better engage with the city. Current policy now includes seeking tourists who stay longer and spend more money in the region; and, more importantly, encouraging tourists to visit a wider area than the main city center, where the current main tourist attractions are located. The new DMO and Wilbert and Duignan (2015) argue that it is only through connecting up spaces and places that currently sit in individualized silos out of view of "normal" visitor streams that a "slow tourism" approach can be sought.

Through embedding a slow tourism approach, aided in part by the "Slow Phases" (SP) framework proposed in the latter section, regions can better redistribute economic spending derived through the visitor economy toward less visible and more locally based businesses and communities and divert visitor experiences away from the more "spectacular" elements of cities. This is particularly important in light of neoliberal globalization; the ongoing shift toward corporate chains through the "clone town" effect, and the valorization effects underway in central urban environments. It is in light of these arguments that we must consider Miles' (2010) critique that the increasing appeasement of global consumers as opposed to local and host communities illustrates how public money can tend to support private interests. We argue that the principles associated with slow tourism offer a potential antidote to this problematic, helped through embedding the SP framework.

The chapter is the part of the output of a three-year collaborative project (*Centrality of Territories*) working with six other western European universities on an urban sustainability agenda focused on small cities. Several in-depth interviews with key informants, including the Chief Executive of Tourism in Cambridge, and regional festival directors, alongside views from major attractions and small businesses underpin the empirical analysis presented. This compliments observational fly-on-the-wall experiences from the authors based on initial experiences sitting on the Advisory Board of the DMO. It is through in-depth detailed analysis of Cambridge's tourism idiosyncrasies and linkage to theories of slow tourism and political economy that this chapter makes a useful contribution.

Background: the Cambridge context

The city of Cambridge in England can be understood as a small city with an official population of some 123,900 in the UK census (UK Government, 2011). It is, of course, well known for its main university, increasingly so in Asia and especially China, where it has become a major brand. However, Cambridge shows that it is not size of population that is so important in terms of influence a city has. In a world perceived as one of increased inter-urban competition and global urban orders – characterized by networks of connection and urban hierarchies – it is as much about reach and influence (Jayne, 2006, p. 5). Indeed, over the past few years Cambridge has been touted as Britain's most successful city in various media stories (Anderson, 2015), though the reasons for this are often couched in vague business investment jargon that fails to grasp wider spatial factors at work.

Cambridge might be thought of as one of many urban growth poles, centers of certain ordering and organizational activities as part of what is termed globalization. Here, we might follow Doreen Massey, who has argued that we need to see that globalization is as much locally produced as the local is globally produced (Massey, 2006). Massey (2006) is also at pains to point out that the global should not be seen as the opposite of the local, with the latter being seen as good and the former as bad, for this is too simplistic and insular a view. We need a broadened sense of place and indeed of a city like Cambridge, away from just an internal view about investors and people such as students and tourists coming to this place and about "our" hospitality. As Massey (2006) also reminds us, geographies of places aren't only about what lies within them (2006, p. 64). There are all kinds of connections that also run out and through "here" – trade routes, investment routes, political and cultural influences that go around the globe and link with the fate of other places. These connections raise questions of responsibility for some of these wider geographies of place, as well as responsibilities for what happens inside this place (Massey, 2006). This has some bearing on the thinking and practice of slow tourism, where the local can easily tend to be valorized as being clearly more authentic and sustainable. Massey's (2006) view is that we should be careful about setting up such dichotomies, and many have also argued that locally produced things are not always the most sustainable, though sometimes they may be, but that needs to be a question that is continually asked. Moreover, when we ask about the sustainability that is often posited as being connected to slow tourism we need to ask questions such as, What is to be sustained, and for whom?

Cambridge might be thought of as a tourist-historic city (Ashworth and Tunbridge, 2000). However, the city and regional economy is diverse, with education and technology companies driving an economy that has been thriving even at times of national recession that emerged from bailout of banks by national government, leading to high demand for housing, and growth in development throughout areas of the city. Indeed it has been estimated that there are about 900 high-tech businesses employing about 37,000 people – close to a quarter of all jobs (EEDA, 2011, p. 2). Some new housing and technology business developments are being led by Cambridge University and Colleges of the University that reflects the continued importance of the University and Colleges in the city and the fact that they are major landowners in the city, and have access to large amounts of capital for investment. In recent years a large Medical Research Council biomedical campus has been developed next to the Addenbrookes hospital. Global pharmaceutical giant AstraZeneca PLC is building a new research site here. New housing and offices have been developed around the railway station, and a £1 billion development is being led by the University of Cambridge in the northwest of the city, creating 3000 houses, research facilities, spaces for 2000 postgraduate students, along with schools and additional infrastructure. Moreover, a separate £1 billion government development of, and around, a new railway station (set to open in 2016) is being completed in the city to service the Science Park and north of the city. Originally created in 1970 by Trinity College (one of the oldest University Colleges), this was the first Science Park in the UK. Moreover, health and education have in recent years become major aspects of the Cambridge economy, accounting for more than 30 percent of employment in the city region (EEDA 2011, p. 3). By comparison, tourism-related employment was estimated to account for about 6 percent of total employment for Cambridge, or about 5,000 jobs (EEDA 2011, p. 121).

In many ways urban tourism reflects the attractiveness of a city generally, and a city that is attractive to tourists is also likely to attract new residents. Apart from employment, tourism provides things that local people can benefit from such as more and more diverse places to eat, specialty shops, as well as helping to underpin events like Strawberry Fair, Cambridge Folk Festival, various food festivals, among other things. However, as the final government appointed East of England Development Agency report on Cambridge (before it was abolished) also argues, "Local attitudes to tourism are ambivalent and have been so for many years: visitors generally seen as adding to city centre congestion and noise" (EEDA, 2011, p. 120). This ambivalence is also reflected in local newspapers and in talking to local residents. Pressures of congestion have been evident in Cambridge for several decades. It might be argued that, being more visible, tourism gets blamed for congestion when it is only one part of the problem that leads to crowding.

Challenges: Cambridge's tourism

Cambridge's economic strength and ability to ward off the harshest consequences of recession can be attributed to several factors. This evidently includes education; specifically English language (EFL) and Higher Education sectors, but also the technological and scientific hub at the Cambridge Science Park and Silicon Fen – and now – health and medical industries with the construction of one of Europe's largest hospitals (Addenbrookes) and the inward investment of AstraZeneca's headquarters. On reflection, given the size and growth of these industries and the continued economic fortification they provide for the city and regional economy, it almost feels as though tourism as an industry could quite well rest on its laurels, helped by Cambridge's reputation as a globally recognized heritage city. Critically speaking, this may have been true until the introduction of the new DMO in what can be considered a challenging moment in Cambridge's tourism system. Emma Thornton, Chief Executive of Visit Cambridge and Beyond illustrates this point:

> One of the real challenges for Cambridge from a tourism perspective is that it is still perceived by many as a day trip destination. The opportunity exists now, through the development of the new Destination Management Organization, which has no geographical boundaries, to develop and promote the narrative of the broader area, therefore encouraging visitors to stay longer, explore further and create more value from our vibrant visitor economy. (Personal Communication, 2016)

With respect to the one-day tourist problematic, Tourism South East (2010) illustrates that out of what they calculated to be 4.08 million annual day and staying visits, just over 3.245 million constituted day visits (Tourism South East, 2010), with a significant 87.4 percent staying between 3 and 9 hours, as shown in Table 13.1.

The introduction of Visit Cambridge and Beyond (VCB) is, in part, driven by central government cuts to local governments like Cambridge City Council, where between 2010 and 2015 local authorities in England have experienced cuts of 40 percent to central government funding as part of ideologically driven austerity policies from the coalition rightist government (Local Government Association, 2014) and the Conservative Government that gained power in 2015. City Councils such as Cambridge have thus reviewed the services they offer and how they offer them. As growing tourism was not a statutory City Council service, but a discretionary one, this sector has been somewhat deprioritized and arguably depoliticized. In October 2014 the Cambridge City Council agreed to review the role of the private sector to take

Table 13.1 Day visitors and staying visitors

			Day visitors				
	Total	*N/A*	*Under 16 years*	*16–30 years*	*31–45 years*	*46–55 years*	*Over 55 years*
1–2 hours	3.3%	0.0%	0.0%	0.7%	0.7%	0.0%	2.0%
3–5 hours	43%	0.7%	0.0%	7.9%	8.6%	7.3%	18.5%
6–9 hours	44.4%	2.0%	0.7%	8.6%	5.3	11.3%	16.6%
10 + hours	9.3%	0.0%	0.0%	1.3%	3.3%	2.0%	2.6%
Total	100%	3%	1%	19%	18%	21%	40%

Source: Tourism South East, *Economic Impact of Tourism: Cambridge. City Results 2010*. TSE Research, Eastleigh, 2010.
Surveys, Accommodation Stock & Visitor Figures 2008 www.cambridge.gov.uk/sites/default/files/docs/Tourism%20surveys%20and%20visitor%20information.pdf

the lead role in tourism development. The resulting DMO was formed and run, in the main instance, by the private sector [80 percent private, 20 percent public funded]. Such private-led partnerships are an aspect of U.K. national government policy, and the City Council in Cambridge has followed this path.

The city's tourism strategy has started – and will continue – to become a prime focus for economic development through stimulating increased visitor revenues, associated multiplier effects and employment opportunities. It aims to provide a boost to small business within – and beyond – the realm of Cambridge's invisible walls, while simultaneously promoting a new brand and destination image, inviting would-be and current visitor to stay longer and enjoy the fruits of Cambridge's traditional but vibrant regional economy and society. This is reflected in the "Vision" of the VCB: "Cambridge will be recognised and celebrated globally as a world class leisure and business destination"; "Visit Cambridge will be the leading voice for the visitor economy for Cambridge and the surrounding area."

The need to move Cambridge beyond the one-day tourist problematic was also reflected in one of the key DMO "Strategic Priorities" for "running targeted marketing campaigns to change perceptions of Cambridge to a short-break destination (not just a day trip) and develop new markets." Recommendations outlined across this study thus strategically align, not only to the current DMO objectives and vision, but to the historically hoped-for but rather discretionary tourism objectives of the City Council as outlined in their *Tourism Strategy* in 2014 as part of the *Cambridge Local Plan* consultation (Policy 8.56) to ensure the city "focuses on the desire to 'extend' the length of stay of visitors" (Cambridge City Council, 2014). As mentioned, the Tourism unit of Cambridge City Council had for some time recognized the problems of an overly centralized and narrow range of attractions. In policy 79 of the *Cambridge Local Plan 2014* concerning "Visitor Attractions" it is stated:

> Proposals for new visitor attractions within the City Centre will be supported where they: complement the existing cultural heritage of the city; are limited in scale; and assist the diversification of the attractions on offer, especially to better support the needs of families. (Cambridge City Council, 2014)

This point is emphasized even more showing political support for: "attractions that draw visitors beyond the City Centre attractions and encourage the development of alternative attractions throughout the sub-region are also encouraged" (point 8.57).

The reasons why the city suffers from short visitation impacts are wide reaching. Firstly, a significant proportion are from the local region and would quite obviously only visit for a day as Cambridge is an important place for activities and services such as shopping and nighttime events and socializing. Secondly, international visitation from London can be seen as both a benefit and burden – attracting tourism to the city, while simultaneously stunting their capacity to stay for longer periods of time. The close proximity to and ease of travel accessibility between Cambridge and London (direct nonstop train service from Kings Cross Station in North London to Cambridge in 46 minutes) are strong reasons for this, whereby the city becomes an easily done day trip, allowing a quick whistle-stop tour of the city by overseas visitors predominantly visiting and staying in London (e.g. in 2012, London attracted two-thirds of holiday visits from international holiday tourists [VisitBritain, 2014]).

The third and final major factor here is how standardization and corporatization of high street shopping may be contributing to a poorer tourism and cultural offering, as one central shopping and leisure area becomes much like that of another (New Economics Foundation, 2010). On the one hand such retail chains can evidently be attractive to regional shoppers and consumers. Yet, it has become common parlance among national and local government and in business policy and strategy, that in order to survive, cities like Cambridge need to continue to adopt an entrepreneurial approach to urban governance to compete for seemingly mobile capital – what David Harvey (1989) refers to as a shift from managerialism to entrepreneurialism in urban governance. Business competitiveness, rather than social justice or equity or citizenship is the internalized logic of entrepreneurial governance, whereby cities make themselves "as attractive to footloose international finance as possible, foregoing any social programs likely to be a burden on business by multinational companies who might otherwise invest in the city" (North & Nurse, 2014, p. 8). The effects of this entrepreneurial governance on the urban experience can be significant, particularly in light of manipulating tourism experiences (e.g. as outlined in the context of [mega]events – see

Pappalepore & Duignan, 2016). Not only are Western capitalist countries such as the UK seeing an erosion of public space in favor of private ownership, but also such policies often make way for more homogenous forms of urban space, particularly the loss of diversity and corporatized standardization of the high street and centralized urban areas (see Miles, 2010).

Alongside these so-called clone town effects, another challenge for Cambridge is the overreliance on central urban visitor attractions. Even at the national level, images of Cambridge projected by VisitBritain are by and large centered on highly centralized, densely populated, commercial urban areas that consist of a few major visitor attractions: (1) leisure activities like punting on the River Cam (listed as number 23 of 101 things to do in England by VisitEngland in a 2013 marketing campaign); (2) the historic cultural tourism of the Cambridge Colleges (e.g. King's College), and (3) Central Market square. Promoted tourism attractions in Cambridge are very much focused on the Cambridge University colleges. A visitor survey of 2008 on "Reasons for visiting Cambridge" did not include a category for the University colleges, though "heritage/museums" was the top reason given by 24 percent of respondents (www.cambridge.gov.uk/tourism). Theatre and concerts were also popular at 16 percent, while shopping and visiting gardens were rated slightly lower.[1]

Secondary attractions

The aforementioned issues may well provide an incentive for a one-day whistle-stop tour of the city by international tourists in particular. However perhaps by virtue of unintended consequence, this limits the length of visitor stay. Interviews undertaken as part of our research having to do with a series of cultural attractions like that of Kettle's Yard museum and art gallery indicate that they feel they are places that would be mainly visited on the second or third day of visits – peripheral and somewhat superfluous to the main perceived tourism offering. In light of these concerns, it is apparent that Cambridge needs to develop more secondary, peripheral and eclectic forms of visitor engagements and attractions. At this point it is also important to note that suggestions to enhance tourism are not to specifically increase overall tourism numbers within the city parameters (as to do so would likely increase the congestion problems the city currently faces), but rather to seek to help change the focus of tourism for some visitors in a manner that widens the geographical visitor footprint. It is to specifically consider how to diversify tourism in the city: (1) enhance visitor experiences, and (2) lengthen stay, thus increasing likeliness to experience more local attractions and services (including accommodation, theatre and local events, restaurants, etc.). Furthermore, the overall aim of a more active visitor management is emphasized.

The above points become of interest if we link these to some current ideas in urban tourism and beyond to practices and ideas around slow tourism. For example, in terms of new variations and trends in what some tourists seek in urban tourism Robert Maitland (2007, p. 27) has argued that, while many cities have taken a supply-side perspective to attracting visitors, there has been comparatively less research into the characteristics, attitudes and want of visitors or the roles they play in shaping new tourism areas. This is reflected in one overt strategic objective by the DMO to "establish a programme of research to understand current visitor profiles and identify growth opportunities." Maitland (2007) suggests that distinctiveness of destinations may be more important than notions such as authenticity to particular aspects of the tourism market. Moreover, some visitors, especially experienced travellers, may want a more eclectic mix of experiences including aspects of the everyday as well as more standardized forms. For example, such experienced tourists may want to see how people live in a city, as well as then staying in quite standardized hotel accommodation (Maitland, 2007, p. 28). That is, some tourists seek some deeper experiences of place, but still wish for a certain reassurance of being in the average semi-luxury or budget hotels that can be found in most cities.

Maitland (2007) goes on to argue there may also be an increasing overlap between what tourists, day visitors, and residents and workers do on their evenings and days off. He suggests this may be seen in the main in polycentric large cities like London. But it may well be the case that this can also be found in smaller cities like Cambridge that attract particular types of cultural, educational, and Visiting Friends and Relatives (VFR) tourists in significant numbers. With respect to the VFR segment, it is likely that as a city with two universities, many migrant workers and international students, VFR totals are significantly undercounted. This is typically true of many cities. Moreover, research on VFR of university cities (Bischoff & Koenig-Lewis, 2007) has shown that universities are large, frequently underestimated generators of VFR tourists, and that VFR visitors typically spend more time in destinations than many other visitors. VFR visitors are therefore visitors that may be seeking wider experiences of the local region as a secondary aspect of their visit and could respond positively to marketing a wider range of attractions to them – though how to do this becomes an interesting question.

Theorizing slow tourism

Dickinson, Lumsdon, and Robbins (2011) argue that there are three identifiable behavioral categories of what can be termed slow tourism. Firstly, there are studies that focus on modes of transport that have lower environmental impacts and less travel. This aspect focuses on alternatives to air and car travel, such as trains, buses, cycling, walking, both to and within a destination, and where the travel to and from the destination becomes part of the holiday. The second emphasizes better tourism experiences, where visitors engage in a deeper experience of place. The third focuses on transport as a tourist experience. Others have argued that slow tourism is better seen attitudinally rather than as a category of behavior, as categorical and behavioral approaches can too easily overlook aspects of slow tourism that appear in what might be termed "fast tourism" (Oh et al., 2016, p. 208). In other words, these three behavioral aspects of tourism may be done together or separately, and there may be differing attitudes to why. In this study we focus more on the second category of Dickinson et al. (2011), that of deeper experiences of being in the destination, as a general aspect of slow tourism, albeit one that coincides with other descriptions of some cultural tourists, and one which is still rather vague. In this we are not seeking to ascertain how tourists travel to destinations, but rather what they do when they get there. As such it reflects a pragmatic and investigative approach to helping develop slow tourism.

The slow movement approach applied to tourism is seemingly a call for a change of leisure life practice – the choice of "fast" versus "slow" – and in doing so to engage in modes of critical consumption that requires some reflection on the type of tourist and place we want to be. Slow tourism is more about savoring experience, as opposed to racing through – where the quality of the experience/visitation is purely determined by fast, efficient, quick, "productive" and plentiful quantity of visits. Miles (2010) notes that global entertainment seduces and pacifies consumers, even perhaps determining the nature of our existence; where social life becomes more about owning and having than about "living." In reality, many tourists may favor aspects of both differentiated local aspects and standardized aspects, as argued earlier. The slow movement also calls for consumers to consider critically analyzing the consequences of their consumption decisions, whereby consumers "use their power of choice to modify market relations, in order to make them fairer and more conducive to a good life for all" (Sassatelli & Davolio, 2010, p. 205). It is here that we consider the need for visitors to shift from what Miles (2010) refers to as "touristic consumerism" for the sake of "having." Sassatelli and Davoli (2010), amongst others, however highlight the political and economic complexities of shifting to a slower mode of consumption – that slow food implicitly promotes a movement which values accessibility for all, but inherently promotes a middle-class lifestyle, inclusive only for those with financial capability to consume "slow" goods and partake in such modes of critical consumption. We must therefore consider these arguments in light of localizing slow tourism in the context of Cambridge city developments. The idea that consumers actively choose smaller producers, over more corporate entities, assumes the ability to afford the often-higher prices that local retailers may charge for goods/services due to their lack of economy of scale. The critical question to pose, then, is how far the shift to "slow" is economically viable for those wishing to partake in critical consumption, particularly in the context of tourism.

Embedding slow tourism

In response to the "fast" way of life and the addressed tourism problematic, planners and practitioners must consider ways to encourage longer and

Table 13.2 "Slow Phases" (SP) model

Phases	Detail
Phase 1 – [slow] resource examination	Detailed exploration and examination of city, town and region resources that incorporate "slow" principles.
Phase 2 – stakeholder alignment	Identification of relevant, influential and strategically aligned stakeholder networks to be incorporated in to the negotiation and communication of the slow tourism agenda.
Phase 3 – strategic and integrated marketing communications	Comprehensive analysis of traditional and digital marketing methods from both theory and practice to promote resources mapped from Phase 1 as well as encourage amplification through effective stakeholder alignment addressed by Phase 2.
Phase 4 – theoretical and practical extension	Continuous review of effective practice and theoretical development to refine and enhance efficacy of embedding slow tourism. This involves frequent reassessment and refinement of analysis conducted Phases 1–3.

deeper visitor engagement. Building on Wilbert and Duignan's (2015) initial four phases of embedding a slow tourism approach, this paper advances the SP framework. This is illustrated by Table 13.2, and provides detailed empirical analysis to flesh out each part to provide a practical and contextual overview of Cambridge's idiosyncrasies.

Phase 1 – (slow) resource examination

The core objective for this phase was to identify all forms of tourism offerings available in and around the municipality of Cambridge, which constituted the values of slow – following a common methodology developed by the participating cities of the network *Centrality of Territories*. This exercise contributed to the mapping of 113 alternative attractions researched from a range of online sources like Tripadvisor, official tourism sites, personal observation and empirical data. This mapping ranged from typical tea gardens, the historic, now-latent comedy scene largely deriving from Cambridge Colleges (e.g. birthplace of Monty Python), right through to educational events and experiential leisure activities (e.g. stargazing in the Institute of Astronomy). The idea that cultural events and festivities showcasing local talent also emerged as a major way visitors to the city can provide a snapshot in to Cambridge's diverse eclectic cultural offering.

The interesting distinction we found, particularly for more peripheral areas from the city centre, is the cultural diversity of the city, a diversity which has been less recognizable in the mainstream marketing of the Visit Cambridge tourism website. As such, diversity does not just point to smaller, local things which might be thought of as traditional in the typical form in which British heritage is marketed (that is as being predominantly white, and of the elites, wealthy, famous) but includes aspects that permeate what is, for want of better term, a small but increasingly cosmopolitan, globally connected city. Those wishing to connect with a wider aspect of Cambridge can find more ethnic and cultural diversity than might be thought, particularly within the peripheral inner city districts of the city. The mapping of slow resources has also identified forms of nature based tourism and historic sites delivered by organizations such as the National Trust and English Heritage dotted around the periphery of the city, as well as the relatively new walking/cycling infrastructure that has been developed in and around Cambridge. The city has a strong cycling culture, which is uncommon for UK cities, though it is still hardly the friendliest of cycling cities as most roads are shared with cars, buses and lorries, and streets are often very narrow.

This cycling and walking infrastructure is supported via a network of stakeholder organizations, such as Sustrans and the National Trust, which develop walking and cycling routes in and out of the city and in turn links with the strategy of the City Council to host Stage 3 of the 2014 Tour de France between Cambridge and London on the 7th of July 2014. The initiative of cycling, bus ways linking the city with surrounding villages, and park and ride schemes, is part of a wider strategy to reduce car congestion in and around Cambridge. Integral to the mapping of phase one was the transfer of slow sites of consumption into a network of other European similarly sized cities. The Geographical Information System (GIS) labeled as *Sevenbeauties* currently houses the initial (and constantly updated) slow resources of both Cambridge and other participating cities, including the lead city of Bergamo in Italy. (For an outline of the GIS system of Sevenbeauties – see Wilbert & Duignan, 2015, p. 210.)

Phase 2 – stakeholder alignment

The responsibility of contributing to and pushing forward slow forms of tourism development falls on the shoulders of a multitude of stakeholders – from community groups, local policymakers to national and globally oriented tourism bodies (see Sautter & Leisen, 1999). This is essential as often urban policy, especially event policies can often be subject to limited community consultation (Cashman, 2002; Miles, 2010). Thus far this appears not to be the case in Cambridge. From the author's experience on the new DMO advisory board, an integrated approach to community inclusion underpins a democratic approach to planning. As part of the author's practical analysis, a mapping of local stakeholder organizations and powerful individual actors with the capacity to drive change were identified. These ranged from the City Council and the DMO, event and festival directors, through to organizations that embody the principles of sustainable development (e.g. Sustrans, and Cambridge Past, Present and Future [PPF]). Interestingly, one interviewer for this project, a bursar of a University college, argued that Cambridge, unlike Oxford, had few attractions beyond the city center and that such things as cycling tourism would be very niche activities. As such, not all stakeholders will share the view that tourism can be extended out of the city center. The interviewee also stated that several colleges were planning visitor centers in or near the colleges to give more of a sense of the current research and investment that such colleges are engaging in, rather than being focused on the past.

Organizations such as Tripadvisor, Lonely Planet and VisitBritain also play a fundamental role in the perception of Cambridge's tourism offerings. Analyzing these social actors' strategic alliances provides an opportunity to share resources, ideas and collaborative power in an agenda that "needs plenty of qualified supporters who can help turn this (slow) motion into an international movement" (Portinari, 1989, p. 1).

Phase 3 – strategic and integrated marketing communications

Given the project is in its initial phases, recommendations provided here consider ways in which the collaborating actors can push forward what is a promising project of enhancing slow tourism approaches for small cities and in the regions around them. Interestingly, the strategic alignment between the project's slow focus and the Council's broader tourism policy agenda emerged throughout 2015. The Cambridge City Council Visit Cambridge & Beyond visitor guide and business membership scheme (www.visitcambridge.org/beyond-cambridge) provides a snapshot in to the range of spaces and places on offer beyond the inner walls of the city, thus promoting at least some of the secondary forms of tourism identified by our Phase 1 resource mapping exercise. As explored earlier, the council's strategy to encourage the hosting of the Tour de France (July, 2014) coherently aligns with both the established problematic of city congestion, and the development of cycle routes in and around the city. The idea that velo-tourism may encourage longer stays as outlined in the strategy for Cambridge tourism mentioned earlier (see pp. 200–201) is being developed in practical tourism and events policy. Moreover, as mentioned in the "Secondary attractions" section, one significant part of the visitors to Cambridge that seem to be both underestimated and little understood, is VFR tourism, especially in light of significant student numbers in the city. University of Cambridge, Anglia Ruskin University, and the more than 30 other English Language Schools (EFL) mean that there are likely to be significant numbers of friends and family visiting students and staff in the city and not just during term time. Also, as mentioned previously, research on VFR tourism has shown that VFR visitors tend to spend more time and non-accommodation-based money in destinations compared to other types of visitors, as well as drawing local residents in to tourism activities (Bakker, 2007; Seaton & Palmer 1997). The notion that VFR visitors may be encouraged to seek wider experiences of local regions, guided by the host, seems likely, but more research is needed on these visitors.

Cambridge also plays host to a variety of events and festivals for its size. This includes celebrating the diverse cultural offering the city has to offer. For example, a growing number of events are focused around food, drink, music, literary talent and scientific discovery that allow visitors and local residents to identify what Cambridge, as a city and the wider region, has to offer. EAT Cambridge 2013, 2014 and now 2015; Mill Road Winter Fair; country shows and science festivals typify these offerings. Interestingly, following recent economic and social impact analysis of the EAT Cambridge 2014 festival, respondents of the study (local independent participating food and drink traders) claimed these types of urban interventions potentially allow local people to engage in critical consumption – particularly the transformative behavior of local people to break routines of choosing chains/online shopping outlets to experience the local more. The idea that both local (domestic and national) consumers may be drawn to the city to enjoy good local food may be an important one for enhancing Cambridge's reputation for slow food. Respondents surveyed for the analysis repeatedly highlighted how the festival showcased "good Cambridge traders" with "positive engagement with local foodies" and helped improve "awareness of the street food scene in Cambridge." With respect to the wider city image, one respondent claims the festival raised the "food profile of the whole city, giving more legitimacy to the idea of Cambridge having a great food-scene." As mentioned in the "Secondary attractions" section, interviews we undertook with some smaller Cambridge attractions, like Kettle's Yard museum and art gallery, expressed a need to have more tourists staying overnight for them to benefit from tourism. Many smaller attractions with smaller profiles would usually only be visited by those staying for several days in the city. This is also recognized by the new tourism destination marketing organization. But persuading people to think of Cambridge as a place to stay for several days has, thus far, proved elusive. Creating a broader identity for Cambridge in terms of a slow approach is what we are seeking to encourage.

Phase 4 – theoretical and practical extension

In these initial phases of the research the authors of this chapter have begun to develop and work through scholarly networks and public engagement. Partnerships are being developed with other stakeholders in Cambridge, in particular the City Council. Presentations at international conferences encompassing both academic and public stakeholders have highlighted Cambridge's context and opportunities, and how academics and practitioners may develop aspects of the slower, more diverse forms of tourism. Methodologies have been discussed and shared in these meetings between different members of the network of small cities, alongside best-practices ideas. The authors have also used local and regional television and radio media appearances to discuss issues pertaining to gentrification effects seen in the inner city areas of Cambridge – making the case for diversifying tourism offerings.

Since the *Centrality of Territories* network inception, we continue to encourage discussion pertaining to slow forms of development – through engagement via policy networks, stakeholder organizations, through event and festival engagements. Though there are hugely interesting possibilities ahead, the challenges of this slower, more sustainable approach to tourism should not be downplayed. To a great extent the dominant focus from the new DMO is on unconstrained growth of tourism. There are moves already developing through the new DMO to seek to diversify tourism in other spaces and places, mainly through marketing initiatives on the Visit Cambridge & Beyond website. Yet, not all local stakeholders will necessarily welcome the diversification of tourism in to the spaces they manage, as can be seen from the concerns that Cambridge Past, Present and Future expressed about the management of Wandlebury Country Park on the edge of the city. They were concerned that a growth in visitors would alter how the park is experienced and would lead to the need to fence off areas from access (interview with Cambridge Past Present Future 2015). Dialogue with local residents, small and micro businesses, conservation organizations and more need to be opened up both to try to reduce concerns, but also to take seriously such projected management problems.

Supporting practice: the role of universities and educational institutions

This section illustrates how slow tourism as a strategy may be brought about through effective strategic and operational alignment between educational institutions and regional tourism policy makers. Building on a recent Association of Business School's (2016) examination, the tourism team at Anglia Ruskin University has fostered successful relationships among the University, local communities of small businesses, festival directors, and key policy makers across Cambridge's DMO, "Visit Cambridge and Beyond." Establishing successful relationships led to the University's attainment of the "Leadership in the Visitor Economy" presented by the Association of Tourism in Higher Education (ATHE) sponsored by England's national body for tourism: "VisitEngland" in 2015.

Strategic alignment has been sought in several ways, and provides a series of ways in which educational institutions can play a major stakeholder role in invoking the SP model. These include the following:

- Involving students in the planning and delivery of major slow food and drink festivals and supporting small businesses.
- Pro bono analysis of regional events and festivals (including EAT Cambridge 2014, 2015 and 2016, and the Cambridge Half Marathon

in 2016) to illustrate the economic and social benefits for grassroots activities that support a slow tourism approach.

- Coauthorship of regional business articles between the University and the DMO to present a "slower" future of tourism management and development for the city and beyond.
- Embedding the tourism team in the development of regional DMO tourism policy, practice and strategy on advisory board and inviting students to be involved on the front end of real tourism issues.
- Embedding the DMO in the development, assessment and guest lectures of the University BSc Tourism Management program. This also includes using the strategic priorities of DMO to support the direction and writing of undergraduate dissertations.
- Involving stakeholder groups (discussed in the "Phase 4" subsection) in the construction of academic publications.

Bachelor of Science (BSc) Tourism Management students play a fundamental role in examining and tackling all aspects of the SP model. Their experience illustrates the beginnings of an antidote to current neoliberal logic and marketization, which is currently manifesting students-as-consumers, that manifests students-as-partners. This serves as both a strategic utility choice for enhanced resource deployment in academic and practical projects, but also as a major initiative toward creating authentic learning experiences which support "constructive alignment" and "deeper learning" through "active learning" and "assessment for learning" strategies. Although this chapter serves not to provide a pedagogic analysis; fostering student-staff collaboration and forging greater connectivity between student, academic and SP model is a vital part of embedding a slow approach in regional contexts.

Directions for future tourism

As the discussion above shows, the short-term aim is to help transform dominant forms of tourism and to widen the potential benefits from tourism in the region by applying a slow model that diversifies and expands geographically tourism offerings. There is the potential then to link up with wider initiatives in Cambridge from groups in the city – such as the Transition Cambridge group that is part of the Transition Towns Network, "working towards a lower energy, sustainable and prosperous future." According to the network,

> In our vision of the future, people work together to find ways to live with a lot less reliance on fossil fuels and on over-exploitation of other planetary resources, much reduced carbon emissions, improved wellbeing for all and stronger local economies. The Transition movement is an ongoing social experiment, in which communities learn from each other and are part of a global and historic push towards a better future for ourselves, for future generations and for the planet. (Transition Network, 2016)

Aspects of slow tourism can be seen to fit with these wider visions in the shorter and longer term. However, tourism is not usually addressed in such network practices as of yet. The longer-term aim of such a slow tourism for Cambridge would be to link in to similar aims as the transition towns.

Note

1   Such visitor surveys tend to be tourist information office and Visitor Informational Centre–based, so will lead to some skewing in types of visitors questioned.

References

Anderson, E. (2015, March 7). Is Cambridge the UK's Most Successful City? *The Telegraph.* Retrieved from www.telegraph.co.uk/finance/festival-of-business/11456262/Is-Cambridge-the-UKs-most-successful-city.html

Ashworth, G. J., & Tunbridge, J. E. (2000). *The tourist historic city: Retrospect and prospect of managing the heritage city.* Oxford: Pergamon.

Bakker, E. (2007). VFR travel: An examination of the expenditures of VFR travellers and their hosts. *Current Issues in Tourism, 10*(4), 366–377.

Bischoff, E., & Koenig-Lewis, N. (2007). VFR tourism: The importance of university students as hosts. *International Journal of Tourism Research, 9,* 465–484.

Cambridge City Council. (2014). *Cambridge local plan: Proposed submission and public consultation.* Retrieved from. http://cambridge.jdi-consult.net/localplan/readdoc.php?docid=171&chapter=9&-docelemid=d3-2933#d32933

Cashman, R. (2002). What is "Olympic legacy"? In IOC (Ed.), *The legacy of the Olympic Games 1984–2000.* Lausanne: International Symposium Lausanne.

Dickinson, J., Lumsdon, L., & Robbins, D. (2011). Slow travel: Issues for tourism and climate change. *Journal of Sustainable Tourism, 19*(3), 281–300.

East of England Development Association (EEDA). (2011). *Cambridge Cluster at 50: The Cambridge economy: retrospect and prospect.* Retrieved from www.sqw.co.uk

Harvey, D. (1989). From managerialism to entrepreneurialism: The transformation of urban governance in late capitalism. *Geografiska Annaler, Series B, Human Geography, 71*(1), 3–17.

Jayne, M. (2006). Conceptualizing small cities. In D. Bell & M. Jayne (Eds.), *Small cities: Urban experience beyond the metropolis* (pp. 1–18). London: Routledge.

Local Government Association. (2014). *LGA briefing: Provisional local government finance settlement 2015-16,* 18th December. Retrieved from www.local.gov.uk/documents/10180-/5533246/LGA+On+the+Day+briefing+Provisional+LG+Finance+Settlement-201516.pdf/4ce0905f-d881-4426-8a7b-9755ec6d26bc

Massey, D. (2006). London Inside-out, *Soundings, 32:* 62–71.

Maitland, R. (2007). Culture, city users, and the creation of new tourism areas in cities. In M. K. Smith (Ed.), *Tourism, culture, and regeneration.* Wallingford: CABI Publishers.

Miles, S (2010). *Spaces for consumption.* London: Sage.

New Economics Foundation. (2010). *Clone Town Britain 2010: High street diversity still on endangered list.* Retrieved from www.neweconomics.org/press/entry/clone-town-britain-2010-highstreet-diversity-still-on-endangered-list

North, P., & Nurse, A. (2014). Beyond entrepreneurial cities: Towards a post-capitalist grassroots urban politics of climate change and resource constraint. *Metropoles, 15.* Retrieved from http://metropoles.revues.org/5005

Oh, H,. Assaf, G. and Baloglu, S. (2016). Motivations and goals of slow tourism. *Journal of Travel Research, 55*(2): 205–219.

Pappalepore, I., & Duignan, M. B. (2016). The London 2012 cultural programme: A consideration of Olympic impacts and legacies for small creative organisations in East London. *Tourism Management*, 54, 344–355.

Portinari, F. (1989). *Slow food manifesto*. Retrieved from www.slowfood.com/about_ us/eng/manifesto.lasso

Sassatelli, R., & Davolio, F. (2010). Consumption, pleasure and politics: Slow Food and the politico-aesthetic problematization of food. *Journal of Consumer Culture*, *10*(2), 202–232.

Sautter, E. T., & Leisen, B. (1999). Managing stakeholders a tourism planning model. *Annals of Tourism Research*, *26*, 312–328.

Seaton, A. V., & Palmer, C. (1997). Understanding VFR tourism behaviour: The first five years of the United Kingdom tourism survey. *Tourism Management*, *18*(6), 345–355.

Tourism South East. (2010). *Economic impact of tourism: Cambridge. City Results 2010.* Eastleigh: TSE Research.

Transition Network. (2016). Retrieved from www.transitionnetwork.org/about/strategy

UK Government. (2011). *2011 Census*. Retrieved from www.cambridge.gov.uk/2011-census

VisitBritain. (2014). *Cambridge Travel Guide*. Retrieved from www.visitbritain.com/ en/Destinationsand-Maps/History-and-heritage/Cambridge.htm

Wilbert, C., & Duignan, M. (2015). Going s-Low in Cambridge: Opportunities for sustainable tourism in a small global city. In E. Caste & F. Burini (Eds.), *Centrality of Territories: Verso la Rigenerazione di Bergamo in un Network Europeo*. Bergamo: University of Bergamo Press.

14 Drinking in the good life

Tourism mobilities and the slow movement in wine country

Donna Senese, Filippo Randelli, John S. Hull and Colleen C. Myles

Introduction

Food and wine, or more broadly, oeno gastronomic tourism combines recreational, entertainment and educational experiences with the potential to engage in positive, often permanent, lifestyle change. As an emergent form of mobility, gastronomic tourism reflects recent megatrends among travelers who desire experiential journeys that provide authentic experimentation of natural and cultural places that enhance wellness and quality of life. The emergence of food and wine tourism in particular has much in common with the main tenants of the Slow Movement for fair, local, quality food production. It is not by coincidence that some of the most successful gastronomic tourism destinations are located in wine regions with a history of wine and food valorization championed by the Slow Food Movement. Slow tourism is guided by an attachment to place (Matos, 2004) that allows visitors a real and meaningful connection with people, places, culture, food, heritage and environment (Caffyn, 2012). Where tourism develops in regions of gastronomic significance, the synergy of slow consumption and slow lifestyle has also been associated with personal well being, relieving the time-space pressures that accumulate in today's alienated capitalist life-world (Harvey, 1989 as cited in Conway & Timms, 2010).

The lure of slow wine and food, gastronomy that is good, fair and local, has been well documented (Dickenson & Lumsden, 2010; Fullager et al., 2012). However, little is known about the tourism mobilities (Urry, 2007) associated with slow gastronomy, especially where it becomes entangled with lifestyle and amenity migration (Bell & Ward, 2000; Hall & Williams, 2013) There is a sense of wellness associated with the consumption of well-rooted gastronomy that can drive the tourist experience and attract migration. The production value of slow gastronomy also captures the political and ethical discourse of sustainable values based in territory, landscape and culture (UNWTO, 2016b). In central Italy, where the Slow Movement originated, tourists and amenity migrants have been drawn to rural communities for decades by the way of life associated with agricultural work, food and wine products and family relationships (Williams, King, & Warnes, 1997). In North America the first certified Cittàslow communities were designated in four of the most important wine and wine tourism producing regions: California (Sonoma), British Columbia (Naramata in the Okanagan Valley and Cowichan Bay) and Nova Scotia (Wolfville of the Annapolis Valley).

Quality of life is linked with the landscapes of *terroir*: geographically delimited spaces of food and wine production, identified by the blend of innovative and living products with natural and cultural resources (Unwin, 2012). A Gallic term, terroir is also a powerful marketing asset for the wine and food industries, producing place identities that have been politically and economically contested (Vadour, 2002). "Terroir travel" (Marlowe, 2016) has emerged simultaneously with the Slow Food Movement as tourists, and consumers more generally, seek out the source of valorized goods and the lifestyles and traditions that produce them. Terroir tourism synthesizes the draw of sustainable, healthy lifestyles with political activism to consume locally and responsibly (Lowry & Lee, 2011). Wine regions capitalize the demand to visit destinations of production where visiting a winery, running a winery, and living in the vicinity of a winery becomes valued among amenity-seeking tourists and amenity migrants (Senese, Randelli, & Hull, 2016).

Our investigation uses the theoretical framework of evolutionary economic geography to examine the Slow Movement as a driver of change in Tuscany, Italy and the Okanagan Valley of British Columbia, Canada. These study sites provide examples of wine production where tourism and amenity migration have taken on common qualities. Other key drivers that facilitate tourism and migration in wine regions are theorized to illustrate temporal and spatial patterns of occurrence. The political and social ideals of slow food and its broad network of members, chapters and designated communities worldwide invigorate the amenities of terroir. The appeal of Slow Food's eco gastronomy of everyday life (Hoeschele, 2010) has a natural offshoot in eco gastronomy of the tourism experience. Therefore, we lay out the evolutionary geography of wine, tourism and migration in Tuscany and the Okanagan, with the emergence of the Slow Movement to understand their synergies.

Theoretical framework

Brouder (2016) describes the analytical lens of evolutionary economic geography (EEG) as a valuable tool in understanding the process of tourism change, particularly in terms of its sustainability. We use EEG to examine the process of tourism transformation alongside other development paths (Boschma & Martin, 2010) in wine regions. Recent studies have used EEG in the analysis of rural transformation towards tourism specialization (e.g. Brouder & Eriksson, 2013; Randelli, Romei, & Tortora, 2014). EEG has great potential to understand change in tourism destinations, where its central concern is focused on the processes of path creation and path dependence which interact to shape geographies of economic development and transformation (Boschma & Martin, 2010). In order to reveal the transformation process towards tourism development, we stress the co-evolutionary process of different drivers of change encapsulated in the Slow Movement and gastronomic tourism: the preservation of natural environments and healthy lifestyles, social and cultural traditions, and the production of quality gastronomic products and experiences.

Our approach to EEG examines the spatial structure of the economy as it emerges from the micro-behaviour of individuals and firms (Boschma & Frenken, 2006) and the macro influences of market driven windows of opportunity and institutional change. The economic landscape is the result of an evolutionary sequence in which innovations are selected because, for some reason, they are a better fit than others to the existing rural configuration (Senese et al., 2016). Currently, market driven windows of opportunity include demands for a healthy, natural lifestyle, and a current of Naturophilia, which has emerged with considerable strength in highly industrialized countries (Cadieux & Taylor, 2013; Hall, Roberts, & Mitchell, 2005; Shaw & Williams, 1994). Similarly, the impetus for fair, quality food products driven by slow tourism is fed by consumer desire to "escape hectic lifestyles" (UNWTO, 2016a) and to "enjoy life's simpler pleasures" (Matos, 2004, pp. 95–96). Similarly, the growth of wine and food tourism demand has been attributed to changing patterns of leisure time and greater segmentation of holidays (Cánoves, Villarino, Priestley, & Blanco, 2004), along with a changing market for quality food products and healthy food supply systems derived out of sustainable natural environments (Oosterveer & Sonnenfeld, 2012).

In both case studies, the emergence of tourism mobilities within an agricultural landscape mark a shift in the predominant historical rural configuration of the economy through the interplay of processes at micro (local) and macro scale. While much of this is the level of market trends, institutional support is also an important driver of that change. The alignment of developments at all scales determines the success of a rural shift towards tourism and its evolution into permanent tourism. The evolutionary approach is not unrelated to the regional political ecology approach, which emphasizes attention to the "chains of explanation" in a given locale (Blaikie & Brookfield, 1987). By considering drivers both up and down scale, patterns and processes in place are more readily discernable (McKinnon & Hiner, 2016). Utilizing the EEG approach, we contextualize the history and evolution of tourism mobilities and their shared landscape under the umbrella of the Slow Movement.

The case of Tuscany

The success of gastronomic tourism in Tuscany is ascribed to the richness of local resources (Telleschi, 1992) that include a varied and beautiful landscape, high-quality food products and a rich cultural life shaped through the centuries by agrarian life, art and architecture (Figure 14.1). From the fifteenth century until the mid-twentieth century, the rural configuration in Tuscany was based on the "*mezzadria*" system, a form of sharecropping. In the Tuscan mezzadria, merchants owned the majority of rural properties close to the urban areas and used the sharecropping system to manage them. Landowners flourished, selling their share of production in the city while farmers kept small farms with housing and sustenance for their families. The iconic Tuscan landscape so important to rural tourism today, took on its typical appearance during the mezzadria with merchant *villas* surrounded by a scattering of sharecropper *case coloniche* (farm houses) amidst mixed crop farming and woodland (Senese et al., 2016). The rural settlements on the Tuscan hills are still composed of villas surrounded by gardens, parks (Azzari & Rombai, 1991) and numerous farmhouses and small villages, surrounded by olive trees and vineyards. This traditional landscape, was valorised internationally in 2004, when the Val d'Orcia, south of Siena, was inscribed as a World Heritage site under Criterion (iv) "as an exceptional reflection of the way the landscape was re-written in Renaissance times to reflect the ideals of good governance and to create an aesthetically pleasing picture" and Criterion (vi) "landscapes where people are depicted as living in harmony with nature, and have profoundly influenced the development of landscape thinking" (Di Giovine, 2008).

All of Italy experienced a deep economic and social crisis in the post WWII period. In Tuscany sharecroppers abandoned their farmhouses to seek out industrial jobs in urban areas. Between 1955 and 1963 the gap between farm

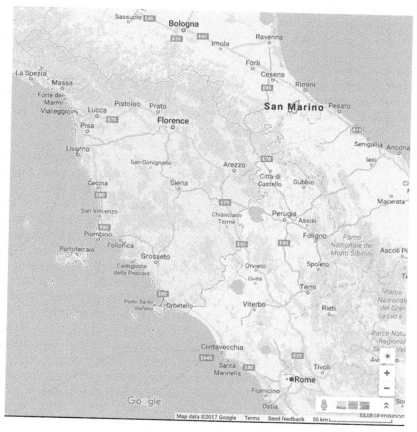

Figure 14.1 Tuscany Region, Italy.

income and industrial salaries continued to widen, reaching 1 to 3.7 in 1955, and 1 to 5.5 in 1963 (Cianferoni & Mancini, 1993). In 1964 sharecropping contracts were declared invalid by the government, and subsequently the 1971 Italian Census of Population showed a depopulation of the Tuscan country-side. Government classified many Tuscan rural regions as "depressed areas" and many rural municipalities lost over 50 percent of their population in the period 1951–1971. With the exception of a few ancient wine families such as the Ricasoli Antinori and Frescobaldi, the re-organization of rural Tuscany then moved with a process of change in landownership. In economic evolutionary terms, the demise of the mezzadria agricultural economy opened a window of opportunity as landowners sold their properties, either to new entrepreneurs or to sharecroppers, who in turn became entrepreneurs. Based on the landscape heritage of the mezzadria there was widespread availability of empty build-ings on farms. New residents began acquiring these empty farmhouses in the 1960s, initially for very low prices and later for increasingly greater sums. These pioneers were predominantly foreigners, amenity migrants who were typi-cally retired and moved from England, France, Germany, Switzerland and the United States. Other pioneers included Italians, who escaped the large, urban, industrial cities of Italy such as Milan, Rome, Naples and even the industrial centers of Tuscany such as Florence, Prato and Siena (Senese et al., 2016). Young Italians, frustrated and worn by the economic crisis of the 1970s, sought jobs and a "refuge" in the countryside (Telleschi, 1992), adding to the growing number of pioneers within this changing rural landscape. The Italian federal government supported this group of young pioneers in 1977 with creation of "young people cooperatives," a move that aimed to recover uncultivated land.

For the most part, foreign migrants within this process of evolutionary change in Tuscany were first attracted to the area as tourists by the beauty of landscape, the pleasant climate and a natural life style based in a much admired rural culture. Their visits eventually led them to buy rural properties in order to have a country house or to become a hobby farmer and or wine producer (Perrin & Randelli, 2007). Many of these migrants brought a wealth of business skills and knowledge of finance that included an international web of contacts. This pioneering set of lifestyle farmers played a leading role in re-development of the wine industry and the developmental transition towards tourism. They shared an intense interest in traditional cultural life as well as a deep interest in local gastronomy arts and crafts. Hines (2010) defines them as "permanent tourists," rural gentrifiers enacting cultural projects akin to those of tourists but doing so with the intention of permanently writing them into the social and physical landscape. By 1985, the wave of international lifestyle migrants earned Tuscany the name Chiantishire, as approximately 5,000 British citizens called the Tuscan countryside home. About half of these amenity migrants were retired, but most all were well educated and wealthy and had moved to Tuscany out of admiration for the way of life associated with agricultural work and family relationships in rural Italy (Williams et al., 1997). Today interna-tional migrants from a variety of countries remain concentrated in rural wine producing regions of the province (Benassi & Porciani, 2009).

The role of institutions at the national level is of considerable importance to Tuscany's rural reconfiguration and highlight the role that changing evaluations of food production led up to the emergence of the Slow Movement. In 1965, after several study tours conducted by farmers and trade unionists in some European countries with advanced tourism development, the National Association of Agriculture and Tourism (Agriturist since 1978) was founded. Since its inception, Agriturist has held a leading role in organizing events and conferences to draw public, political and media attention to the possibilities of agricultural tourism. In 1973, Terranostra was founded by the National Confederation of Farmers to provide support and attention to the problems of small farms not supported by Agriturist. In 1976, Alturist (now Green Tourism) was born out of the initiative of an alliance of a group of farmers. Alturist defined their role as an institute in support of the farm and the environment, for the defense of the countryside and for promotion of cultural and recreational activities within it.

Agrotourism was discussed in various conferences and events dedicated to the farm with the aim of spreading awareness among farmers and highlighting the important role of tourism in supporting agricultural income. Elsewhere in Italy the autonomous province of Trento passed a law "Actions to farm" in 1973, allowing farmers to provide on -farm accommodation. A few months later, the autonomous province of Bolzano passed the law "Outline for rural tourism" that limited the number of beds to 8 at each farm. Simultaneously, at the microlevel, some pioneers experimented by hosting tourists on their farms. Tuscany led the process of path creation. In 1975 Agriturist published the "Guide for Rural Hospitality," the first rural tourism database in Italy that identified 80 farms throughout Italy with accommodation (about 500 beds) and 18 of these farms were in Tuscany. The number of pioneer farms in Tuscany increased dramatically after 1975 and by 1984 there were 171 farms in the region experimenting with tourism. Due to the continuing agricultural crisis, farmers saw the opportunity to increase their income and find a profitable use for many empty buildings. In this preliminary stage, regional law on tourism accommodation was lacking in Tuscany and hospitality was of low standard. At the time, tourism was based nearly exclusively on lodgings: rooms rented in the owner's private home or independent lodgings, both on the farm and in private houses.

During this period Agriturist, Terranostra and Alturist played a leading role in making both farmers and other governing bodies in Italy aware of new paths to tourism. With the national law on "Farm Accommodation Regulations" in 1985, the period of agrotourism experimentation ended in Italy and *agriturismo* was born. The agriturismo law provided a framework that strictly defined the context and transferred the responsibility for tourism on the farm from the central government to the regional legislative bodies. After the autonomous provinces of Trento and Bolzano, Tuscany was the first to legislate *agriturismo* legislation. The regional law (n. 36/1987) stipulated that tourism should be only a secondary activity alongside that of agricultural production. Above all, the relevance of the Tuscan law was that it officially included tourism in farm activities, while preserving its *status* of agri-firm. This is very important in the European context because it allowed farmers to invest in tourism and gave them access to a large set of policies and funds designed for the development of agriculture.

The Tuscan agriturismo law also pointed farmers to the new path to tourism. The success of pioneers attracted other farmers and residents to follow them. In this stage of growth, the micro-behaviors of local firms reinforced new trends on the macro-level. The Slow Movement politicized traditional food preservation and increasingly brought local contexts of rural production to the international stage, especially among wealthy urbanites. Here, two important trends collided at the macro level as an impetus to success: first, European funding for multifunctionality within agriculture, and second urban people looking for a natural lifestyle in the countryside (Béteille, 1996; Champion, Coombes, & Fotheringham, 1998; Romei, 2008). Since 1987 the regional government of Tuscany had invested European funds for agriculture in rural areas to set up and then improve *agriturismo*. With the availability of this additional financial support, farmers had the opportunity both to restore the old sharecropper farmhouses and later to provide them with additional tourism amenities such as swimming pools, restaurants and sport facilities. In the short period 1988–1991, 196 farm restorations were financed to use for accommodation with 11.3 billion (approximately 6 million Euro) of Italian lire (Telleschi, 1992, p. 72).

This period of transition overlapped with the emergence of Slow Food in Italy globally, and reflects the social, political and cultural ideals set forth in the Slow Food Manifesto. The focus of Slow Food and growing agritourism in Tuscany has remained steadfastly fixed on traditional and typical gastronomic production and lifestyle. In 1999 the Slow Food Presidia project was established to help unique, traditional food products have an economic impact and guarantee a viable future. By coordinating marketing and promotion, establishing quality, authenticity and production standards and promoting local consumption, the Presidia project brought the traditional gastronomic products of Tuscany to a global audience. The Slow Wine Guide quickly followed suit, marketing Italian wineries that "conjured up a sense of place and the eco-sustainability of the cellar" (Gariglio & Giavedoni, 2015). The 2015 Slow Wine Guide awards 28 Tuscan wineries with the honor of the snail indicating that the winery interprets Slow Food values, sensory perceptions, territory, environment and identity and also offer good value for money (Gariglio & Giavedoni, 2015, p. 10).

While the Slow Movement grew globally, its imprint on rural tourism in Tuscany became more entwined with agrotourism when international businesses and increasing numbers of foreign migrants began to invest in rural accommodation. Entrepreneurs invested in farmhouse restoration and in doing so supported small local firms and traditional craftsmen working as masons, carpenters, joiners, plumbers, electricians and so on. As the number of tourists increased, so the price of houses and farms started to rise and international investment continued. Related tourism services such as tourist information and public transportation began to be offered by local municipalities. Local entrepreneurs followed suit as restaurants, car rental agencies and taxi services emerged to service growing tourist demand for local, typical goods and traditional lifestyles in the rural experience economy (Senese et al., 2016).

At this stage, the integration of tourism improved through the construction of social and cultural networks that enabled actors to develop resources such as local traditions, art forms, celebrations, experiences, entrepreneurship, and knowledge (Saxena & Ilbery, 2008) much of it based in the agricultural and gastronomic sector. In order to encourage repeat visits and longer stays, many farms provided a number of activities related to nature, rural pastimes and specialized agricultural products such as wine tasting, cooking classes, horse-riding, trekking, truffle hunting and foraging. Bed and breakfasts in the small communities that serve the agricultural economy also provided private lodging, and rural resorts also emerged and have experienced continuous growth to service the demand of tourists.

Today tourism remains a stable driver of rural configuration in Tuscany as the initial pioneering wave of slow food and wine tourists with demands for good, fair and local food and wine has become part of the mainstream, reaching a volume of visitation approaching mass tourism levels. Existing entrepreneurs have diversified their offerings with further investments in the quality of accommodations, professional accreditation of their employees, web based marketing and on the range of services and facilities they offer including restaurants, guided tours and internet facilities. At this stage of maturity, tourism, food and wine production are almost inseparable in Tuscany. Eventually tourism may produce more income than agricultural activities, because it is more profitable, and because younger entrepreneurs prefer to focus on the business tourism than the business of agriculture. However, the influence of the Slow Manifesto in defense of local production and the culture of farm life and lifestyle remains central to both the tourism and agriculture industries. Institutional planning remains crucial to ensure short and long-term community benefits. The principles for good community planning and the Slow Movement seem to coalesce here under the broader umbrella of an eco-gastronomic lifestyle, including attention to authenticity and quality, education, conservation and protection and partnerships between local agents (Saxena, Clark, Oliver, & Ilbery, 2007).

The case of the Okanagan

Like Tuscany, tourism mobilities associated with the Okanagan oeno gastronomic industries have a long history driven by the draw of a good life in a beautiful landscape: the heart and soul of the slow movement's utopian eco gastronomy. An evolutionary economic geography of agriculture, wine and tourism in the Okanagan reveals patterns of economic and social change, crisis and resilience that mirror in many ways, the evolution experienced in Tuscany. The Okanagan Valley is one of many north-south running valleys between the Coast Mountain Range to the west and the Monashee Mountain Range to the east in southern British Columbia. The 200-kilometre valley contains a series of long, narrow, deep lakes surrounded by rolling uplands with kame and outwash terraces and, an assortment of glacial and alluvial features (Senese, Wilson, & Momer, 2012). This natural configuration provides home to a mosaic of habitats, a unique and diverse assemblage of plant and animal species, wetlands, grasslands, Ponderosa pine and subalpine forests (Cannings, 2000). Quite simply the Okanagan provides a stunning natural backdrop to a rich oeno gastronomic landscape. The Okanagan is recognized as one of the most beautiful winescapes in Canada (Aspler, 2013) and as part of the Thompson Okanagan Tourism Region welcomes 3.5 million visitors annually, generating over CAN$1.7 billion for the regional economy and employing approximately 15,000 residents (Hull, 2016; TOTA, 2012). The *Travel Experiences Guide for the Thompson Okanagan Region* promotes the local flavors of the region's artisanal, handcrafted food and wine, the dozens of cultural heritage sites, the diverse array of learning programs, the wellness offerings to balance mind, body, and spirit, as well as eco adventures in the mountains, lakes and rivers (TOTA, 2015). The physical environment and unique natural capital are recognized as main motivators for visiting the region (Carmichael & Senese, 2012) (Figure 14.2).

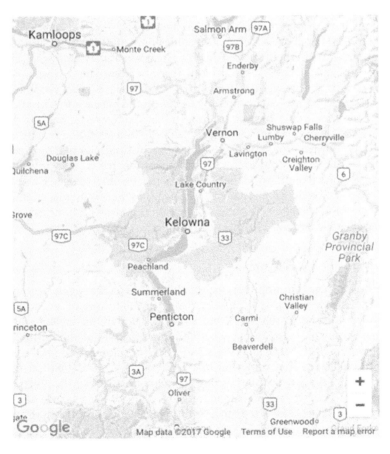

Figure 14.2 Okanagan Valley, British Columbia, Canada.

The Okanagan agricultural ecumene and the appeal of the "good life" have been used consistently throughout the history of European settlement in the valley. The warm dry climate provided by the valley's position in the rain shadow of the Coast Mountain range encouraged tender fruit and market gardening and despite its isolation, European settlement of the Okanagan began in the mid 1800s. Since that time the Okanagan regional economy has relied on extensive agriculture and central positioning among the province's mining and forestry settlements. Early agricultural settlers from Europe and North America were attracted by advertising with glowing descriptions of the valley as the "land of fruit and sunshine," "the garden of Canada," "the lost garden of Eden" and as a "newfound earthly paradise" (Grand Pacific Land Co. Ltd, 1912 as cited in Wagner, 2008). Early developers understood that promotion of the tree fruit industry could serve as an ideal engine for development for the region (Wagner, 2008, p. 28) and encouraged migration through agricultural potential to a wide audience. The advent of rail and steamship transportation at the turn of the century made more intensive farming, especially tree fruits viable, as perishable commodities made their way to the larger populations in the lower mainland of British Columbia. These transportation developments also provided an ease of access for growing numbers of tourists from Vancouver and the lower mainland as well as Alberta and central Canada. Rich agricultural resources that cultivated an otherwise vast wilderness resonated with settlers and tourists, constructing a western Canadian version of the rural idyll.

The ability to cultivate wine grapes and the lifestyle associated with wine production has also been used to encourage tourism and settlement in the Okanagan. Oblate Missionary Father Charles Pandosy first planted wine grapes in the Okanagan in Kelowna during the 1850s. Later there was extensive planting of labrusca varieties in the post Prohibition era (1912–1922) and the first commercial winery, Calona Wines, opened in Kelowna in 1932. Experimentation with French hybrids and vinifera varietals, including the Becker project of 1977–1982 proved that premium quality grapes could ripen in the Okanagan. Still, climate played a role in a struggling wine industry as severe freezes wiped out much of vinifera varieties in 1968 and 1978 (Senese et al., 2012). In 1989 institutional influences triggered the next phase of development. Preferential tax treatments of the Canadian wine industry, in place since the 1930s, were removed. This resulted in crisis, and opened windows of opportunity for the Okanagan wine. Signing of NAFTA (North American Free Trade Agreement) in 1989 meant that Canada's wine industry needed to adapt quickly to a more competitive environment (Hira & Bwenge, 2011; McGuire, 1993). Grape growers were paid $8,100 per acre to pull out undesirable grape varieties and replant in vinifera varieties. In total, 2,400 acres were pulled and replanted leaving only 1,000 acres of premium vinifera vines. This began a swift rural reconfiguration of land use in the Okanagan as the number of wineries increased consistently with wine pioneers ready to balance the risk of climate disasters against the risk of satisfying market demands (Belliveau,

Smit, & Bradshaw, 2006). Early wine pioneers of the era had arrived from Switzerland, Austria and Germany, producing largely cool climate Germanic varieties such as Riesling, Ehrenfelser and Gewurztraminer. Locally established farming families of the Okanagan also recognized the potential of the industry and started planting grapes. Early pioneering growth in the wine industry was then encouraged by the tide of wide scale social change associated with the demand for more natural lifestyles. Urban-to-rural migration of wealthy urbanites to the Okanagan also grew during this era, attracted by the promise of living in an environmentally pristine place, opening a winery, and living the good life in the rural idyll of the Okanagan (Hopgood, 2016).

In the 1980s the globalized economy devalued primary resources and revalued consumption industries in the new post-Fordist economy with impacts on agricultural and land use in the Okanagan. Massive restructuring in resource industries in many parts of British Columbia meant job losses, mining and mill closures (Halseth, 2005), leaving a trail of small, mostly rural ghost towns in the interior of British Columbia. Rural decline in British Columbia was facilitated through an intentional policy program that viewed hinterland areas as a "resource bank" from which to fund provincial infrastructure and services, without adequate attention to rural reinvestment (Markey, Halseth, & Manson, 2008). Rapid growth of urbanization in larger centers worked hand in hand with globalization at this time and together, these broad social trends left rural resource towns in crisis but also paved a road with opportunity in its reconfiguration of the economy. When food crops were devalued in the wake of globalized economies, they were increasingly replaced with amenity crops such as wine grapes, ginseng, medicinal plants and herbs. Farmers also recognized the tourism value of such crops and began to understand the growth of agrotourism as a possible tool in farm succession. This scenario provided the perfect storm of rural economic crisis and pioneers recognizing an opportunity at the local level with widespread social change at the macro level. Here the mantra of Slow Food lifestyles linked to eco gastronomy began to catalyze consumers who increasingly demanded local products as a resistance to globalization and as a reaction against increasingly urbanized lives (Parkins, 2004; Miele & Murdoch, 2002).

During the same period institutional changes further influenced opportunities for rural reconfiguration towards wine and tourism in the Okanagan. Population pressures grew at the rural urban fringe of cities across British Columbia, as most arable land in the province is located close to urban areas. In Southern British Columbia, limited arable land met a rush of urban to rural migration with the escape to the countryside in the 1970s. In 1973 the Provincial Government of British Columbia reacted to urban encroachment into agricultural land with the Agricultural Land Reserve (ALR). The ALR represented an attempt to address dwindling farmland through land preservation; however, it also simultaneously politicized the landscape, as outraged farmers (Yearwood-Lee, 2008) were then unable to sell agricultural land at the rural urban fringe to investors eager to develop sprawling suburbs.

Institutional change of the ALR forced farmers and other entrepreneurs to consider alternate means to make farming viable and agrotourism grew as a way to support farming life. In 2002 BCAgriTourism was formed to support and regulate agritourism and amendments were made to the ALR to further regulate the growing industry. Agrotourism regulations in B.C. are similar to those in Tuscany. In B.C. agrotourism regulations land must be assessed as a farm, the tourism activity must be seasonal or temporary and must be secondary to farming activity (West Coast Environmental Law, 2016).

Falling food commodity prices, ALR regulations and the growing promise of agrotourism accelerated a conversion of orchard to vineyard in the Okanagan. This was especially apparent in the small to medium plots of land adjacent to build up areas of communities up and down the valley. These sites proved to be ideal locations for not just wine grapes but also wine tourism, as they allow relatively easy access to tourism infrastructure, and transportation with connections to major tourism markets in the Lower Mainland of B.C. and the U.S.A. (Carmichael & Senese, 2012). The rural-urban fringe of cities like Kelowna and Osoyoos, where almost 50 percent of the ALR land base is within the city boundaries, witnessed remarkable growth in winery development at this time complete with tourism facilities such as tasting rooms and restaurants. Jim Wyse, proprietor of Burrowing Owl winery in the South Okanagan wrote the first winery accommodation guidelines for the provincial government in 2002 and the winery bed and breakfast was born in British Columbia.

The desire to stay at a winery and experience a lifestyle that was increasingly valued as healthy grew at this stage of development especially among the aging baby boom cohort closing in on retirement. Increasing health consciousness, the quest for spirituality and the desire to escape from the accelerated pace of life contributed to the growth of wellness tourism (Senese et al., 2016) that also produced transformation of lifestyle mobilities associated with the Okanagan. Conflated with gastronomy, this also marks the increasing influence of a globalized slow movement that became increasingly galvanized in the cultural landscape of the region. Peters (2007) notes similar patterns of change in the cultural landscape of El Paso de Robles California brought about by a shift in agricultural production from cattle ranching to viticulture which he refers to as the "purple belt" that triggered tourism development followed by increasing population growth which rapidly pushed development into sprawling suburbs.

In the 1990s the "French Paradox" linked health benefits to red wine consumption and gave further support to the notion of wellness and lifestyle associated with wine (British Columbia Wine Institute [BCWI], 2016). This contributed to the rising demand for red wines and subsequent growth of vineyards to the hot, dry South Okanagan where red wine grapes are best cultivated. As the wine industry grew southward in the valley, a greater variety of vinifera grapes, including reds, requiring greater heat units like cabernet sauvignon were planted with success. The success of serious red wine production coincided with a changing succession of wine industry migrants as wine makers, entrepreneurs and proprietors soon arrived from a variety of new destinations like Australia, South Africa, California and New Zealand. Today, there are almost 200 wineries in the Okanagan, and more than 10,000 acres in vinifera production (BCWI, 2015). More than 80 percent of Okanagan wineries are owned by recent migrants to the valley (since 1990), almost 40 percent of those migrants have made the move internationally while the remaining majority of winery proprietors are recent lifestyle migrants from the large urban centers of British Columbia and neighboring Alberta (Senese et al., 2016). Like the pioneers of Tuscany, many of these new winery proprietors are experienced business people, though very few have any experience in the wine industry. Professionals from the world of finance and wealth management or some other form of professional occupation own more than 70 percent of wineries in the Okanagan. Many of these proprietors first visited the valley as tourists and have built second homes at the winery or vineyard and commute from their primary homes in the large urban centers of western Canada.

In 2009 the Slow Movement came to the valley officially, when Cittàslow International accredited the town of Naramata in the Central Okanagan, as a Slow City. Discover Naramata, the local tourism organization, pursued the accreditation on behalf of local community members, tourism operators and the 26 wineries located in the small town. The main goal of Cittàslow is to promote the philosophy of the Slow Food Movement, and apply the concept of eco gastronomy to everyday life (Lowry & Lee, 2011). Naramata was the second accredited Cittàslow destination in North America, following the first accreditation in another wine region of BC Cowichan Bay on Vancouver Island. Slow Food Thompson Okanagan became a convivium of the international Slow Food Movement in 2012. Like the Naramata experience with Cittàslow, members of the tourism and wine industries of the Okanagan pursued the Thompson Okanagan accreditation as a convivium. In 2013 the Thompson Okanagan Slow Food convivium hosted the Annual Meeting of Slow Food Canada, which is considered to be the most important bilingual food organization in the country.

While the valley has been promoted as a year-round playground by the tourism industry (Aguiar, Tomic, & Trumper, 2005) and a favorable place to retire (Teixeira, 2009) for many years, the influence of the Slow Movement on mobilities is most evident in development of a terroir brand that promotes health, wellness and tradition built out of the cultural capital of the wine and agricultural industries, and the natural capital of the environmental setting. The region is known for a combination of attractions, wine and culinary tourism, outdoor adventure and wellness experiences (Hull, 2016) that reflects the concepts of eco gastronomy and continue to influence lifestyle-based mobilities. A population boom accompanied growth in the wine industry and promotion of the terroir brand. The valley has maintained a population growth rate of 2.9 percent for the last several decades, the highest growth rate in the province. Net migration continues to increase, hovering around 3 percent. The proportion of residents who are elderly and retired now exceeds 24 percent, the highest in Canada, and 46 percent of income earned in the valley comes from non-work, investment and pension income (Invest Okanagan, 2016; BC Stats, 2016 as cited in Senese et al., 2016). Land use pressures from population growth and the lifestyle demands of migrants, has resulted in continued urban and suburban encroachment on agricultural land despite the ALR. Attempts to densify urban centers continue, but residential, resort, recreational development continues to envelope the countryside, mirroring market demands of tourists and migrants. Sprawling suburbs with names like Vineyard Terrace built by development companies who have also co-opted the brand, such as Wine Country Homes and Vineyard Custom Homes, surround vineyards. Wellness resorts, ziplines and cycling trails offer unfettered access to the agricultural heartland. Lifestyle suburban developments, complete with vineyard, have been planned, or are being built in every jurisdiction of the valley for a market of aging baby boomers intent on living the good, healthy rural life in wine country.

Conclusion

The synergy of oeno gastronomic tourism with the Slow Movement is clearly shown in both Tuscany and the Okanagan although any direct impacts in one direction or the other are difficult to discern. Through the lens of EEG we encounter common development paths in both cases that have collided en route to reconfiguration of rural land uses and lifestyles in wine country. However, those paths are not linear, nor are they orderly. In the case of Tuscany, pioneers of lifestyle migration energize development paths towards tourism, while in the Okanagan tourism drove the paths towards lifestyle migration. Windows of opportunity were created by economic transition in both cases, but where institutional support in Tuscany appears as a catalyst for changing paths towards agritourism, institutional support in the Okanagan is more reactionary, legislating development that had already taken place driven by those pioneers of the industry. This may be attributed to the differing scale of institutional support that was national and international in Tuscany and provincial in the Okanagan.

In each case, there is much evidence to suggest that the foundations of eco gastronomy in the Slow Movement both reflect and promote widespread change in market demands for fair, local, healthy choices among tourists. The wine industry in both places has acted as a willing conduit to these changes in demand, especially through development of tourism, but also through the industry's ability make agricultural production resilient in changing times. The natural and cultural capital associated with the wine industry appears to satisfy the invigorated social ideals of the Slow Movement and its eco gastronomy of everyday life. However, its success has also wrought continued problems of population pressure on agricultural land and lifestyle, especially in the Okanagan, where it continues without a foreseeable solution. The good life in wine country as espoused through the eco gastronomy of the Slow Movement is, therefore, not without its problems and continues to be worthy of study.

Acknowledgments

We wish to acknowledge the generous support of the Universita` degli Studi Firenze, Dipartimento di Scienze per l'Economia e l'Impresa and Sonnino International Education in Montespertoli, Tuscany.

References

Aguiar, L. L., Tomic, P., & Trumper, R. (2005). Work hard, play hard: Selling Kelowna, BC, as year-round playground. *The Canadian Geographer/Le Géographe Canadien, 49*, 123–139.

Aspler, A. (2013). *Canadian wineries.* Toronto: Firefly Books.

Azzari, M., & Rombai, L. (1991). La Toscana della mezzadria. In *Paesaggi delle colline toscane.* Venice: Marsilio.

Bell, M., & Ward, G. (2000). Comparing temporary mobility with permanent migration. *Tourism Geographies, 2*, 87–107.

Belliveau, S., Smit, B., & Bradshaw, B. (2006). Multiple exposures and dynamic vulnerability: Evidence from the grape industry in the Okanagan Valley, Canada. *Global Environmental Change, 16*, 364–378.

Benassi, F., & Porciani, L. (2009). *The dual profile of migration in Tuscany*, Universita` di Pisa, Dipartimento diStatistica e Matematica, Applicata all'Economia, Report n. 315.

Béteille, R. (1996). L'agrotourisme dans les espaces ruraux européens. *Annales de Geography, 592*, 584–602.

Blaikie, P. M., & Brookfield, H. C. (1987). *Land degradation and society.* Abingdon: Methuen.

Boschma, R., & Frenken, K. (2006). Why is economic geography not an evolutionary science? Towards an evolutionary economic geography. *Journal of Economic Geography, 6*, 273–302.

Boschma, R., & Martin, R. (2010). *The handbook on evolutionary economic geography.* Cheltenham: Edward Elgar.

British Columbia Wine Institute BCWI. (2016). *Annual Report 2016.* Retrieved from www.winebc.org/file/Information

British Columbia Wine Institute BCWI. (2015). *Annual Report 2015.* Retrieved from www.winebc.org/file/Information

Brouder, P. (2016). Evolutionary economic geography: Reflections from a sustainable tourism perspective. *Tourism Geographies*, 1–10.

Brouder, P., & Eriksson, R. H. (2013). Tourism evolution: On the synergies of tourism studies and evolutionary economic geography. *Annals of Tourism Research, 43*, 370–389.

Cadieux, K., & Taylor, L. (2013). *Landscape and the ideology of nature in exurbia: Green sprawl.* New York, NY: Routledge.

Caffyn, A. (2012). Advocating and implementing slow tourism. *Tourism Recreation Research, 37*, 77–80.

Cannings, R. J. (2000). The South Okanagan Valley: A national treasure at risk. *Proceedings of a Conference on the Biology and Management of Species and Habitats at Risk*, Kamloops British Columbia Ministry of Environment Lands and Parks and University College of the Cariboo.

Cánoves, G., Villarino, M., Priestley, G. K., & Blanco, A. (2004). Rural tourism in Spain: An analysis of recent evolution. *Geoforum, 35*, 755–769.

Carmichael, B. A., & Senese, D. M. (2012). Competitiveness and sustainability in wine tourism regions: The application of a stage model of destination development to two Canadian wine regions. In P. Doughtery (Ed.), *The geography of wine* (pp. 159–178). Netherlands: Springer.

Champion, T., Coombes, M., & Fotheringham, S. (Eds.). (1998). *Urban exodus.* London: CPRE.

Cianferoni, R., & Mancini, F. (Eds.). (1993). *La collina nell'economia e nel paesaggio della Toscana.* Florence: Accademia dei Georgofili.

Conway, D., & Timms, B. F. (2010). Re-branding alternative tourism in the Caribbean: The case for "slow tourism." *Tourism and Hospitality Research, 10*, 329–344.

Dickenson, J., & Lumsden, L. (2010). *Slow travel and tourism.* London: Earthscan.

Di Giovine, M. A. (2008). *The heritage-scape: UNESCO, world heritage, and tourism.* Lanham, MD: Lexington Books.

Fullagar, S., Markwell, K., and Wilson, S. (Eds.) (2012). *Slow tourism: Experiences and mobilities.* Bristol: Channel View Publications.

Gariglio, G., & Giavedoni, F. (2015). *Slow wine guide 2015.* Turin: Slow Food Editore.

Hall, D. R., Roberts, L., & Mitchell, M. (2005). *New directions in rural tourism.* Ashgate, Hants.

Hall, C. M., & Williams, A. (Eds.). (2013). *Tourism and migration: New relationships between production and consumption* (Vol. 65). Dordrecht: Springer Science & Business Media.

Halseth, G. (2005). Resource town transition: Debates after closure. In *Rural change and sustainability: Agriculture, the environment and communities* (pp. 326–342). Oxfordshire: CABI Publishing.

Harvey, D. (1989). *The condition of postmodernity* (Vol. 14). Oxford: Blackwell.

Hines, J. D. (2010). Rural gentrification as permanent tourism: The creation of the "New" West archipelago as postindustrial cultural space. *Environment and Planning D: Society and Space, 28*, 509–525.

Hira, A., & Bwenge, A. (2011). The wine industry in British Columbia: Issues and potential. *American Association of Wine Economics Working Paper No. 87*.

Hoeschele, W., 2010. Measuring abundance: the case of Cittaslow's attempts to support better quality of life. *International Journal of Green Economics, 4*(1), pp.63–81.

Hopgood, D. (2016). Summerhill Pyramid Winery 25th anniversary. *Taste, 18*, 4–7.

Hull, J. S. (2016). Wellness tourism experiences in mountain regions: The case of sparkling Hill Resort, Canada. In H. Richins & J. S. Hull (Eds.), *Mountain tourism* (pp. 25–35). Wallingford, UK: CABI International.

Invest Okanagan. (2016). *Okanagan Valley Economic Profile 2015.* Retrieved from www.investokanagan.com/resources

Lowry, L. L., & Lee, M. (2011). CittaSlow, slow cities, slow food: Searching for a model for the development of slow tourism, travel & tourism research association. *42nd Annual Conference Proceedings: Seeing the Forest and the Trees-Big Picture Research in a Detail-Driven World.*

Markey, S., Halseth, G., & Manson, D. (2008). Challenging the inevitability of rural decline: Advancing the policy of place in northern British Columbia. *Journal of Rural Studies, 24*, 409–421.

Marlowe, B. (2016). Organic Oregon: An emerging experience in terroir tourism. *Proceedings XI International Terroir Congress* (pp. 183–188). Willamette Valley, Oregon.

Matos, R. (2004). Can slow tourism bring new life to Alpine Regions? In *The tourism and leisure industry: Shaping the future* (pp. 93–103). New York, NY: Haworth Hospitality Press.

McGuire, D. M. (1993). *The political economy of the grape and wine industry in British Columbia and impact of the free trade agreement.* Working Paper, Okanagan University College, Kelowna, British Columbia.

McKinnon, I., & Hiner, C. C. (2016). Does the region still have relevance? (Re)considering "regional" political ecology. *Journal of Political Ecology, 23,* 115–122.

Miele, M., & Murdoch, J. (2002). The practical aesthetics of traditional cuisines: Slow food in Tuscany. *Sociologia Ruralis, 42,* 312–328.

Oosterveer, P., & Sonnenfeld, D. A. (2012). *Food, globalization and sustainability.* New York, NY: Earthscan.

Parkins, W. (2004). At home in Tuscany: Slow living and the cosmopolitan subject. *Home Cultures, 1,* 257–274.

Perrin, C., & Randelli, F. (2007). Aree rurali e residenti stranieri: Un confronto fra chianti e campagne francesi. *Rivista Geografica Italiana, 114,* 67–92.

Peters, G. L. (2007). The changing cultural landscape of El Paso de Robles. *Yearbook of the Association of Pacific Coast Geographers, 69,* 74–87.

Randelli, F., Romei, P., & Tortora, M. (2014). An evolutionary approach to the study of rural tourism. *Land Use Policy, 38,* 276–281.

Romei, P. (Eds.). (2008). *Turismo sostenibile e sviluppo locale.* Padova: CEDAM.

Saxena, G., Clark, G., Oliver, T., & Ilbery, B. (2007). Conceptualizing integrated rural tourism. *Tourism Geographies, 9,* 347–370.

Saxena, G., & Ilbery, B. (2008). Integrated rural tourism a border case study. *Annals of Tourism Research, 35,* 233–254.

Senese, D. M., Wilson, W., & Momer, B. (2012). The Okanagan Wine region of British Columbia, Canada. In P. H. Dougherty (Ed.), *The geography of wine. Regions, terroir and techniques* (pp. 81–94). London: Springer.

Senese, D. M., Randelli, F., & Hull, J. S. (2016). The role of terroir in tourism led amenity migration. *Proceedings XI International Terroir Congress,* Willamette, Oregon, 189–194.

Service BC, BC Stats. (2016). *Demography, Vital Statistics, Population Estimates and Projections.* Retrieved from www.bcstats.gov.bc.ca/StatisticsBySubject/Demography

Shaw, G., & Williams, A. (1994). *Critical issues in tourism.* London: Blackwell.

Telleschi, A. (1992). *Turismo verde e spazio rurale in Toscana.* Pisa: ETS Editrice.

Teixeira, C. (2009). New immigrant settlement in a mid-sized city: A case study of housing barriers and coping strategies in Kelowna, British Columbia. *The Canadian Geographer/Le Géographe Canadien, 53,* 323–339.

TOTA. (2015). *Thompson Okanagan travel experiences guide.* Vancouver: Government of British Columbia. Destination BC.

TOTA. (2012). *Embracing our potential: A ten-year strategy for the Thompson-Okanagan region 2012–2022.* TOTA, Kelowna, British Columbia, Canada.

Unwin, T. (2012). Terroir: At the heart of geography. In P. H. Dougherty (Ed.), *The geography of wine. Regions, terroir and techniques* (pp. 37–48). London: Springer.

UNWTO. (2016a). *Global report on the transformative power of tourism,* Affiliate Members Report, Vol. 14.

UNWTO. (2016b). *Global report on food tourism.* Associate Members Report Four, Madrid, Spain.

Urry, J. (2007). *Mobilities.* Cambridge: Polity.

Vadour, E. (2002). The quality of grapes and wine in relation to eography: Notions of terroir at various scales. *Journal of Wine Research, 13,* 117–141.

Wagner, J. R. (2008). Landscape aesthetics, water, and settler colonialism in the Okanagan Valley of British Columbia. *Journal of Ecological Anthropology, 12,* 22.

West Coast Environmental Law. (2016). *Agri-tourism*. Retrieved from wcel.org/agri-tourism

Williams, A. M., King, R., & Warnes, T. (1997). A place in the sun international retirement migration from Northern to Southern Europe. *European Urban and Regional Studies, 4*, 115–134.

Yearwood-Lee, E. (2008). *History of the agricultural land reserve*. Legislative Library of British Columbia, Victoria British Columbia.

15 Conclusion

The promises and pitfalls of slow

Michael Clancy

Introduction

As Paul Knox reminds us, the true distinction between fast and slow living resides not with the Slow Movement, but rather globalization. Only 15 percent of the world's population lives within the fast world, which is characterized by global capitalism, advanced technology, rapid communication and globally branded consumerism. The remaining 85 percent are implicated and affected by it but are not full participants (Knox, 2005). It follows that Slow Food, Slow Cities, tourism and larger Slow Movement largely take place among that 15 percent. This is not to suggest that this makes the movement somehow unimportant; few, if any lifestyle or social movements are universal. What remains at stake is the significance of these activities. As consumption movements are they simply forms of symbolic communication, or are they more politically significant? How do we interpret Slow?

The spread and promise of slow

One way to assess the phenomenon comes it examining what might be called its horizontal spread – its movement into new areas, and here there has been clear diffusion (money, education, design, religion, gardening). But also testimony to the success of the Slow Movement in many wealthy, postindustrial societies that today many elements of slow within the three areas examined in this book have gone mainstream and done so in many cases without the slow label. In the area of food, for instance, farm-to-table restaurants, which seek to reconnect food producer with consumer while replacing global food chains with local ones, have popped up everywhere. Indeed, concepts such as foodsheds, foodways, food chains and food miles derive directly or indirectly from the Slow Food movement. Increasingly regions market themselves as tourist destinations through regional traditional food and wine offerings, including those prepared in such restaurants. Hudson Valley, New York, parts of Canadian British Columbia and the Cotswolds, UK, all exemplify this trend, where wild produce and seasonable organic ingredients and products from local artisans find their way to table in Michelin-starred restaurants

(Crapanzano, n.d.). Even among those restaurants that don't bill themselves as farm-to-table, increasingly many menus still note local ingredients by purveyor.

In part these restaurants are simply responding to growing curiosity among their diners as to where their food comes from, another broader trend that has gone mainstream over the past two decades. Increased health and environmental concerns, along with more knowledge about animal welfare, global food production chains and mass food production more generally, have all led to greater consumer demand for local, sustainable food.

Farmers markets are an additional manifestation of this trend. As Vecchio (2009) shows, with the exception of a few countries these local markets in the United States and Europe once all but disappeared after the appearance of the supermarket. In the early part of this century, however, they have returned with gusto. According to the United States Department of Agriculture, the number of farmers markets in the U.S. more than quadrupled between 1994 and 2014 to more than 8,000 (USDA, n.d.). Similar trends have taken place throughout Western Europe. Citing industry sources, Vecchio estimated that the total market for local and regional food was worth $4 billion in 2002 in the U.S. (2009, p. 3). More recently the USDA estimated that same market to be valued at $12 billion in 2014 and projected to hit $20 billion by 2020 (USDA, n.d.). Vecchio reports that since the appearance of the first new food market in Bath in the U.K. in 1997, some 450 similar markets appeared in the U.K. by 2004. They arose both as a response to consumer demand and also as an alternative means for distribution by producers frustrated with low farm prices (Holloway & Kneafsey, 2000; Sims, 2010; Spiller, 2012). Local and organic foods have also become much more visible in mainstream markets throughout the U.S. and Europe in recent years (Knox & Mayer, 2013). In my local supermarket, part of a global chain owned by a Dutch multinational, seasonal fruits and vegetables are labeled as such and often placed near the entrance doors among the 42,000 items found in a typical grocery store.

Governments have also gotten on board, citing this new demand for local food. In the UK, the government's Policy Commission on the Future of Farming and Food wrote a 2002 report that stated, "One of the greatest opportunities for farmers to add value and retain a bigger slice of retail prices is to build on the public's enthusiasm for locally-produced food, or food with a clear regional provenance" (Cited in Sims, 2010, p. 106). In the United States, the USDA reported in 2012 that roughly 8 percent of farms (nearly 164,000) were selling products directly, through mechanisms such as farmers markets, farm stands and other direct-to-consumers marketing channels (Low et al., 2015). The 2002 Farm Bill authorized the USDA to support farmers markets and local food production networks through federal competitive grants. In Europe the EU LEADER Programme has similarly funded this type of food production as part of its broader mandate to promote rural economic development. In addition the European Commission funded a Facilitating

Alternative Agro-Food Networks (FAAN) program to examine local food networks within the EU.

An additional indicator of the renewed interest in food production and distribution – at least in the USA – has been the growing attraction by younger generations to farming, gardening and broader food production. Some 50 percent of Millennials in the United States claim to be foodies and the largest single buyer of organic produce are parents aged 18–24 (Turow Paul, 2016). Farming, once a rapidly declining activity in the United States, has continued to become more concentrated, and the average age of farmers continues to increase. Yet to some degree this is being mitigated by a cohort of Millennials –many of them highly educated –who are turning to small-scale, mostly organic farming. For some this is a lifestyle choice, moving away from faster paced cities into the countryside. Others, however, have been instrumental in expanding urban agriculture (Dawson & Morales, 2016; Hess, 2009; Mincyte & Dobernig, 2016). Millennials have also been a leading force toward other craft food and drink movements such as cheese, pickles, butchery and beer and cider production. Similar patterns have been reported in France, where young urban professionals have quit their jobs in cities and moved into small, organic farming, contributing to national market estimated at €7 billion annually (Morenne, 2017).

In addition to food and drink, many of the slow principles inherent in the Cittáslow movement have also gone mainstream. As Manela (this volume) summarizes, these amount to some 55 criteria grouped within six areas: environmental policy, infrastructure, quality of urban fabric, encouragement of local products, hospitality, and community. In addition, Cittáslow is directly tied to Slow Food. Its creation was inspired by the Slow Food movement, and one requirement that continues to exist for all slow cities is the presence of a Slow Food convivium, or promise to activate one. Overall the goal of Cittáslow is improved livability for residence under a vibrant, sustainable economic model. In the Global North, cities, once centers of industrial production, continue to be reimagined and restructured as finance, technology, and creative economy centers. In part this represents a new economic development strategy under a changed local and global business environment (Mayer & Knox, 2006; Sánchez-Moral, Méndez, & Prada-Trigo, 2015; Servon & Pink, 2015). Planners have come to realize that arts and culture, entertainment and green spaces are integral to this process. For some (Polèse & Stren, 2000; Tocci, this volume) this is tied to the idea of smart cities, and as Duignan and Wilbert (this volume) point out, these amenities and attractions draw residents and tourists alike.

The original Slow Cities movement began in large part as a response to automobile and bus traffic in five small Italian towns that was viewed as disrupting the quality of life for residents. Today, transport and traffic issues have become central to cities and towns all over the world. Alternative means of mass transit, municipal cycling programs and expanded bicycle lanes, and pedestrian-only shopping streets (POSS) have risen in cities and towns.

Pioneered by Venice and Copenhagen, in Europe broader car-free zones have become ubiquitous in major cities but also mid-sized towns. Major cities such as London, Paris, Mexico City, Oslo, Madrid and Barcelona have all limited auto traffic in central urban spaces. The South Korean city of Suwon, a city of one million residents, experimented with an expanded car-free zone for 30 days in the historic neighborhood of Haenggung-dong in 2013 and subsequent reports suggest car traffic had declined two years later (Valmero, 2015). Several of the values associated with Slow Cities also fit into the so-called New Urbanism movement that seeks to create more livable cities through urban design that allows for better living and sustainability through greater housing density, creation of green public spaces, accessible transport and walkability (CNU, 2015; Gehl, 2013).

Many of these same concepts have come to revitalized small cities and towns. Knox and Mayer (2013) point out the fastest growing areas in the U.S. in recent years to be towns of 10,000–50,000. Ironically, much of their appeal comes from revitalization after decades of decline tied to globalization, deindustrialization and suburbanization. More recently, many have become attractive by creating many of these same quality of life amenities and slower lifestyles (Mayer & Knox, 2010). Many market towns and historical transportation centers have been revitalized as brownfields have been repurposed, town centers reinvigorated, housing stock renovated and public spaces improved. In sum, principles associated with Slow Cities – greening cities, making cities sustainable, improving transport, creating greater livability – have become dominant themes in modern urban planning. They also inform other subsequent movements, such as Transition Towns, which also seek local solutions to economic and environmental issues in the era of advanced global climate change and the possibility of peak oil (Servon & Pink, 2015).

As noted in the opening chapter, Slow Food and Cittáslow are much older and institutionalized than the slow travel and tourism phenomena. Yet many elements of slow tourism are tied to these movements themselves. As Lavarini and Scramalgia, Corvo and Matacena, and separately Senese et al. (all this volume) and others (Fletchall, 2016; Hall, 2006; Montanari & Staniscia, 2009) point out, slow tourism demand is often linked to aspects of slow food and drink as well as place. As noted above, hospitality and tourism is one of the six categories for evaluation within the Cittáslow network, and in many cases towns seek Cittáslow status in large part as a means to promote tourism. What can be claimed is that slow tourism forms part of what Mowforth and Munt (2008) call "new tourism," which they define as including green, sustainable, responsible, and low impact. In addition to being post-Fordist in nature (Poon, 1993), new tourism is a response to problems that have arisen from the previously predominant form of tourism: mass tourism. "They include environmental, social and cultural degradation, unequal distribution of financial benefits, the promotion of paternalistic attitudes, and even the spread of disease" (Mowforth & Munt, 2008, p. 95). The newer forms of tourism aim to avoid these problems and in some cases help to solve them.

Although definitions of slow tourism are still contentious, for many the term includes both green and socially responsible elements.

Possible pitfalls

As suggested elsewhere in this volume, together Slow Food, cities and tourism represent alternative lifestyles and a reaction to a fast world. While they are overlapping phenomenon, sharing many features, there are also important differences. Food and tourism are each alternative consumption movements, while efforts revolving around slow cities and territories are more comprehensive, involving work, leisure, home life, transport, pollution and public spaces. Slow Food and Cittáslow place emphasis on reconnecting people with each other, counteracting social isolation produced under modernity. Both the slow city and slow tourism movements involve themselves with space and place making. Following Dunlap's (2012) work on the Slow Food movement, it may be argued that both Slow Food and tourism are a reaction against societal developments of leisure but also of their time more generally. Preparing and eating food may constitute a leisure activity under some circumstances but it is always one of physical necessity.

What the three movements share is a concern for daily life activities – where and how they take place, their physical and spatial surroundings, and meanings associated with them. As I note at the outset of Chapter 5, this places them within the realm of lifestyle politics (Haenfler, Johnson, & Jones, 2012; Pink, 2008; Pink & Servon, 2013; Portwood-Stacer, 2013; Shotter, 1993). This involves, in part, making sense of the world and making the world through practice. This is not to suggest that powerful structures do not matter, but rather that, "working inter-subjectively, individuals negotiate their lives and intervening cultural power in more complex and uncertain ways" (Crouch, 2007, p. 50). While Crouch applies this approach to tourism, Pink and Servon suggest this is also true for individuals navigating urban spaces. Writing of Cittáslow, she argues here people are practicing sensoriality "found in the routine, ongoing, and habitual experiences of the everyday" (Pink & Servon, 2013, p. 454). Ultimately this practice serves to create new meanings and ultimately new spaces and senses of place (Knox, 2005).

As many contributors to this volume make clear, one clear promise appears to come in response to these individual lifestyle demands: various economic opportunities for individuals, firms, towns and regions. Many who emphasize slow food, tourism and territories suggest the emergence of fairer and more cooperative relationships between producers and consumers. In a sense this is an effort to humanize commercial activities and make them more personal. While many of the authors here appear optimistic regarding the possibilities of slow as a tool of sustainable economic development for cities, towns or entire regions (Duignan and Wilbert; Tocci; Lavarini and Scramalgia in particular in this volume), several issues remain. One is accessibility. Hsu (2014) suggests that treating time dichotomously is problematic, in that the social acceleration process that the Slow Movement has reacted against is not monolithic. Cresswell (2010) and Germann Molz (this volume) similarly discuss differential mobilities within a larger politics of pace. What Southerton and Tomlinson (2005) refer to as the "time squeeze" is experienced differently across class and gender lines (also see Mattingly & Sayer, 2006). This raises the question of who can access "slow," especially in its consumerist forms. Some have derided Slow Food in particular as elitist and with little larger social significance, "too expensive for ordinary people, just the latest trend among foodies and gourmands" (Schlosser, 2002, p. 11, as quoted in Hall, 2012, pp. 62–63). To its credit, the Slow Food organization has worked to increase access of slow, local healthy food beyond those groups through a number of global and national campaigns in schools, Presidia, Slow Food Gardens and other initiatives.

No parallel initiatives have come to the forefront in slow travel and tourism thus far. This may be because slow travel and tourism involve leisure consumption, and also because the movement is younger and less institutionalized. Nor, however, has this issue been adequately raised in the academic literature on the subject. At first glance, accessibility within the slow city movement appears to be less of an issue because many urban spaces are public in nature, but as many cities have become more popular affordability and gentrification have followed. National housing crises have hit the U.K. and Ireland, and cities such as London, New York, Dublin, Copenhagen, Vancouver, San Francisco, Sydney, Toronto, Berlin and others have become increasingly unaffordable (Lees, Shin, & Lopez-Morales, 2015; Porter & Shaw, 2009). Although the Cittáslow movement focuses on small cities and towns, to the extent that it is successful in urban regeneration through promoting cultural authenticity and economic and environmental sustainability, the same issues of accessibility are likely to arise. As Gunduz, Oner, and Knox (2016) point out, Slow Cities are susceptible to the same branding, place marketing, and amenity seeking migration as other places. Do their new status for distinctive place identities simply make them another item of consumptive desire?

Although class, access and affordability make up one set of possible pitfalls, they are not the only ones. A separate but related challenge for slow territories and cities is that of the dichotomy of slow and fast. Because slow practices and spaces gain status and meaning through their posed opposite, "fast," they require the very speed they react against. One result is the construction of bifurcated places – constructed authentic sites residing spatially outside of the modern. Here there is a certain nostalgia for the traditional, the authentic, in a manner that is becoming a sort of Luddite zoo in an otherwise hyper-modernized world. This is an issue raised in some of the literature on heritage and ecotourism. Sites become tourist attractions due to their perceived (or constructed) backwardness, or as Johnson (1999, pp. 191–192) argues, their status not just as "empty spaces" but also "empty time."

238   *Michael Clancy*

Conclusion

The contributions in this book have shown that the Slow Food, slow cities and slow travel and tourism phenomena come as reactions to capitalism and modernity with their focus on consumption and speed, and their perceived deleterious effects on the quality of life – what Ritzer calls "the globalization of nothing." In this sense they concur with Markwell, Fullagar, and Wilson's (2012, p. 228) claim that those who participate are taking part in resistance against what they call the "homogenizing forces of globalization". And yet we also know that "Slow" is still a part of that very system and cannot escape it. Nor are these anti-consumerist movements. Instead they are best thought of as alternative experience movements, but because so much experience today has become commodified, they constitute direct (food and tourism) or indirect (cities) alternative consumption movements.

As such, it is not a surprise that interpreting the meaning and significance of the Slow Movement has been difficult. For some critics its focus on personal pleasure makes it self serving and elitist (Cresswell, 2010; Tomlinson, 2007). Its emphasis on the self limits any potential. Slow Food USA was dogged by this allegation of elitism for many years. One response under then-head of the national organization Josh Viertel was a $5 Challenge – the challenge to make slow food affordable, roughly the same price as a McDonald's Happy Meal. Viertel resigned under pressure in 2012 and later wrote an essay suggesting that broadening the movement and reasserting the "fair" aspect of Good, Clean, Fair needs to be a central facet to the movement's survival. "Can you both fight for the farmer and fight for the eater, or do farmers and eaters have competing agendas?" (Viertel, 2012).

In contrast, for optimists, those involved in Slow might be though of as part of what Ray and Anderson (2000) refer to as Cultural Creatives, 50 million strong in the United States (plus many more globally), a group of change makers who work through nontraditional activist means to commit their lives to progressive change (Groenendaal, 2012). At the heart of this eclectic group is a set of shared values that include seeking authenticity, reflection, mindfulness, engaged activism. An interesting aspect of the CC label is that it identifies members from the outside and openly, approvingly labels them an educated elite. If Mintz (2006) is correct in identifying core Slow Food members as "a limited number of people, most of them in the West, most of them educated people of some means" (p. 10, cited in Sassatelli & Davolio, 2010, p. 203), then they are certainly to be assigned to that larger group. Central is the connection between personal experience and global change. It is the Cultural Creatives who are most active in lifestyle politics – focusing on the everyday, the routine, as both a statement of personal politics and a means for creating change on a larger scale.

The appeal of all this, of course, is the promise of renewed agency in a hypermodern, globalized world where many feel less agency all the time. Elsewhere Pink refers to this as *indirect* activism (2012, p. 109, her emphasis) in that rather than confrontation, it engages through example. Here Haenfler et al. (2012) work on lifestyle movements is particularly useful. They suggest these eclectic movements – ranging from voluntary simplicity, pledges of virginity, Promise Keepers, vegans – amount to diffuse cultural movements that politicize the self and daily life. As such, they overlap with traditional contentious politics models such as interest group politics, traditional and new social movements, but also differ from them in important ways. By politicizing ordinary daily practices people are able to create new personal identities. Their actions make up small-scale change initially and lead by example, but hope to spread these practices more widely so they create new economic institutions, cultural practices and political change (Haenfer et al., 2012). In this way they amount to what Micheletti (2003) refers to as "individual collective action."

While sounding a bit like a contradiction in terms, individual collective action might be thought of as a continuum, with some lifestyle behaviors much more on the individual end and others closer to the collective. In some ways Slow Food has come the furthest here in moving from the individual to the collective. Early rhetoric in the movement emphasized individual pleasure of consuming but in recent years there has been much more focus on social aspects and economic ties. The Ark of Taste specifically places emphasis on protection of traditional food, practices, lifestyles and livelihoods – and with it global justice, biodiversity and environmental protection – over personal pleasure (Sassatelli & Davolio, 2010). Cittáslow is also a collective manifestation of Slow Food in that the movement was originally inspired by Slow Food and embraces Slow Food principles. By applying them to public spaces it moves beyond individual lifestyle practices and becomes more collective. When cities, villages or towns engage in activities such as carnivals, festivals, contests etc., they demonstrate a commitment and further the emphasis toward "the good life" for members of the community. It is not surprising that slow travel and tourism, constituting the youngest and least institutionalized of the three phenomena dealt with in this book, has the furthest to go. Whether it moves from the individual consumerist edge of this continuum remains to be seen. All three will continue to evolve and deserve our attention as lifestyle movements. Ultimately, as social scientists, our assessment of the Slow Movement, spearheaded by food, urban lifestyles and travel and tourism, may be shaped more by our own biases than anything else, specifically our views on individual agency versus powerful structural forces in the world.

References

CNU. (2015, April 20). *The charter of the new urbanism.* Retrieved from www.cnu.org/who-we-are/charter-new-urbanism

Crapanzano, A. (n.d.). *England's latest farm-to-table mecca, the Cotswolds.* Retrieved from www.travelandleisure.com/articles/cotswalds-england-dining-destination

Cresswell, T. (2010). Towards a politics of mobility. *Environment and Planning D: Society and Space, 28*(1), 17–31. Retrieved from https://doi.org/10.1068/d11407

240   *Michael Clancy*

Crouch, D. (2007). *The power of the tourist encounter.* In A. Church and T. Coles (Eds.), *Tourism, Power and Space.* London: Taylor and Francis, pp. 45–62.

Dawson, J. C., & Morales, A. (2016). *Cities of farmers: Urban agricultural practices and processes.* Ames, IA: University of Iowa Press.

Dunlap, R. (2012). Recreating culture: Slow Food as a leisure education movement. *World Leisure Journal, 54*(1), 38–47.

Fletchall, A. M. (2016). Place-making through beer-drinking: A case study of Montana's craft breweries. *Geographical Review, 106*(4), 539–566.

Gehl, J. (2013). *Cities for people.* Washington, DC: Island Press.

Groenendaal, E. (2012). Slow tourism initiatives: An exploratory study of Dutch lifestyles entrepreneurs in France. In S. Fullagar, K. Markwell, & E. Wilson (Eds.), *Slow tourism: Experiences and mobilities* (pp. 201–213). Bristol, UK: Channel View Publications.

Gunduz, C., Oner, A. C., & Knox, P. L. (2016). Social resilience in Aegean slow cities: slow city Seferihisar. *Universal Journal of Management, 4*(4), 211–222.

Haenfler, R., Johnson, B., & Jones, E. (2012). Lifestyle movements: Exploring the intersection of lifestyle and social movements. *Social Movement Studies, 11*(1), 1–20.

Hall, C. M. (2006). Introduction: Culinary tourism and regional development: From slow food to slow tourism? *Tourism Review International, 9*(4), 303–305.

Hall, C.M. (2012). *The contradictions and paradoxes of Slow Food: environmental change, sustainability, and the conservation of taste.* In S. Fullagar, K. Markwell, and E. Wilson (Eds.), *Slow Tourism: Experiences and Mobilities.* Bristol: Channel View Publications, pp. 53–68.

Hess, D. J. (2009). *Localist movements in a global economy: Sustainability, justice, and urban development in the United States.* Cambridge, MA: MIT Press.

Holloway, L., & Kneafsey, M. (2000). Reading the space of the farmers' market: A case study from the United Kingdom. *Sociologia Ruralis, 40*(3), 285–299. Retrieved from https://doi.org/10.1111/1467-9523.00149

Hsu, E. L. (2014). The slow food movement and time shortage: Beyond the dichotomy of fast or slow. *Journal of Sociology, 51*(3), 628–642. Retrieved from https://doi.org/10.1177/1440783313518250

Johnson, N. (1999). Framing the past: Time, space, and the politics of heritage tourism in Ireland. *Political Geography, 18*(2), 187–207.

Knox, P. L. (2005). Creating ordinary places: Slow cities in a fast world. *Journal of Urban Design, 10*(1), 1–11. Retrieved from https://doi.org/10.1080/13574800500062221

Knox, P. L., & Mayer, H. (2013). *Small town sustainability: Economic, social, and environmental innovation.* Basel: Birkhäuser Architecture.

Lees, L., Shin, H. B., & Lopez-Morales, E. (2015). *Global gentrifications: Uneven development and displacement.* Bristol, UK: Policy Press.

Low, S., Adalja, A., Beaulieu, E., Key, N., Martinez, S., Melton, A., … Jablonski, B. B. R. (2015). *Trends in U.S. local and regional food systems: A report to Congress* (USDA Report to Congress No. AP-068). Washington, DC: USDA.

Markwell, K., Fullagar, S., & Wilson, E. (2012). Reflecting upon slow travel and tourism experiences. In S. Fullagar, K. Markwell, & E. Wilson (Eds.), *Slow tourism: Experiences and mobilities* (pp. 227–233.). Bristol, UK: Channel View Publications.

Mattingly, M. J., & Sayer, L. C. (2006). Under pressure: Gender differences in the relationship between free time and feeling rushed. *Journal of Marriage and Family, 68*(1), 205–221. Retrieved from https://doi.org/10.1111/j.1741-3737.2006.00242.x

Mayer, H., & Knox, P. L. (2006). Slow cities: Sustainable places in a fast world. *Journal of Urban Affairs, 28*(4), 321–334.

Mayer, H., & Knox, P. L. (2010). Small-town sustainability: Prospects in the second modernity. *European Planning Studies, 18*(10), 1545–1565.

Micheletti, M. (2003). *Political virtue and shopping: Individuals, consumerism, and collective action.* New York, NY: Palgrave Macmillan.

Mincyte, D., & Dobernig, K. (2016). Urban farming in the North American metropolis: Rethinking work and distance in alternative food networks. *Environment and Planning A, 48*(9), 1767–1786. Retrieved from https://doi.org/10.1177/0308518X16651444

Mintz, S. (2006). Food at moderate speeds. In R. Wilk (Ed.), *Fast food/slow food: The cultural economy of the global food system* (pp. 3–12). Walnut Creek, CA: Altamira Press.

Montanari, A., & Staniscia, B. (2009). Culinary tourism as a tool for regional re-equilibrium. *European Planning Studies, 17*(10), 1463–1483.

Morenne, B. (2017, January 17). Life on the farm draws some French fleeing urban ennui. *The New York Times*, p. A4. Retrieved from www.nytimes.com/2017/01/17/world/europe/france-small-farming-organic.html

Mowforth, M., & Munt, I. (2008). *Tourism and sustainability: Development, globalisation and new tourism in the third world* (3rd ed.). London, New York, NY: Routledge.

Pink, S. (2008). Sense and sustainability: The case of the Slow City movement. *Local Environment, 13*(2), 95–106.

Pink, S. (2012). *Situating everyday life: Practices and places*. London: SAGE.

Pink, S., & Servon, L. J. (2013). Sensory global towns: An experiential approach to the growth of the slow city movement. *Environment and Planning A, 45*(2), 451–466. Retrieved from https://doi.org/10.1068/a45133

Polèse, M., & Stren, R. E. (2000). *The social sustainability of cities: Diversity and the management of change*. Toronto: University of Toronto Press.

Poon, A. (1993). *Tourism, technologies and competitive strategies*. Wallingford: CAB International.

Porter, L., & Shaw, K. (2009). *Whose urban renaissance?: An international comparison of urban regeneration strategies*. London: Routledge.

Portwood-Stacer, L. (2013). *Lifestyle politics and radical activism* (1st ed.). New York, NY: Bloomsbury Academic.

Ray, P. H., & Anderson, S. R. (2000). *The cultural creatives: How 50 million people are changing the world*. New York, NY: Harmony Books.

Sánchez-Moral, S., Méndez, R., & Prada-Trigo, J. (2015). Resurgent cities: Local strategies and institutional networks to counteract shrinkage in Avilés (Spain). *European Planning Studies, 23*(1), 33–52.

Sassatelli, R., & Davolio, F. (2010). Consumption, pleasure and politics. *Journal of Consumer Culture, 10*(2), 202–232. Retrieved from https://doi.org/10.1177/1469540510364591

Schlosser, E. (2002) Foreword. In C. *Kummer, The Pleasures of Slow Food: Celebrating Authentic Traditions, Flavours and Recipes* (pp. 10–11). New York: Chronicle Books.

Servon, L. J., & Pink, S. (2015). Cittaslow: Going glocal in Spain. *Journal of Urban Affairs, 37*(3), 327–340.

Shotter, J. (1993). *Cultural politics of everyday life: Social constructionism, rhetoric, and knowing of the Third Kind*. Milton Keynes, UK: Open University Press.

Sims, R. (2010). Putting place on the menu: The negotiation of locality in UK food tourism, from production to consumption. *Journal of Rural Studies, 26*(2), 105–115. Retrieved from https://doi.org/10.1016/j.jrurstud.2009.09.003

Southerton, D., & Tomlinson, M. (2005). "Pressed for time" – the differential impacts of a "time squeeze." *The Sociological Review, 53*(2), 215–239.

Spiller, K. (2012). It tastes better because … consumer understandings of UK farmers' market food. *Appetite, 59*(1), 100–107.

Tomlinson, J. (2007). *The culture of speed: The coming of immediacy*. London: SAGE.

Turow Paul, E. (2016, November 11). Beyond kimchi and kale: How millennial "foodies" are challenging the supply chain from farm to table. *Forbes*. Retrieved from www.forbes.com/sites/eveturowpaul/2016/11/11/how-foodies-are-slowly-upending-the-ag-supply-chain/

USDA. (n.d.). *Local and regional food systems*. Retrieved from www.usda.gov/wps/portal/usda/usdahome?contentid=usda-results-local.html

USDA. (n.d.). *Number of U.S. farmers' markets continue to rise (chart)*. Retrieved from www.ers.usda.gov/data-products/chart-gallery/gallery/chart-detail/?chartId=77600

Valmero, A. (2015, October 23). *After hosting "ecomobility" festival, cars are back but less loved in Suwon. Citiscope*. Retrieved from http://citiscope.org/story/2015/after-hosting-ecomobility-festival-cars-are-back-less-loved-suwon

Vecchio, R. (2009). *European and United States farmers' markets: Similarities, differences and potential developments*. Presented at the 113th EAAE Seminar: A Resilient European Food Industry and Food Chain in a Challenging World. Crete, Greece.

Viertel, J. (2012, January 23). The soul of Slow Food: Fighting for both farmers and eaters. *The Atlantic Online*. Retrieved from www.theatlantic.com/health/archive/2012/01/the-soul-of-slow-food-fighting-for-both-farmers-and-eaters/251739/

Index

For Product Safety Concerns and Information please contact our EU
representative GPSR@taylorandfrancis.com
Taylor & Francis Verlag GmbH, Kaufingerstraße 24, 80331 München, Germany

www.ingramcontent.com/pod-product-compliance
Ingram Content Group UK Ltd.
Pitfield, Milton Keynes, MK11 3LW, UK
UKHW021617240425
457818UK00018B/607